FEAR OF
OUR FATHER

FEAR OF OUR FATHER

A True Story of Abuse, Murder, and Family Ties

LISA BONNICE AND STACEY M. KANANEN

BERKLEY BOOKS, NEW YORK

THE BERKLEY PUBLISHING GROUP
Published by the Penguin Group
Penguin Group (USA) Inc.
375 Hudson Street, New York, New York 10014, USA

USA | Canada | UK | Ireland | Australia | New Zealand | India | South Africa | China

Penguin Books Ltd., Registered Offices: 80 Strand, London WC2R 0RL, England
For more information about the Penguin Group, visit penguin.com.

FEAR OF OUR FATHER

A Berkley Book / published by arrangement with the authors

Berkley Books are published by The Berkley Publishing Group.
BERKLEY® is a registered trademark of Penguin Group (USA) Inc.
The "B" design is a trademark of Penguin Group (USA) Inc.

For information, address: The Berkley Publishing Group,
a division of Penguin Group (USA) Inc.,
375 Hudson Street, New York, New York 10014.

ISBN: 978-0-425-25873-6

PUBLISHING HISTORY
Berkley premium edition / June 2013

PRINTED IN THE UNITED STATES OF AMERICA

10 9 8 7 6 5 4 3 2 1

Cover design by Jason Gill.
Interior text design by Laura K. Corless.

ALWAYS LEARNING   PEARSON

We dislike talking about our experiences. No explanations are needed for those who have been inside, and the others will understand neither how we felt then nor how we feel now.

VIKTOR E. FRANKL, QUOTING SENTIMENTS
EXPRESSED BY FORMER AUSCHWITZ PRISONERS,
MAN'S SEARCH FOR MEANING

CONTENTS

INTRODUCTION

by Lisa Bonnice

I met Stacey Kananen less than two months after the police found her mother's body buried in her Orlando, Florida, backyard. I had just escaped the "real world" to live the Jimmy Buffett lifestyle, after working for five years in an NBC-affiliated newsroom as their MSNBC affiliate producer. I lived at and worked for Gulf Coast Resort, a nudist resort near Tampa. Stacey was the girlfriend of Susan Cowan, my boss's daughter. Susan was going to be assisting her mother in managing the resort, and Stacey was to be in charge of the restaurant.

Gulf Coast Resort was a small, close-knit community of about one hundred houses and eighty RV sites—the kind of place where everyone knows everyone else's business, like a naked Mayberry—and we had all heard about what had happened in Orlando. Stacey was being crucified in the media, even though she was not arrested. Everyone at the resort was dying to be the possessor of the world's best gossip, but the gravity of the tragedy prevented most people from asking Stacey too many personal questions.

Understandably, Stacey didn't share any details about the crimes or the rumors that began surfacing about the horrible abuse that had been heaped upon her by her father. We were strangers to her, and it really was none of anyone's business. She confided in a few friends as she got to know everyone, with bits and pieces, but no one at the resort learned the full story until her murder trial, years later. Even then, only a small portion of Stacey's life story was told—just enough to ensure a verdict of "Not Guilty."

All hell broke loose in May 2007, when police officers swarmed the resort after her brother pleaded guilty to two murders and accused her of helping him. For the next few days, reporters parked their live trucks outside the gates of the resort and were denied entrance, so news helicopters flew overhead because it was the only way for them to get pictures for the evening news. Stories of the lesbian accused of murdering her parents and fleeing to a nudist resort, in their viewing area, were just too titillating for the press to ignore.

As I got to know her, I was witness to Stacey's amazing ability to survive anything that was thrown her way. She endured endless depositions and hearings, gossiping gawkers, and the hurtful doubts about her innocence by even friends and family. Her own brother was accused of a crime so heinous that it would snap the mind of an ordinary person.

Between the time I met Stacey in February 2004 and her trial in March 2010, I watched, as objectively as possible, as this incredible woman waded through the story you're about to read. I attended her bond hearings and trial, and have no doubt that the verdict was fair and accurate.

Stacey had no interest whatsoever in writing a book until six months after the trial, once some major therapy and healing work was begun. I had cajoled her on numerous occasions, as the story was unfolding, twisting and turning, "If you ever want to write a book about this amazing story, *please* let me be your coauthor!" I didn't realize, at the time, just how bad it was, growing up in her family. She kept that information to herself. I was mostly fascinated by the intriguing story line I was witnessing. Once the trial commenced, and I realized how profoundly the Kananen family was abused, I dropped the subject out of respect for what she went through. But then, in August 2010, she approached me and said she had decided to write a book and wanted me to help her. As we worked on the book, through the untold hours of interviews and research, I was humbled by the trust Stacey showed in me, sharing with me painful and personal stories, which in the telling allowed me a deeper insight into her inner psyche.

I have a very large respect for Stacey Kananen and her passionate vision of becoming an advocate for abused children. I wish Stacey nothing but success in achieving her dream of helping to find nonjudgmental, humane solutions for families, including the abusive members, to find a way to live in peace and nonviolence.

PROLOGUE

I lived with my father for twenty-two years—from the day I was born until the day he disappeared on September 11, 1988. He was later found buried under the cement floor of his own garage in Orlando, Florida. He had been killed by a single bullet to the head. He was such a hateful son of a bitch that no one reported him missing. His body wasn't found until fifteen years later, on December 22, 2003, three months after my mother mysteriously disappeared, also on September 11, when a search for her began. His body was discovered hours before they found my mom's body buried in my backyard. Her death was a horrible tragedy. His, not so much.

Out of those two decades with my father, the hardest were the five months that we lived in Viola, Arkansas, when I was eleven. During these months, he was especially out of control. He had always been extremely violent and cruel—beating any and all of us, oftentimes just on a whim—but now his violence was tinged with madness. The violence itself hadn't necessarily escalated, but his enjoyment of our suffering had. I'd seen him kick my mother in the head until she was unconscious. I'd seen him play Russian roulette with a loaded pistol against my brother's ear. I was afraid, every single day, that he was literally going to kill someone in our family. He told us he could and would, and we believed him.

He had already moved the five of us—himself, my mother, my brother, my sister, and me—from state to state a few times, always giving us only a couple hours to pack for each move. I got off the school bus one January afternoon in Minnesota to find we were moving to Arkansas. Until then, I had lived up north in Monson, Maine, and Clarissa, Minnesota, so I was used to hearing the accents of New England Yankees or Minnesota Swedes. My grades started slipping once we moved to Arkansas because I couldn't understand my sixth-grade teacher's Southern drawl.

I was always motivated to do well in school because high marks meant fewer beatings. With my face buried in my textbooks, hidden away in a cramped bedroom I shared with my sister, Cheryl, who is older than me by two years, I was less likely to be singled out than whoever might be in the living room while he sullenly drank his vodka in front of the TV. I learned at a young age to become invisible.

But once I started sixth grade in Arkansas, I attracted

unwelcome attention to myself, completely by accident. My new teacher asked us to turn to a page in our English books, and I had no idea what she said, her vocabulary was so full of "yawls" and "chirrens." Once she noticed that I wasn't flipping pages, she flew at me like an angry bee, assuming that I was misbehaving.

I wasn't used to being in trouble in school, so I panicked and reacted the way I did at home when I sensed danger: I froze, went to my inner numb place, and started counting syllables on my fingers, waiting for it to be over. I had taught myself to count out how many syllables were in the words I was hearing in order to distract myself from painful physical experiences. Before I knew it, I was in the principal's office. There, I found out why my teacher was so angry.

Terrified, I explained what happened, but he was convinced that I was just being a smart-aleck Yankee brat. When he picked up the phone to call my parents, I burst into tears and begged, "Please don't call my parents. I'm sorry. I'll do what the teacher says."

What I was afraid to say was, "Please don't call my parents because if my father hears that I got in trouble in school, he'll beat me. He's been molesting us kids for as long as I can remember. My life is a violent hell, and since we've moved to Arkansas, his abuse has ramped itself up to surreal levels. And if you tell him I misbehaved, it may literally be the last time you ever see me."

Miraculously, the principal agreed to put down the phone. I was assigned a guardian angel in the form of a "study buddy" who helped me through the rest of sixth grade. The surface wound had received a bandage, but the underlying cancer had not been diagnosed or treated.

In hindsight, I can see that the incident in the principal's office was one of many possible turning points in my life. It created one of those "if only . . ." moments that I sometimes wonder about: How would my life have ended up if only that principal had recognized my panic-filled cry for help? If only I had felt safe enough to tell him why he couldn't call my house, could the abuse have been stopped? If so, who could I have become, if I had a normal life?

"If only . . ." is a big subject. If only the laws were different back then, then my mother might not have eventually been murdered. If only that principal—or anyone else, for that matter—recognized the signs of abuse and had intervened in some way, then my brother might not be in jail right now for killing both of our parents. If only I'd felt that someone, anyone, could rescue us, then I might have spoken up. If I had, I might not have been raped for the first time by my father—shortly after this incident— with the cold barrel of a loaded gun in my mouth.

CHAPTER 1

If Only . . .

March 12, 2010, should have been the happiest day of my life. It was the day that I was declared "Not Guilty" by a jury of my peers. Three years earlier I was charged with first-degree murder in the killing of my mother—a crime committed by my brother, Rickie, who told police that I helped him kill our parents. After three years under house arrest, with a GPS tracking device strapped to my ankle, I was finally set free. I honestly believed, while hoping and praying for this very moment, that to be exonerated would be the greatest moment of my life and my troubles would be behind me.

I was wrong. Now that the trial was over—and the distractions of building a legal defense were out of the way—I could see, with a fresh pair of eyes, the devastation that growing up as Richard Alfred Kananen Sr.'s daughter had left behind. It was like looking at a bombed-out war zone. Nothing was left and I had to rebuild my life from scratch. My parents were dead. Rickie was in jail and my sister, Cheryl, was convinced of my guilt. I still had Susan, my life partner of over twenty years, but even that relationship was strained to the point of almost breaking from the stress of the trial. My future looked pretty bleak, on what should have been the "happiest" day of my life.

For the first time ever, I decided to go to therapy. Until then, I kept the bizarre story of life with my father bottled up inside of me because I saw no need to talk about it. I only told, on the witness stand, the absolute bare minimum of my life story—just enough to make sure that I was exonerated—and then only at the insistent urging of my defense attorney. It was done. The abuse was over. I survived it, and I preferred to move forward, never looking back.

I could tolerate the frequent headaches, caused by being slammed up against so many walls; the ulcers, from eating myself up inside; the painful and difficult menstrual cycles, from the damage done to my internal organs by years of sexual abuse. I could tolerate being unable to sleep deeply, as long as nothing evil happened anymore during the night. All of that I could live with, because it was mild in comparison to how I got to be that way. As long as my life was no longer in danger, life was a piece of cake and I was fine.

Therapy was difficult, at first. It was bad enough that I was forced to share intimate life experiences in a trial that aired on national television, stories that I had never even shared with Susan, because I never wanted her to feel my pain. Now I had to tell it all to a stranger who wasn't about to let me get away with my lifesaving avoidance techniques and coping mechanisms. I found it more difficult to talk about these incidents than to actually experience them. When they were happening, they were suddenly and violently forced on me—so they couldn't be avoided—but to think about them later and tell someone, *I* had control over whether they got to be relived.

It was easier to live through the pain and brutality and try to forget about it than it was to analyze ways that I had somehow allowed it to happen. Never mind that the first time I was molested, I was four and I couldn't fight my father off. Never mind that he was a madman who did, literally, whatever he wanted. Never mind that even my mother, a full-grown adult, was too frightened to defy him when he came toward her own children.

Never mind all that: I still felt it was my fault that I had been abused. If only I had done something to stop him. If only I had told someone along the way. If only I had run away when I was old enough. I could drive myself crazy, second-guessing, and that's why I finally decided to go to therapy, so I could stop torturing myself with the question I'd never find an answer for: "If only . . ."

The problem with "if only" is that abusers have their own "if onlys": "If only you would do what you're told, I wouldn't have to hit you." We who are abused are told that we're getting what we deserve. We learn that no one would help us because no one would believe us. And if we did dare to ask for help and it backfired, we had better be prepared to face the consequences of death, or worse. In my father's house, there really was a "fate worse than death." There were times I wished he would just kill me and get it over with.

People who haven't experienced abuse have trouble understanding. They ask questions like, "Well, why didn't you just leave? I would never have put up with that!" Worse yet, some accuse my mother by saying, "If I was your mother, I would have done everything I could to protect my kids! What sort of horrible mother lets her children be raped and beaten?" Those who have not experienced the trauma of abuse simply don't understand that people like my mom know that the consequences for defending the children could be worse than what the kids are already experiencing. What happens if he kills her, for example, and who will keep her children from even worse abuse? At least she can take a beating for them once in a while, or tend to their wounds after he's done with them. Abusers have the power to convince their victims that there is nowhere to go, no one who cares, and no one who would ever help. And what happens if she does leave? There's the knowledge that he will *absolutely* track her down and punish her in ways more heinous than she can imagine. Of that, there is no doubt, at all.

There are those who just don't understand the mind games that people like my mom play in their own heads, just to get through the day. Typically, victims convince themselves, "It's not that bad. We're still alive. It could be worse." They build these bizarre little internal worlds where they honestly believe that. They're gradually eased into these awful scenarios, like lobsters in a cooking pot: "Yes, it's getting a little hot, but I'm sure it won't get any hotter." Before they know it, they can't escape and they get boiled alive.

Most important, people who've never been abused don't understand that a woman who is courageous enough to stand up to and leave a severely abusive man is probably not going to get involved with him in the first place. Abusers don't make it very far into relationships with people who won't take their crap. It's a twisted cycle that can't be understood from the outside, and talking to a therapist who didn't grow up this way is a difficult and shame-filled process.

When I saw an article in the newspaper in October 2010, seven months after my trial, about a two-year-old girl who had been returned to her abusive parents after fighting for her life in the ICU, I felt all those years of bottled-up rage that I was not allowed to feel for myself come pouring out. According to the story, "Doctors found fractured ribs, a severed pancreas, bite marks on her buttocks and thigh, and a fork-shaped burn on her knee."[1] She was returned to her home because there was no way of knowing which parent had hurt her! That's when I knew that I was correct in my decision to share my story to help save kids like me and families like my own. Otherwise, all of our suffering will have been and will continue to be in vain.

---

1 Alexandra Zayas, "Child Abuse Case Is Dropped," *St. Petersburg Times*, October 20, 2010, p. 3B.

CHAPTER 2

A Safe Haven

Susan and I moved to Hudson, Florida, north of Tampa, in February 2004, several weeks after our lives in Orlando exploded with tragedy and horror. My older brother, Rickie, was arrested two days before Christmas for murdering both of our parents, Richard Sr. and Marilyn Kananen. The murders happened fifteen years apart: Our father's body was buried under my parents' garage floor in 1989, after spending several months in a freezer. Mom, who lived just down the block from Susan and me, disappeared in September 2003 and—without my knowing— was buried in my own backyard that same year. I couldn't bear to live in that house or in Orlando.

A couple hours west on State Road 50, Susan's parents, Ed and Ann Kirk, who were embroiled in an ugly divorce at the time, both owned Gulf Coast Resort, a nudist resort in Hudson. This wouldn't have been my first choice for a place for us to start over, but it was our only option. We needed to go somewhere where at least one of us had family. I couldn't hold down a job, given the state of mind I was in. I had also just been released from the psych ward after trying to commit suicide—my brother, knowing the police were onto him, had convinced me that I would be implicated in the murder and suicide was our only option. Fortunately, the Orlando police, who were following us, found and rushed me, almost dead, to the hospital where I was treated and Baker Acted (involuntarily admitted for observation). Rickie, who was conscious when they arrived, was taken to jail after a brief checkup in the ER. That night, after Rickie implicated himself in both murders, Orange County Sheriff's Office crime scene technicians dug up my backyard to find Mom's body, after they dug up Mom's garage floor to find our father's desiccated corpse.

I needed to move away from the toxic environment I had found myself in, and so we made our way from Orlando to Susan's mother's house in Hudson.

Ann ran the resort from her three-bedroom home in the nudist housing development adjacent to the resort because it was hard for her to get to the office due to a severe case of cervical spondylosis, aggravated by her own injuries from past physical abuse. The disease took over her spine and left her unable to walk. Ann was disabled, physically, but not mentally. She was sharp as a tack and just as prickly.

Gulf Coast Resort, or GCR, and the adjacent housing subdivision, City Retreat, covered about a hundred acres.

The resort had RV sites, rental units, and tent sites. Add a pool, hot tub, clubhouse, the office/restaurant, and lots of live oak trees draped with Spanish moss, and that pretty much describes the park. City Retreat included mostly prefab homes and double-wide trailers, many of which were only occupied when their "snowbird" inhabitants traveled south for the winter. Contrary to what most people think, there was not a lot of excitement, just people living their everyday lives without clothes.

Until we moved there, I hadn't spent much time at the resort. I didn't see anything wrong with nudism, necessarily, but I also didn't yearn to participate. Susan and I had created a life for ourselves and settled into a beautiful home a couple of hours away, in Orlando, where my mom, sister, brother, and I all continued to reside after my father "left" in 1988. I met Susan shortly after his disappearance, so I had more of a reason to stay in town. Susan and I both found jobs at Disney World, and we liked Orlando, so we settled there. But following my mother's murder, living in the cute little house in Orlando where we had moved less than a year earlier to be closer to Mom and a couple miles from Cheryl's family numbed me to the core. I had to get out. I couldn't bear looking at the backyard or even out the front yard, from where we could see Mom's house. We had spent so much time fixing up our home and now it was a graveyard.

The summer before my mom's disappearance, Rickie, Susan, and I had spent months landscaping the yard. We pulled up the rotted, old boards that made up a walkway around the pool and replaced it with white gravel. It was starting to look just as we wanted, and we hosted pool parties for the family. Because we had such a great time working together, Rickie and I decided to launch a landscaping business, with Cheryl's husband, Chris. We were just working on starting the business when Mom disappeared.

Rickie, who helped pay bills by taking on jobs as a freelance electrician, started purchasing the tools and supplies we'd need and opened a couple bank accounts. He handled everything because, as he explained to me, he had experience opening his own business. I was relieved and glad to let him do it because I still had a full-time job and it was nice to have someone with experience taking care of all of the details. We didn't have any clients yet, but I was excited and hopeful—and incredibly naïve about what Rickie was really doing with those bank accounts. It was all of the money juggling that he was using them for that made the police suspect me, along with him, in my mother's death.

On New Year's Eve 2003, a few days after I was released from the hospital, Susan and I were heading to GCR in Hudson to visit Ann. As we tried to leave the house, we saw news trucks camped out in front, waiting to get some footage or an interview. But as soon as we looked out the front living room window and saw that they had gone to my mother's house down the block, we hopped in the car. Unfortunately, we had to drive past Mom's house to get to the freeway, and when they saw us, they hauled ass after us.

Susan zipped in and out of freeway traffic on I-4, with

me screaming at her from the passenger seat to slow down. Once we lost them, I said, "I can't go back to work at Disney. I don't want to be in this house. I can't deal with all this drama." I needed to quit my job and leave the house that now reminded me of my painful loss.

She announced, "I already decided, we can move to my mother's." During that New Year's trip, Susan and I agreed to move in February to Hudson, which would give us about a month to pack up our lives and take care of any loose ends. Susan went back to work for a month, and I only traveled from the bed to the kitchen to make coffee in the morning, to my chair in the living room until she came home in the evenings. I didn't answer the door or the phone while she was gone. I wanted to be left alone. The dreadfulness of the situation brought back old coping mechanisms—shutting down and retreating inward—which were so thoroughly taught to me by my father, whom we kids fearfully referred to as "the monster" when he wasn't within earshot.

But even those old tools, which served me well all those years, couldn't drown out the thoughts that kept screaming out that my mom was dead. "My mom is dead, *murdered* by my brother. He buried her *right there*, in my *backyard*! And I'm the one who brought Rickie back into her life. I'm the one who tracked him down after he was gone for so long and found him living in squalor, after his marriage broke up. It was me who invited him to live with us, to thank him for trying to protect me from our father as we were growing up. God, if only . . ."

That same January, Cheryl had a service for our mother,

who had been cremated. I asked my attorney, Michael Gibson, whom Susan and Ann hired because Ann insisted on it, if I could attend the service. Michael advised me not to. He asked me, "Do you want to start a scene?" Of course I didn't, but I wanted to pay my respects and mourn my mother's awful death. Unfortunately, I also had to consider whether I would be looked at as being guilty if I didn't attend. Yes, I wanted to keep the peace, but I didn't want them to be suspicious of me just because I didn't go to the funeral. He said, "I wouldn't go. If they come and harass you about it you tell them your attorney said you weren't going." Meantime, my father's remains had been cremated, but neither Cheryl nor I wanted to take them when they were offered to us. I don't know what became of them.

No matter how hard I tried to shut out the unbearable agony of what had happened in my own house, within my own family, I just couldn't do it. Just like I couldn't protect my mom all those years while my father treated her so cruelly and inhumanely, I couldn't protect her from her own son, whom I had invited to move in with us when he needed a place to stay. I tortured myself nonstop with "if only . . ."

I threw myself into the task of moving, but part of that dreaded process was tackling Rickie's room, so Susan helped me in the evenings. In his closet, I found four of my credit cards, which I never used—I only had them for emergencies. They had my signature on the back. I put them away and wondered, "What was he doing with these?"

I ignored the porn that I found and looked through his file cabinets to find out about our business bank account and his own account for Emerald Electric, to which he had added me as a signer. All of the banking information was gone. Then Susan found a handwritten manuscript for a book that he was writing, titled *The Scales of Justice*. I was only able to read the first few sentences before I became sick to my stomach and had to put it down. It was a dreadfully graphic description of how it feels to choke someone to death and watch the life leave the person's body. Susan said, "We have to give this to the police."

She called to tell them what we had found, and Detective Mark Hussey came by to pick it up. I asked him if the police had the missing bank account records, and he said, "We don't have any of those records. We thought you were hiding them." I walked Hussey—an officious, square-headed man with a face like a bulldog—to my kitchen, and I said, "I bet they're all in that shredder," which was overflowing. Rickie had been up shredding papers a couple nights before he was arrested for our parents' murders. I didn't think anything of it. Susan shreds papers; it's no big deal.

Early in January when—thank God—Susan was home, Rickie's public defender, Gerod Hooper, knocked on the door. Rickie had been in jail for a couple weeks and had stopped eating and taking the meds they were feeding to him. He was being examined to see if he was competent to stand trial and was putting on quite a show: starving himself, smearing himself with his own feces, and claiming to hear our father's voice. He wasn't doing well and his lawyer hoped I would help. I couldn't do it. *I* could barely choke down a sandwich and wasn't doing much better than he was. Even if I wasn't so mad at him, I wouldn't have done him any good.

Then, to make matters worse, we got another visit in late January as we were finishing up packing the house, from Detective Hussey. At the time, I was unsure how he felt about me because when Susan and I asked him, weeks earlier, about getting my truck and Susan's computer back, he wasn't very friendly. Everything was moving so fast, and I was still trying to figure out what was happening. So when he showed up again, I didn't know what to think.

He saw that we were packing and he said, "I see that you're moving, and I don't blame you. However, there is no statute of limitation on murder, and I will arrest you one day."

I responded to him that I was going to call my attorney, Michael Gibson. He replied by saying that Michael knew he was there. I refused to let him see how his words affected me, but after he drove away, I freaked out and called my lawyer, asking why on earth he would let Hussey visit me like that and not at least give me a heads-up that he was coming. Gibson said, "I don't know anything about this. If it happens again, don't let him in the house and call me."

Even so, I knew that I would now be living under Hussey's constant scrutiny. On this visit and during subsequent interactions, he was scary, intimidating, and apparently out to get me. Everything I did or would do in the future would be suspect, and slanted to fit into his ideas of who I was.

The constant barrage of journalists, the threats and accusations—and, worse yet, my mother's horrible grave in my backyard—made it impossible to attempt to wrap my mind around what had happened to my family, and thankfully Susan and I were able to get out of there, but not before letting all of the appropriate officials know where we were going, with addresses and phone numbers so it wouldn't look like we were skipping town. We packed up our things and moved to Hudson.

Although I didn't know it at the time, as we were packing up our life in Orlando, preparations for our arrival at Gulf Coast Resort involved the entire staff. One of the rental units, an old one-bedroom mobile home on the lot next to Ann's house, was not in use because it needed extensive repairs. Up until then, it had been used mostly for storage, so it was close and stuffy in there. There was a bigger place in the park, a small one-bedroom house, that we could move into, but it was being rented until the end of the season when the snowbirds went home, so we were going to stay in the trailer until the house was vacant that spring.

When Susan and I first arrived at Gulf Coast Resort, I didn't know about the resort's gossip grapevine, and that everyone knew everything about everybody. They knew who was screwing who, who was late on their rent, who drank too much—you name it, they knew it. In February, when snowbird season was in full swing, there were plenty of people around to gossip about the news stories and articles that were filtering in from Orlando. And I had just unwittingly become fresh meat, the subject of incredible speculation. They were presented with their very own real-life murder mystery, and I was the unfortunate and unwilling star.

GCR residents had read and heard about my attempted suicide in their local paper and from Orlando newspapers online. News reports came out on December 23, 2003, the day after Rickie persuaded me, in my fragile state, to join him in ending it all. Unfortunately, resort residents in Hudson had their heads filled with ideas about me and my family before I was able to settle in there. Once they caught wind of what was happening to the resort owner's daughter's girlfriend, they checked the online news reports daily. Some even set up Google Alerts to e-mail them anytime my name was mentioned in the news. The Orlando media quoted neighbors and others who just wanted to share their theories on the murders and my family. Some said that my mother didn't want me living near her and that she felt like I was watching her. In fact, my mother had said these things about Rickie, but when these people were questioned about it with my name thrown into the mix, I was added in to their statements. In the eyes of the media, the public, and my future neighbors, I was already guilty.

An *Orlando Sentinel* article called Rickie a "ne'er-do-well" who killed our mother for her money—$250,000, which she had inherited from her father when he died just before Rickie came to live with us. They also said that Rickie had been planning my mother's murder for weeks before her death.

Worse yet, they talked about that aborted suicide attempt in December. The papers didn't mention the fact that Rickie walked away from it unscathed and I was hospitalized for days. They focused on one line, taken out of context, that I wrote in my suicide note, "We had a part in Mother's leaving." Those words would haunt me for years.

It bothered me that people thought of Rickie as a "ne'er-do-well." They didn't know him as a person and were making judgments about him with practically no information. While I was angry with him in a way that words can't express for killing our mother and implicating me in it, he was still my big brother, whom I loved. The mixed feelings I felt for him, and still feel for him, are one of the hardest things to deal with.

He wasn't a "ne'er-do-well"; he was mentally ill! It had become obvious, since December 2003, that he was deeply disturbed. He spent twelve pages of his manuscript rewriting the strangulation scene, and it just got more gruesome.

While he lived with me and Susan, we were blind to his mental illness. I didn't see the signs that he was going off the deep end. "Normal," to me, wasn't the same as normal to everyone else. Normal, in our family, was having a father who would make us sit in a chair and throw sharp knives for us to dodge, just for fun, and hold our mother's head underwater in the pool, in front of us, until she was almost dead. If we dared to interfere we got it just as bad as she did. In comparison, Rickie looked downright saint-like and sane.

Ann knew the resort was a gossipy place and I was fresh meat. Once I realized, in the days after I arrived, that I had a ready-made reputation at the resort, I stayed holed up in Ann's house for a week or so while we waited for the trailer next door to be finished because I didn't want to come out. I wasn't about to let anyone see the anguish I was feeling. And no one was going to see me cry. This was my modus operandi; while growing up in the Kananen house I learned that showing fear or emotion guaranteed a more thorough and vicious beating. My father's psychotic frenzy fed on reactions that he saw as weakness.

CHAPTER 3

The Earliest Years

I mostly remember my dad's enormous size—he was over six feet tall, and weighed more than three hundred pounds—his military-style haircut, and his terrible voice. His personality was a cross between the drill instructor from the movie *Full Metal Jacket* and the Terminator, with his ruthless and relentless brutality.

There was instant violence in this man. He could suddenly turn on you and tear you apart, sometimes for no reason at all. He beat us, just for his own kicks. If he felt like smacking someone around, whoever was in the room would do. Other times, all it took was for something minor to go wrong, like lumps in the mashed potatoes, and he'd start looking around for the nearest scapegoat to blame and take his anger and aggression out on. He had the same blank, dark stare and he never smiled. When he escalated to violence, it didn't change. He always just had those . . . black eyes.

For the most part there was no "Nice Daddy." But some days were better than others. In fact, the only way I could tell whether it was going to be a good or a bad day was by what he was drinking in the morning. If he was drinking coffee, it wouldn't be too bad. And if he was drinking a milkshake, it meant that he had been drinking hard the night before and was too hungover to function. He'd then spend the day sleeping and we didn't have to be subjected to his anger. But if he started the morning with vodka, look out. We all knew someone was going to get it that day, even though each of us would try to avoid him like the plague.

Remember when you were a child and you were afraid to go to bed at night without the night-light on, or begged for the door to be left open a crack? Remember how afraid you were of the monsters under your bed, or the boogeyman looking through your window, waiting for you to fall asleep so he could break in and carry you away? Remember how badly you wanted your parents to come and rescue you? My father *was* that boogeyman. He *was* that monster under the bed—*in* the bed. No mommy or daddy was going to come and rescue us because it was Daddy who was causing the pain and terror, and Mommy had been beaten into submission, too afraid to try to rescue us. Every night, every single night, we all turned in knowing that someone in the house may be attacked, dreading the sound of footsteps stopping outside our own door and a turning doorknob. The longer it had been since my father's last nocturnal visit to my room, the more the suspense became unbearable, because he was sure to come in, eventually. Usually he would wait until the bleeding had stopped from the previous incident, but not always.

There's a well-known painting called *The Scream*, by Edvard Munch, which depicts a man on a bridge, shrieking in anguish. Munch said about his painting, "I sensed an infinite scream passing through nature." If you could look at this painting, and empathically feel what the artist felt, you might know what it was like to be experiencing pure terror—constant, never-ending sheer terror, even in the moments when there is no one torturing you, because you know it's only a matter of time before it begins again. You wear a normal-looking face, but your inner face is screaming. This is how I felt every day of every year of my childhood. It is why no single happy memory exists.

There wasn't a lot of talking and reminiscing going on in our household, and we were kept out of contact with any relatives who might have been able to tell us about our parents or ancestors. I don't even know the names of my father's parents. My mom's older brother, Larry, told me after Mom died that my father hated females because he watched his dad work until the day he died, and my father didn't agree with supporting women. Knowing this piece of information adds a piece to the puzzle, because our father never held down a job. He worked a little when they first got married and when I was born, and when we were in Maine he started filing for disability. He had a "bad back."

Mom didn't talk very much. She was a ghostlike figure throughout the years, taking care of the house and keeping it immaculate—it was the only thing in the house she had any control over. She tried, like everyone else, to stay invisible. We all stayed out of his way, preferably in another room, and never started a conversation with him unless absolutely necessary. I have no idea what attracted Mom to him in the first place. I remember seeing pictures of my parents on CNN's *In Session*. There was a photo of my father, presumably from his late teens or early twenties, that I had never seen before. The picture, which was shown when my trial was aired, revealed a very handsome young man of average build. Seeing him looking young and handsome was very jarring to me, as I only ever knew him as fat and scary. Another picture of Mom and a very young Rickie showed that Mom was quite beautiful. It is entirely likely that it was purely physical attraction, as young love so often is, so I guess I could understand what drew a naïve teenage girl to him.

While they didn't go to the same high school, they married when she was in her teens, and my brother, Richard Alfred Kananen Jr., was born only a month after her eighteenth birthday. A good Irish Catholic girl, she married the boy who got her pregnant, and he never let her live it down. We heard it all the time. He acted as though she tricked him, and he took no responsibility for being one of the necessary parties to that pregnancy.

I've learned that, in many abusive relationships, the abuser holds back his or her true self until the abusee is well under control, so it is conceivable that Mom didn't know his true nature until it was too late to get out, like that lobster in a cooking pot I mentioned earlier. Teenage girls sometimes put up with abuse if their man "loves" them. If he was beating her, then apologizing, "Oh baby, I'm so sorry, it'll never happen again, I was just so upset," she may have felt so much love from him in his remorse and tenderness that she stayed for the next time. "It'll never happen again" happens again and again, and after a while abusive men stop saying that. They realize she's not going anywhere—they have her now. They start saying, "Oh, it's *gonna* happen again if you cross me." Considering her very young age and the times, it's possible that my mom simply didn't know to watch out for the red flags that experienced, adult women recognize.

If other early pictures of my parents still exist, I am entirely unaware of them. My mom's collection of family photos was thrown away when Rickie was clearing out her house after he killed her, so most of our family history ended up in a landfill.

I can only imagine what Rickie had to endure for eight years, until Cheryl was born in 1964. At least once she and I were born, the abuse was spread around a little more and he didn't have to take it all himself. Even though his manuscript was supposedly fiction, I recognize our father's personality and some stories from our childhood. His book told a story of a little boy named Richard, whose father, named Dick, beat his mother to the point of unconsciousness after she interfered in a "learning lesson"—a severe thrashing—that the father was administering to the boy.

In Rickie's novel, the father realized, once he saw her bloody and unconscious on the floor, that he had gone too far, and he told the boy to take a pitcher of orange juice out of the refrigerator and drop it on the floor. The boy was then told to call an ambulance and tell the EMTs, when they arrived, that his mother had slipped in the spilled juice and hurt herself. In the meantime, the father left the house. He returned after the ambulance had arrived and pretended to be surprised and horrified to find his wife so gravely injured. Rickie ends that story with a poignant observation, another thing I recognize as the kind of thing our father would do after an incident like that, that Dick gave the boy a "look of triumph . . . smug arrogance."

This story was not fiction. I heard about it from my mother—she said it happened sometime before I was born.

It broke my heart to read that story in his manuscript, because I know those characters very well. But even worse was the section immediately after that story, where he tells of the little boy's conversation with his mother, after she comes home from the hospital. She tells him that he has to learn to hide everything from his father, in order to avoid a brutal "learning lesson." The two of them agree to a sort of pact, to never let Dick know what they are thinking or feeling, and Richard makes the mother promise to never get in between them again, to never protect her son from his father. He also makes her promise to never cry again until they are free. He tells her, in a monotone voice, that he loves her but he will never say it again. They are now playing a game to win her freedom from Dick. The little boy then walks down the hall, sees his reflection in the bathroom mirror, and shatters it with his fist, as the mother cries for the loss of her child's soul, "his caring for humanity."

At my trial in 2010, Rickie told a story on the witness stand about the time he and our father were fixing a car. My brother didn't do something right, so my father dropped the jack and set the car right on top of my brother. He told Mom, "Don't help him. Let him figure it out." I don't know how he got out. I never heard. My mother told me that story. She just stood in the entryway into the house and watched. She didn't know what to do. I never understood how she could just stand there and do nothing, even though I know how much she feared him.

By the time I came around it was just understood: you watched what he did and when you got emotional it got worse. When you didn't, the "learning lesson" subsided more quickly. He wasn't getting any joy if he wasn't getting any tears. But if Rickie's story in his book, about the pact that the boy made with the mother, is true—and I don't know that it is—I don't understand why he hated my mother enough to kill her, if they had made these agreements. Whether they actually had that conversation or not, there seemed to be something in him that wished that they had. But I guess I'll never know.

These stories happened before I was born, and my father had already been in and out of prison in Arizona, convicted of four counts of forgery and sentenced to seven to ten years. He spent three years there, from 1962 to 1965, before he managed to be released on appeal, due to a technicality over the legality of the police search. For God only knows what reason, Mom went back to him when he got out.

If only . . .

CHAPTER 4

Monson, Maine

State Road 50, in Florida, runs east–west from the city of Weeki Wachee—with its live "mermaid" shows on the Gulf Coast—to Cape Canaveral and the Kennedy Space Center on the Atlantic Coast. The land mass is narrow enough that, on a clear day, Space Shuttle launches could be seen from the Gulf side of the state. To drive from one coast to the other takes less than three hours, as long as you don't get stuck in traffic in Orlando, which lies just a little east of center, closer to the Atlantic.

Both Gulf Coast Resort, in Hudson, and the house I shared with Susan on Okaloosa Avenue, in Orlando, are just a few miles south of SR 50, so it's a pretty easy shot to drive from one to the other. In 2003, Mom still lived in the house she bought with my father in 1977, near the intersection of Okaloosa and Alachua Street—just around the corner from me, Susan, and Rickie. Walt Disney World, where Susan and I both worked, is about thirty miles south.

We loved working for Disney and had been employed there for over ten years when Mom was killed. I worked in food service, an area of expertise in which I particularly excel. If I worked in your restaurant, you could rest assured that it would be spotlessly clean and absolutely ready for a health code inspector's surprise visit. This was a trait I picked up from Mom, who was obsessively clean. In fact, she was fanatical about keeping her house in order. It was this work ethic that I brought with me into any restaurant in which I worked, since I was seventeen at my first job at McDonald's.

Susan worked mostly in the Disney retail shops. She is, by nature, a happy person, and her loud and friendly laugh made customers feel welcomed. Susan is a natural at customer service, with her fun-loving delight in all things girly. She thrived, working among the toys and figurines and cute Disney apparel.

Those peaceful years between 1988 and 2003, between my father's disappearance and my mother's death, reflected Disney's theme as "The Happiest Place on Earth." I finally had the life I always wished for during my wretched childhood: my father was gone and Mom was safe and nearby, and her dad moved down from Massachusetts in 1989, after his wife died, to live with her. My grandpa was a very sweet old man, and we finally got to know him, after years of isolation from our extended family. I found a loving relationship when Susan and I met shortly after my father disappeared, my sister lived just a few miles away with her husband and three kids, and no one went out of their way to hurt me. Susan and I were doting aunts, especially with Cheryl's son—the boy who had my heart—Daniel. I loved seeing Daniel and his sisters having a normal, happy life.

Susan and I loved Disney, and our cute four-bedroom bungalow was a shrine. Every shelf, nook, and cranny was stuffed to overflowing with Disney figurines and knick-knacks. Mom's house was similarly packed with Disney souvenirs, as we all spent many happy days there, oftentimes taking Cheryl's kids with us to the theme park.

Susan's favorite character was Mickey Mouse, and the personality she showed others reflected that choice. Seemingly happy-go-lucky and guileless, Susan was always full of sunshine and smiles, unless you pissed her off (then her Inner Ann came out and she became her mother's daughter). People tell me that I more accurately reflect my favorite character, Donald Duck: I guess I'm a little more sassy and suspicious.

Because my past was riddled with land mines and ambushes, my high-strung reflexes always kept me on guard. Even in my sleep, I was stiff as a board, ready to spring out of bed to flee, if necessary. My earliest life experiences caused the development of my constant and diligent fight-or-flight mode. Even as a toddler in California, where I was born in 1966, I knew life was dangerous. My father had not yet started using me as his punching bag, but I certainly witnessed him slapping Mom and Rickie around.

The violence in our home got so bad that our apartment

complex manager, Clarence—whose wife made wonderful cookies that she shared with us kids—told Mom that if she ever needed a place to escape, she could count on them. Instead, our family moved to Maine. My father had a keen sense of when neighbors were on to him, and he had no problem uprooting the family and moving across the country with us.

It was in the picturesque little town of Monson, Maine, that my family spent the next few years, from about 1969 to 1974, and where my personal hell began. Monson, a town of a few hundred people, lies near the northernmost end of the Appalachian Trail and is one of the last stopping points for supplies before heading north for the last stretch of that famous hike.

One particular day in the summer of 1973 was a day when Monson residents might have been debating whether to close the windows and turn on the air-conditioning because the temperature was just this side of too hot. Elton John might have been singing "Crocodile Rock" on one station, or "Tubular Bells" might have been playing on another. It would have been a lovely day for a swim in Lake Hebron at the community beach just south of town. That's what would have appeared to be happening with us two little girls, who were on the shore of the lake, with our dad.

If you were a resident of Monson, you might have recognized us as one of the families who lived up on Tenney Hill Road. If you were a neighbor, you might have known that the younger girl on the shore, the towheaded blonde with pigtail braids, was six-year-old Stacey, and the older girl was her eight-year-old sister, Cheryl. You'd also have known that their mom would have been at work because it was the middle of the week and their dad stayed home with the kids, living off of disability. You might have even formed your own opinions about that disability, especially after seeing him load and unload his teenage son's fishing boat out of the back of his pickup truck all by himself.

Either way, you probably would have gone on about your everyday life because what the Kananen family did was none of your business. After all, poor, sweet Marilyn had it hard enough, and Richard was not the kind of man you messed with, because you were a little afraid of him. He was a heavy drinker, and the sounds that came out of that house told you that he smacked his family around. It was obvious that they were desperately poor and could use every penny they could get. In a town that small, it was hard to not know which families were on government assistance, and if Richard wanted to risk defrauding the government, well, that was no skin off your nose.

After all, none of us kids or our mother ever complained about any abuse. No one ever had any bruises to show for all of the suspicious noises. There was no way for anyone outside of the home to know that our father was very good at what he did. He knew how to hit and not leave bruises in visible areas. He knew how to knock the wind out of you by thumping you "just so" in the chest in a way that left no mark. And he knew how to make you so afraid of opening your mouth that you didn't dare talk back, protest, or—God forbid—tell anyone.

All three of us kids had learned to dread summer vacation. Any time off from school, including Christmas and

Easter break, didn't mean "no more pencils, no more books." It meant being home, alone, with our father.

Mom worked Monday through Friday, while he stayed home. Her presence certainly didn't prevent him from doing whatever he wanted, but her absence made him more bold in lording his power over us kids, especially the sexual abuse, which he did behind closed doors—even if that closed door meant locking Mom out of the house while he had his way with whichever of us was unlucky enough to strike his fancy that day. No school meant he had all day to play his cat and mouse games, and we had no break all summer from his sadistic abuse until school began again in the fall.

That gorgeous afternoon, just before my seventh birthday, Cheryl and I climbed into our father's pickup truck when he ordered us to get in and sit down. We sat quietly as he drove to the public shoreline area of Lake Hebron.

It wasn't a beach as much as a pleasant, grassy break in the trees that hugged the shoreline all the way around the lake. There was no pier, just a small patch of sand at the water's edge. Locals could drive their boats to the shore of the lake and launch from there, and picnickers would throw down their blankets on the grass and swim in the crystal clear water. About thirty feet from shore was a floating deck that experienced swimmers would use as a diving platform into water that was deep enough to be safe for diving, but not so deep that they couldn't see the bottom.

Father backed his truck up to the shore and curtly ordered us out. His bad back didn't stop him from heaving the fishing boat from the back of the truck and into the water. The three of us climbed in, no one saying a word. He started the little outboard motor and steered his way to the diving platform, where he told Cheryl and me to get out. Neither of us knew how to swim, so we were very careful climbing out of the wobbly boat as we silently made our way up onto the deck. Cheryl, who was bigger than me, got out first and helped me to clamber out of the boat, up the ladder and onto the searing hot wooden platform.

Not daring to dance our burning feet off of the hot deck, we watched, confused, as our father turned the boat around and headed back toward shore. We had no idea what was happening, and we had no reason to trust him, so fear began to set in. He shouted back to us, over the noise of the motor, "If you want to come home, make your way to shore. You're either going to swim or you're going to starve. Or you're going to drown if you can't make it."

Cheryl and I sat at the edge of the platform for a long while, as he waited in the truck drinking a beer and smoking a cigar, until we realized he really wasn't coming back for us. We knew it was either sink or swim, and we had to get to shore before he left us there and went home. We knew he'd do it, too, if we took too long. Plus, we were only wearing shorts and T-shirts, and the Maine nights were cold, even in the summertime. We knew we'd end up sleeping out there, because he wouldn't tell Mom where we were and we didn't dare to ask anyone else for help. To ask for help, to draw attention . . . well, even at our tender ages, we knew better than to do that.

We finally climbed cautiously into the cool water, clutching the ladder, hearts pounding and filled with dread—seeing the bottom far, far away—and pushed off from the deck, instinct kicking in with a furious natural impulse to dog-paddle. We learned quickly, after a few slips of our heads below the surface, how it burns to inhale water. That pain spurred us forward, our little arms and legs churning away. Cheryl would sometimes get ahead of me, but when she noticed that there was too great a distance, she would roll over on her back and float, waiting for me to catch up. She had learned that trick from watching Mom swim: when you get tired, turn over and float.

It was a long, arduous struggle toward shore. It felt like miles away—our lungs stinging and sides aching, sheer panic moving us forward—but we eventually made our exhausted way back to the truck, only to find our father was furious.

It was chillingly clear to me that he had been hoping we wouldn't make it. He was mad that we were still alive! Yes, two fewer mouths to feed would sound appealing to him, and he could always say that he was trying to teach us to swim and we accidentally drowned. But did he really hate us so much that he wanted us dead?

He hauled the boat back into the bed of the truck and slammed the door behind us after we climbed into the cab. All he said was, "Shut up. Don't talk," and when we got home, he simply barked, "Change your clothes."

Up until this event, my response to his behavior was usually fear. But it was this day, at the tender age of six, that I felt a shift. I remember feeling, for the first time, reciprocal anger and hatred for my father, and a stubborn refusal to die—a child's equivalent of "Fuck you!" to the man who demanded obedience simply because he was bigger. "Fuck you, you can't kill me. No matter what you throw at me, fuck you, I'm going to live."

By this time, he had already been tearing me apart with his sexual abuse for almost three years. The first time was on my fourth birthday, in 1970. My father sat me on his lap and introduced me to sips of beer. Then after I was drunk, he began the first in a series of cruel attacks that would continue until his disappearance and death eighteen years later, in 1988.

There are some men who violate children by pretending it's a game, a "fun, little secret" that they keep with their "special friends." They rationalize it by telling themselves that they love children. There was none of that with my father.

His attacks were brutal and painful. He wasn't in it for the closeness, as inappropriate as even that may be. This wasn't sex; it was violence that just happened to involve body parts that are supposed to correspond with sex. He made it clear that he owned us kids and our bodies, and whatever he wanted to do to us, no matter how excruciating, was to be tolerated and not argued with. There is no easy way to say this, but at this point he wasn't yet raping me by entering me with his penis. He was using objects, tools, whatever was handy. "Getting me ready," is what he called it. Ready for what, I wouldn't know until we moved to Arkansas.

It's events like this that make forgiveness next to impossible. I hesitate to even tell these details because I do not wish for any of these stories to be even mildly sexual in tone, or to give anyone ideas. I do not wish for pedophiles or child molesters to read what I went through and experience even the slightest bit of arousal. This was not sex and it was by no means consensual. This was torture and there is no excuse for it, no matter how they wish to rationalize their behavior. The only glimmer of possible understanding that I can feel is to realize that a huge number of child abusers were once abused themselves, and are trying to make their experience okay by inflicting it upon someone else. They wish to release the horror of their own abuse by passing it on. All I can say is, I pray that anyone who feels the urge to do such terrible things to a child seeks and finds help before they act on those devastating and irreversibly damaging urges.

I realize now that, as we kids were being owned and physically damaged, so were our psyches. We were taught that we were nothing but playthings to a sadist. By attacking us internally, in the guise of sexual behavior, he was reaching the core of our deepest sense of self, teaching us from the inside out that our humanity was nonexistent to him and, therefore, to us. As tiny, defenseless beings, all we could do while this giant man wielded his terrifying attacks upon us was to lie there and take the searing pain, and try not to cry or scream. To react in this way, the way the human body automatically and naturally responds to torture, only fed his creepy frenzy and made it hurt more.

I wasn't my father's only prey. Rickie testified at my trial that he, too, was subject to our father's sexual abuse. I believe him because more than once I saw my father coming out of Rickie's bedroom fastening his pants, a move I recognized and understood.

Cheryl would state under oath that her memories ended with being led into the bedroom and the door closing behind her—her psyche would allow her no further recollection of what may have happened to her after the door was closed. I, however, remember seeing my father fondling my older sister. Beyond that, I cannot say what happened to Cheryl behind those closed doors, and I respect her privacy enough to not speculate on her experiences with him. I can only assume they were similar to mine. We never talked about it, growing up, and once he was gone, we put our past behind us and didn't bring it up.

It was toward the end of our time in Monson that the family home went up in flames. I have only vague memories of the event, but Mom told me later that all of the family photos that existed, up to that point, burned with the house. Rickie was already in his late teens by this time. He testified at my trial that our father had set our house in Monson on fire and left us kids inside to die. His implication was that our father lit the house ablaze not just for insurance money, but to rid himself of his burdens. Rickie said on the witness stand, in a dull and unaffected voice, that he was the one who saved us girls. He's the one who climbed a ladder, broke the windows, and helped us escape. He said that when he looked to see our parents sitting in the family car, watching, he saw Mom laughing.

Cheryl also testified with her memories of that same story, but with one big difference. Cheryl remembers our parents having a fight, and Mom being severely beaten. She recalls looking out the window of the burning house and seeing our mother in the car, screaming.

CHAPTER 5

The Minnesota Years

After we left Maine in the summer of 1974, we moved to Clarissa, Minnesota. My father loved not having neighbors nearby who might decide to interfere in his activities. We lived four miles from town on a ten-acre farm. That was distance enough to keep us isolated.

We got there the summer before I started third grade, and the abuse escalated. Both my mom and brother had jobs, since Rickie had just graduated high school in Maine. He had his room, we had our room, and I don't remember him ever, ever, being down in the living room watching TV with the family. He always went to his room as soon as he got home. He just stayed to himself.

Cheryl and I were home during the day with my father, so we suffered the majority of his sadistic treatment. My sister, clever thing that she was, made friends quickly and was frequently able to finagle weeklong visits away from home, which left me alone. Oddly, I didn't hold it against her, leaving me with him like that. We all sort of fended for ourselves, although even at six years old I was always concerned about protecting my mother. I took many beatings for her, over the years—as I'm sure Rickie and Cheryl did, too—and even antagonized a few to protect her. Maybe we all instinctively knew that if he killed Mom, we would be left alone with him and—even though she didn't protect us—she was a layer of insulation between us and him. As long as she was alive, we stood a chance. Without her, we'd be dead. I always felt responsible for what was happening to my mom because my father often said I was the accident child: if I wasn't born, they might have been divorced. Whether that was true or just his way to rip me apart, it stuck with me all my life, and I felt constant existential guilt.

Everyone in our house was just trying to survive. We weren't cutthroat, we didn't throw one another under the bus, and we didn't get somebody in trouble to see if they'd get beaten instead of us; we all just tried to stay quiet and invisible, so that maybe we'd get through the day. But while Cheryl was escaping to her friends' houses, and I was alone with him during the week, he would try to have intercourse with me. I was too small, so he would get angry and frustrated, and just jam anything he could find into my vagina. I don't know if he did the same things to Cheryl or not. She and I never talked about it.

If he did not assault her, sexually, I would be very surprised, because one winter my parents were having an extremely violent, bloody fight and, because it cost too much to heat the upstairs, Cheryl and I were sleeping downstairs on cots in our parents' bedroom. He beat Mom severely and forced her to sleep outside, in an old chicken coop that we had transformed into a playhouse (thank God it had a wood stove). At bedtime, Cheryl asked him where Mom was. He said, "She's not here, but you can come to the bed and be the woman of the house." Fortunately, he was too drunk that night to go any further than that. I wish I could say that my personal experience with sexual abuse ended with disgusting, smart-assed comments like that, but it did not. Because of things I was forced to do, I have been unable to swallow pills since I was in about fourth grade. And that's all I have to say about that.

Our father must have had some kind of power over Rickie: maybe it was, "If you fight back I'll kill your mom and sisters." Even though we weren't close in the way many siblings are, I guess in our own way we were close because we looked out for one another. If one of us was getting in trouble, the other would figure out a way to end it. That's the only kind of relationship we ever had.

Rickie was extremely thin until he was well into adulthood. He graduated high school at about 125–130 pounds, and he's over six feet tall. He was tall and gangly, but all muscle. He could pick up one of those big cast-iron stoves, by himself. That says a lot, because if I had my brother's size and strength, I never would have let my father get away with what he did. I remember watching my brother carry huge tire chains into the field where a tractor was stuck and when he got there he was slapped around.

He went to college in Wisconsin for a short time. He says he quit because my father called him and said, "Either you come home or I'm going to kill everybody." I can see my father doing that. I really can. He played that game with all of us. "Either you stay or everybody's dead. Someday I'm going to kill everybody." We all heard that. We all knew that. Leading up to our first Christmas in Clarissa, Mom told me to write to Santa. Excited, I sat right down and wrote a letter. When Christmas Eve came, my father grabbed his shotgun and told me that when Santa landed he would kill him. At about 1:00 A.M., I heard gunshots. When I got up in the morning, I saw blood on the roof and in the yard. I found out later it was animal blood, and he made Rickie put it there, but I thought Santa was dead and the reindeer were killed.

Christmas seemed to trigger him into behaving especially badly. When I was in sixth grade, and Cheryl was in eighth, we were at the dinner table and Cheryl picked up her glass to take a drink, unfortunately with her pinky in the air. She wasn't doing it to "put on airs," but that's how our father saw it. He flew into a rage and decided that she was banned from the dinner table for three weeks, and she would not be allowed to celebrate Christmas. He stormed over to the Christmas tree and stomped on all of her gifts, jumping up and down on them like a child throwing a tantrum, screaming, "Oh, you think you're better than us? You're some princess!" I was furious that he stomped on the gift that I got for her because it wasn't easy to come by gifts for one another.

We didn't have Barbies. Cheryl had a Mickey Mouse doll, with a pull string that made it talk, and I had a Donald Duck that talked, too. We had board games and books, tiddlywinks and jacks, no real toys. We had a tetherball and badminton. I think we just went through the motions. Just something to kill time—"We're home from school. Instead of hanging out in the house, let's go out and play badminton." Out of sight, out of mind. Mom, Cheryl, and I would sit at the kitchen table and play board games.

We learned from harsh experience to take care of our stuff. You didn't leave a toy in the yard if you wanted to keep it. You didn't leave a ball in the yard. You took care of your stuff, you put it away, and everything had a home. Your clothes were washed and dried, and when Mom came back from the Laundromat you damn well better be there to put them away or my father would get involved. The house was spotless. Mom used to wake me and Cheryl on Saturday mornings to help with the housework. My job was to dust every picture frame, and not make a noise, because if my father was sleeping you didn't want to wake him.

Sadly, one of the fondest memories I have of my big sister was during these Minnesota years, when I was in fifth grade. Our parents had been fighting, without respite, for days. He had beaten Mom badly, and just wouldn't stop. Most of the time we were all able to tolerate the violence and live through it, but for some reason this time it just got to me and I couldn't take it anymore. I was sobbing so hard I could barely catch my breath. Cheryl scooped me up on her lap and told me that we can't choose our parents. This is the life that they chose and we can't change how we live. And even though the memory makes me want to cry all over again, it warms my heart to think of my sister taking care of me like that.

It was that comment that made me change my attitude, and taught me to just suck it up and take it. Up until then, if he would beat or molest me, I would cry when he left the room, but never in front of him. When she made that statement she made me realize, "You're right. We can either make the best of it and survive it, or just give up."

I learned, "It is what it is. I'll stare at the ceiling until this is over with." It ends quicker, by being passive. In my sister's case, she'd let it build and keep antagonizing until he exploded on her. My sister decided to be the demonstrative one and I was the passive one in the house.

Cheryl was always a lot stronger than I was. She, in her own feisty way, fought back against his tyranny. She found ways to get out of the house for extended periods by making friends and getting herself invited over. We didn't have friends come to our house very often, because it was too uncomfortable. Even though I didn't fully realize until high school that our household wasn't like everyone else's—we had no way of knowing that all dads weren't like that behind closed doors—I still knew that other kids thought it was strange at our house. We didn't have conversations about anything. We spoke only when necessary.

On the rare occasions that either Cheryl or I could have

somebody spend the night, it was awkward. My friend Karin, who grew up to be a reporter for the local newspaper, wrote an article about one of those nights after she watched my trial on television. She wrote that she didn't remember anything in particular that was unusual about our household, except that she was uncomfortable there and that she treated me differently the next day. She says that I told her that this is why I never had friends over.

She said that, when she saw my trial, I hadn't changed much—that my hair was shorter than the long blond braids I used to wear in school, but that my face still held a sweet, doe-eyed innocence. I look at pictures of myself from those years, which Karin e-mailed to me, and I see myself just as she described, a sweet-faced little girl with long blond hair, with a bright, innocent smile. Little did anyone in my class know what was happening to me at home. I put on such a brave face at school, for two reasons: sheer necessity and actual relief at not being in the line of fire for a few hours.

Karin said what any of our friends must have felt, in what she wrote. It was an uncomfortable feeling and she couldn't figure out what it was. I don't remember the events of the night she wrote about, but I know how my household was. You sat at the table, you didn't speak, you only did what you were told you could do after dinner. He didn't change the rules if you had people over; it didn't matter—his rules were his rules. The only difference was he wouldn't explode and rant and rave and hit people. So it was just awkward. We probably went through a half hour, forty-five minutes of dinner without anyone saying a word. Immediately after dinner, we'd clean up and go upstairs to our room, unless we were told we had to watch TV that night. People don't live their lives that way. They talk to their parents about what went on in school or church that day. We didn't talk about squat and we didn't go to church.

During my childhood, I would say I believed in God, as long as you didn't ask me that in front of my father. We didn't talk about religion in my house. My father hated the Catholic Church. Then a very nice gentleman moved to town, a nondenominational minister. He opened a little church, and my father liked the man: he didn't preach religion to my father, so he let my sister and me do some activities with him for a short while. He took that away from us because we started changing. I think we got more at peace with things in the house, and it was what it was, and he couldn't get the same reaction out of us, so he decided, well, maybe you don't need to be going there anymore. After that, I never thought about God much, other than to wonder what sort of God would allow us to have a life like we had.

My father must have done something to earn a reputation around town with the local ministers, because one night he and my mother were coming home from a bar and he literally drove right into a ditch, in a snowbank, because he was so drunk. One of the local preachers drove by and stopped to help until he saw who they were. They had to beg the preacher to help get them out because he was scared of my father. He went and got them some help, but wouldn't help them himself.

Our father drank vodka when I was older, but he ran the gamut of everything: beer, wine, amaretto, brandy, scotch, and finally vodka became the cheapest at the end. Rickie's novel manuscript was pretty accurate about the specific procedure for fixing our father a drink: fill a tall glass three quarters full of booze with a splash of water. He'd go through at least one large bottle a day, both in Rickie's book and in real life. You'd go into the kitchen and get ice cubes, and wouldn't break any of those ice cubes. You'd better not be able to fit another ice cube but couldn't let the ice stick up above the rim of the glass. It was very precise. And you didn't make it wrong because he'd fling it across the room.

By the time I was halfway through sixth grade, we could probably count on four or five days a week being really bad and still have a couple of good days in the week. Once you get beaten to the point where your attacker knows you can't take anymore, you have to heal before you can take more beatings, or you're going to end up in the hospital and then you're going to have authorities involved. That's just how it is. At some point, bodies have got to heal. You can't keep getting sexually assaulted or you're going to have problems and you're going to have to go to a doctor. Unfortunately, most abusers know this game. I hate to call it that, but it's a game in their minds—just a game.

The only time any of us went to a hospital was when my mother had to have surgery on her feet. Not because he did something to her; she couldn't walk. Her toes were curling in so they had to take off the baby toes of both of her feet. It was some kind of deformity. Otherwise, no doctors. We healed on our own. Whoever needed to heal, for whatever reason, were the ones that got protected for that day. He may have even known who could or couldn't take any more. It may have been something he directed. As time passed, and I got bigger, I could withstand more intense sexual assaults. They became more violent, with my father using many foreign objects to penetrate me.

He was also becoming very brazen, shooting off guns whenever the mood struck. Sometimes he'd take a shotgun and hit Mom across the head with it. Russian roulette with a pistol was a favorite game of his. He would play with each of us separately and his response was always the same, "I guess today is your lucky day." Only it didn't feel lucky. That particular mind game was the hardest of all. Many times I was torn between fear of death and hope that I would die, to be free of this hell.

Every day there was a loaded pistol in one of the rooms, often right on the kitchen table during dinner. If not, he could walk in the bedroom and put his hand on a loaded gun in less than two minutes. He fired them into furniture. A lot of our furniture had bullet holes. It just became part of life. Yeah, there are bullet holes in the furniture. No big deal.

My father actually called the White House once and threatened to kill the president. He told them he had a sawed-off shotgun. Within a couple hours the state police arrived at our farm. Unfortunately for our family, my father—the con artist—convinced the police that he was harmless and just playing a prank.

This is one reason we were never able to get away from him. The police would come to the door and hear, "Oh, everything's fine," and leave. We didn't take that chance in the middle of the country. There were too many guns, and too few witnesses. So we just let the abuse go. It became everyday life. We were in pain all the time. We were the only kids in class who hated summer vacation.

Now he knew no one would believe he was dangerous. He was becoming skilled at hitting us where no one would see the marks on my sister or me, but he didn't care if people in town saw my mom hurt. No one would ever do anything to stop him, not in this small town. He would tie my brother up in snow-tire chains and make him stand outside. He would make my sister and me sit at the kitchen table and throw all kinds of objects at us, including sharp knives. Sometimes these objects would hit us and leave marks or bleeding, but sometimes if we moved our heads quickly enough we wouldn't get hurt. He gave himself points for making us bleed. My mom, on the other hand, I think he wanted to kill. He would beat her almost unconscious, tie her up sometimes, and shoot off a gun to just miss her. At times, she used to beg for him to kill her. In Minnesota, this lasted for three years until my father decided that it was time to move again.

I was in sixth grade, Cheryl was in eighth grade. We were riding the bus home and when it came to our house we saw the U-Haul truck. That was the moment we knew we were moving, and we both started crying. Yelling quick good-byes to our friends who were still on the bus and promising to keep in touch, even though we knew that we probably couldn't, we stepped off the bus. My father was screaming at my mother for sending us to school because he had told her to keep us home. He was hollering and throwing things at my brother because he wasn't loading the truck quickly enough. When my sister and I approached, we were given two hours to pack our rooms and help pack the sheds. Many personal items and family memories were left behind because, in my father's eyes, we were done packing.

Before I knew it, we were in our vehicles and began driving straight south into the night. No one knew where my father would decide to stop the U-Haul. We drove many hours without stopping even to eat. Our destination became a farm in the outskirts of the town of Viola, Arkansas, where we would spend the most volatile six months of our lives. Thank God we all lived to leave that farm in Arkansas, where fear turned to hatred when he finally got his way and raped me for the first time.

CHAPTER 6

Susan Goes First

Our first days at GCR were spent just trying to acclimate ourselves to our new surroundings and new life. I didn't leave the house much, but Susan would go to the pool from time to time. She was more used to the nudist life than I was, and she enjoyed laying out in the sun. I stayed dressed, pretty much all of the time, unless I wanted to use the pool. That was the only place on the grounds where nudity was required. Otherwise, I wore clothes.

We weren't at Gulf Coast Resort two weeks when an officer entered the diner, whose entrance doubled as the guest check-in desk, to deliver the first subpoena. He came in the front door, as various nudists sat casually eating their breakfasts, and all eyes turned to the man in uniform. Susan's brother, Robert, was working that morning, so he signed for it and called Susan at Ann's house to come and get it, as the resort guests practically exploded with curiosity.

It was an order for Susan to appear in Orlando for a deposition in the case of *State of Florida v. Richard Alfred Kananen, Jr.* I felt a jumbled sense of terror, shame, and a desperate desire to make it all go away.

We drove to Orlando on March 2, about two weeks after the subpoena arrived, and while Susan was being deposed, I sat in the car mortified. My brother was on a hunger strike, in the hospital, with a feeding tube and forced medication. Because of the questions Rickie's attorney, Gerod Hooper, asked Susan, we were beginning to get an idea of what sort of case the prosecutor was building against him, because up until Mr. Hooper asked these questions, we weren't really sure what was happening with Rickie's case. He asked her about my mother's garage, to find out if there was any indication at all that there might be a body buried under the cement floor, and she told them that the garage was always neat and clean, with a carpet on the floor. For years the garage was sort of a playroom for Cheryl's kids. Mom didn't park her car in there at all.

Then the attorney got down to the nitty-gritty, trying to find out if Rickie and I had been plotting to kill Mom. She told him, "Richard was angry about the father, on how he was abused and taught to be a criminal at an early age. From what I understand, the father had the son do criminal things, like robbing and stealing. Now, as far as the mother, he felt the mother did not protect him."

When Hooper asked about the suicide note, and specifically the line I wrote about having a "part in Mother's leaving," she explained exactly what I meant. "When Stacey left the police station, she was confused, distraught, upset. When they pulled away from the police station is when Richard supposedly told her that he killed the mother. And that because they are always together and because of him having Stacey open up bank accounts, that Stacey would be implied [sic] as having to have something to do with it. He convinced her that nobody would believe the truth, and that I wouldn't love her anymore. Therefore, she should kill herself. At that moment, I believe she felt she had no reason to live, knowing her mother was murdered. I don't believe she had anything to do with it."

Through Hooper's questioning that day, we learned that Rickie had been writing checks from Mom's account and was pretty free and loose with his spending. He gave some money to me and Susan to pay for his past room and board, since he had lived there free for several months, saying he won the money in the Fantasy 5 lottery. Susan used it to pay off her car, and I put a down payment on a new truck, trading in my old one, which was having major problems. She told Hooper, "He told us he won the Fantasy 5. We didn't know anything different until the police told us otherwise. And sometimes these things are like a movie. When you see the end of the movie, then you think back to earlier scenes. You say, oh, my God, that's what was happening."

And that's exactly how it felt. In retrospect, we could see that all of these little things were, by themselves, no big deal. But when you add them up, they look very fishy. I first began to realize this on December 22, 2003, when the police were questioning me about Rickie's activities, and that realization scared the hell out of me—all of these little things he was doing were making *me* look guilty. Especially when they pulled out a check made out to me for $2,500 from my mother's account with "Christmas" written on the memo line. When they asked Susan about it, she looked at the endorsement on the back of the check, paused, and said, "This may not be her signature. She always signs with an M. She always signs Stacey M. Kananen, always." The check had been signed "Stacey Kananen," with no "M." It looked like my handwriting, or at least close to it, but that's not how I sign my name. Ever.

Before letting her go, Hooper asked her about some trouble that Cheryl had been having with Daniel, and family scuttlebutt that Mom might be trying to have Daniel come live with her. In August 2003, a month or so before Mom's death, Cheryl became very angry at me, Mom, and Rickie, for confronting her about stories that Daniel had told us about her temper. She gave us a letter telling us to butt out, and that she and her family were seeking counseling. I respected her wishes and we didn't speak much between that time and when Mom disappeared. She was very angry with me already when Mom died. I don't know if that has anything to do with why she ultimately turned against me or not, but it's not like we were on happy terms when this nightmare began.

When the attorney asked Susan about this, she told him, "Daniel was upset with his mother, Cheryl, that she was not treating him properly . . . Marilyn might have said to Cheryl that she would take the kids away . . ." This, I believe, is the reason that Rickie told Daniel that he would kill Cheryl if Daniel wanted him to. At least, that's what Daniel told police back in December of 2003, just a few months before Susan's deposition.

CHAPTER 7

Daniel

When Mom's body was found, Daniel was only twelve years old. He was called in to talk to Detective Hussey, on December 16, after reporting to Cheryl that Uncle Rickie had admitted to murder. Cheryl was present during that interview because Daniel was a minor.

Rickie told the boy, sometime between moving in with us and Mom's murder, that he had killed our father. Daniel stated, in the innocent way only a child could say it, "He told me, 'He's dead. Let's just say that no one stopped me this time.' When he was a kid he tried to do the same thing, but my grandma stopped him. He was always really mad at my grandma for saying that she still loved him and for not really doing anything." Daniel continued, "He said, 'I shot him blow-to-blow . . . like, short range.'"

He told Hussey that Rickie said he traveled around the country saving children from their abusive fathers. He would go to the door as a "pizza man" and once he was sure that the wife and children were out of the building, he would go inside, "take care of the man," and plant drugs in the house.

Rickie told Daniel that our father said that Rickie was going to be just like him, and Rickie had started believing it. He told Daniel that he never wanted to be like our dad, and proceeded to give a demonstration of one of our father's typical temper tantrums. Daniel told Hussey that Rickie was carrying some tools and a ladder, and, "He threw the screwdriver across the yard. He threw the hammer and it broke the fence. He threw the ladder and he just started yelling and cussing. He hit the wall and threw rocks, and he had to stop because he was getting into it."

I was present when Rickie was demonstrating to our nephew what our father was like. We were all working outside, in the yard—something we loved to do together— and I wasn't paying much attention to their conversation. Suddenly I heard my father's voice screaming harsh words, and I just about jumped out of my skin. I whirled around and saw that it was Rickie, doing an uncanny impression of "the Monster."

Because Rickie had admitted to the boy that he had killed our father, Hussey asked him during that interview if Rickie ever talked to him about his grandmother or where he thought she went. Daniel indicated that he hadn't seen Rickie much since Mom disappeared, but he said, "Once he gave me like a look like, he knows where she is. He knows how to do crimes really good. He basically told me he knows how to do whatever without getting caught, 'cause that's how his dad raised him."

When I read the transcript of his interview, my heart broke all over again, because Daniel told stories of Rickie teaching him how to commit all sorts of crimes, from theft to kidnap for ransom to robbing banks by threatening to murder the children of the bank's customers.

Most eerie of all, however, was the psychic vision that Daniel told police that he had of my mother's death. He said, "I saw her worrying, like she was breathing hard. Then she fell and actually hit the floor."

The conversation then turned to the timing of Cheryl's wedding in 1988 to Chris Bracken, Daniel's father, which "coincidentally" fell just a couple weeks after our father disappeared. "He got killed by my uncle, it was like two weeks before their wedding. That's what he told me. Because the wedding would never have gone like it did and my grandfather would've never came down."

Hussey asked, "He didn't tell you a date when he thought he killed your grandfather?"

"No, he didn't."

"And he used the word kill? He did say that?"

Daniel replied, "He said, 'Well, nobody stopped me this time.' And I said, 'You killed him? How?' He's like 'Why would you want to know? Blow-to-blow, I already told you.'"

Hussey continued, "Anything else that he's said to you that was unusual?"

"He told me that his dad raped him."

"Okay," Hussey said. "How'd he start that conversation?"

Daniel told Hussey that he asked Rickie what's the worst thing that happened to him, "He said, 'My dad raped me.'"

"And that's the word he used?"

The boy continued, "Yeah, and he said 'He'd shoot at me. He used to put one bullet in one of the spinning chambers, he'd spin it, click, click, click, click, click, 'Oh, you got lucky this time.' And spin it, click, click, click, click, click, 'Oh, you got lucky again.' Click, click, click, 'Oh man, this is your lucky day!' He said, in Minnesota, one time he actually really shot at him. He said he shot at him before, but missed him on purpose just to scare him. But the other time he said he nicked his arm. He has a scar on his shoulder."

Hussey asked, "Is there anything else that you can think of?"

The boy thought for a moment and said, "Well, I know that for a while I thought my uncle had something to do with it. The look he gave me told me that he did something or he knew something. He's been mad at her for a long time."

"Did he ever tell you that? I mean he told you in so many words that he . . ."

Daniel continued, "I told him, 'You know Grandma still loves you, right?' He's like 'Don't tell me that, don't tell me that! I'm still mad at her.' I asked, 'Is it because she didn't do anything while he was abusing you?' He said,

'Because she still loves him after all that he put us through.' He really hated his dad."

Hussey said, "Tell me a little bit about your Aunt Stacey."

"My Aunt Stacey is the best. She's awesome. She's like my grandma, loves Disney. But I did notice when my uncle started hanging around more she changed. Trying to live up to a big brother's expectations, like acting different. You know, trying to be all tough, kind of. Like my uncle cussed a lot. My aunt didn't. And then my aunt actually started cussing. And I didn't notice that before he showed up."

I was surprised to learn that Daniel thought my personality had changed like that. I wasn't even aware of it. I can only guess that maybe hanging around with Rickie again after all that time brought out a hard edge that I must have developed growing up. Over the years, with Susan in my life and without abuse, I had been able to relax and just be myself. I didn't need to be defensive or hard. But maybe having Rickie around again triggered old behaviors. Whatever it was, the boy had noticed it and I had not.

Daniel continued, "You know about my mom when she gets mad at me and stuff." I can only assume he was having a hard time talking to a cop about what was going on at home, with Cheryl sitting right there. "Rickie, Grandma, and Stacey kind of teamed up to try to stop her. And they started getting closer and closer and my aunt basically kind of imitated my uncle."

After telling Hussey that we bought the house down

the street from Mom's house because he asked us to, Daniel got back on track. "My uncle knows how to fake a person's death. He knows how to kill a person, make it look like they committed suicide or accidental death. I know he's really good at crimes. And he could've easily killed my grandma. He could've got one of his friends; he has a lot friends that do crimes. He could've gone in, Tased on my grandma then taken her in her car, put a whole bunch of clothes in it, buried the clothes with her."

Hussey prompted him to continue, "Uh huh."

"Then taken the car and got it impounded or he could've gotten rid of all the stuffed animals in the back, the license plate, whatever." (Susan's license plate was stolen from her car shortly after Mom disappeared.)

"Why would you put this scenario together?" Hussey asked.

"Because I know what my uncle is capable of. And I know he's really smart when it comes to this stuff. And I also know that he was really mad at my grandma. But the only thing that holds me back is I also know that he's a really good person. And he always told me he would never hurt a child or a woman. But I don't think she would leave no matter what."

Hussey asked, "But did he ever tell you that he knew how to fake somebody's death and make it look like they ran away? Did he tell you that specifically?"

"He told me if a person wanted to fake their death to get out of stuff, he could do it. Or he could actually kill somebody and make 'em look like they ran away."

"Okay, so he did tell you that?"

"Yeah."

"When? Was it just one of the times you were with him?"

"Probably. It wasn't with my aunt, I know that. I don't know what she knows."

"You haven't talked to her much since your grandmother's been gone," Hussey stated.

"I haven't been allowed. I got in trouble for giving them my cell phone number." Daniel had been in trouble for sharing his phone number with me and Susan.

Detective Hussey was ready to wrap it up. "Anything else you can think of?"

"When my uncle has problems," Daniel said, "he likes to be ambitious. He don't like to sit there and talk about it. He likes to save the world. He's on a mission trip. He wants to do everything brutally. Like if he has a problem with someone doing something, he wants to do it his way. Do it mean and nasty. That's what he wanted to do to Mom."

"When did he tell you that?"

"He told me that he has a problem with my mom because he always had to deal with men."

Hussey interrupted, "I'm not following you."

"The only thing holding him back is that she was a woman. He viewed her like one of the abusive men that he takes out of the houses. It was my call," Daniel explained.

"He told you that? It was your call whether or not to do something with your mom?"

"Yeah." Daniel said, "It's my call when, if I wanted it. Then when my dad stepped in, he told him, it's my call. And my dad said, no, no, no and that's why we went to the pastor as soon as possible."

Hussey wrapped up the interview, making sure first that Daniel knew the difference between the truth and a lie. And even though Cheryl and I still aren't speaking, my heart still breaks for her, having to sit in the room and hear her child tell such horrible stories about things that happened when she wasn't around to protect him from our brother's madness.

CHAPTER 8

A Witness for the Prosecution

It took another month or so after Susan's deposition for my subpoena to arrive. In the meantime, I started to work at Gulf Coast, in the kitchen, and facing everyone. The restaurant, which was actually more of a diner even though we all called it "the restaurant," was open air, like a Waffle House, where everything is done in plain view of the customers. I worked behind the counter, taking orders, cooking, serving food, washing all the dishes and pots and pans, keeping the place spotless for any surprise Board of Health inspections, answering the phone, and taking care of guests who were checking in at the resort. It was my job to make nice with everyone while they ate, and keep the customers satisfied. I ran all aspects of the diner, including storeroom inventory and ordering supplies, and manned the front desk, while Susan took care of all of the administrative duties from either Ann's house or the office, adjacent to the restaurant. Susan's brother, Robert, who normally ran the kitchen, had broken his foot, so I was pressed into service long before I was ready, but this was a family business, and when family needed you, you set aside your own comfort and chipped in.

I told Susan that if we were going to make it, I'd have to act like nothing happened and just function normally, whatever normal was. It was awkward at first, not wanting anybody to ask any questions. How would I say, "I don't want to talk about it," in a polite, customer-service way? Luckily, I didn't really have to. The people were friendly and I didn't care that they were nude. They didn't make it an issue, and neither did I.

Susan and I both knew that everyone was watching every move we made. I was comfortable at Ann's because nobody would say anything in front of her. But once I had to start working, I knew Ann would say, "Suck it up," because that's just how she was. I was just another person, with another interesting story, in the "naked city."

One couple, Bob and Kay, made my life miserable. Bob was a shit-stirring gossip. He'd go from one house to the next, collecting news and telling people whatever he gathered along the way. Bob and Kay were in the hot tub, shortly after I arrived at GCR in February, with Dan and Franda. Because voices carry in the great outdoors, and the restaurant was not far from the pool area *and* Bob never was known to keep his voice down, I overheard— from the restaurant's back porch while I was on break one day—Bob telling them that Ann had a murderer working in the kitchen. I liked Dan and Franda, and after I noticed Franda acting oddly a day or two later I pulled her aside and said, "Do you have an issue with me? I know what Bob said." She said, "Oh, he just talks shit all the time. It don't mean nothing to nobody."

I said, "Well, when you want to hear the truth come and see me someday," but she was honest and said she was uncomfortable around me, with all the stories flying around.

"Okay, you've seen me around here for a couple months. Do you really think I can be as good an actress as I'd have to be to really be the murderer Bob says I am? I know that there are psychopaths out there who can fool people, but let's get real. Could I really be that good?"

"Well no, I don't think so," she agreed.

"I'm going to challenge you. If I'm ever put on the witness stand, if this ever goes to trial, and you can catch me in a lie, you let me know." And then I went back to work.

I became a workaholic, but that's what kept me sane. I worked hard before my mom's death, but not to the same degree. I used to work for ten hours at Disney, where they demand perfection and I was happy to give it to them. My hours were unusual—sometimes predawn, sometimes more civilized—and they changed frequently, depending on what they needed from me. It was hard to get into any sort of real rhythm, but I was young and strong and could handle it, so I'd bust my rear end for them, and then have fun and go to movies, dinner, theme parks, but I didn't have any desire for a social life anymore. I was grieving for Mom. Then it would hit me from time to time about *how* she died and the grief would be multiplied tenfold.

Some of the older women took me under their wings, like Gail, whom Ann hired to work in the kitchen with me. She helped with all of the same things I did, taking orders, cooking, washing dishes, and she was invaluable on Friday and Saturday nights when we would make dinners for the whole resort, which usually received a huge turnout. I couldn't have done it without her. Gail and her husband, Bob, lived nearby on the Withlacoochee River, where they had a fishing boat. She was a fisherman's wife, and her face showed her years. Her raspy voice told of years as a smoker, and her asthma inhaler was never far away. She became a very dear friend to me, and I confided in her many of my fears and concerns about what was going on in my family, because I knew she wouldn't tell anyone what we talked about. We became very close, but she died of cancer before the trial. Her death was just one more blow, a surrogate mom taken from me, just when I needed her.

One of the Canadian snowbirds helped me make a cake that my mom used to make, a chocolate mayonnaise cake. We were talking one day in the restaurant about our favorite desserts, and I mentioned that I loved this recipe and didn't have it anymore. She told me she had a recipe for that type of cake, and brought it in one afternoon after the lunch rush so we could give it a try, together. She had the same recipe my mom had—I recognized the recipe as we made it, and it tasted just the same. I, fortunately, ended up with a lot of surrogate moms, including Ann, in her own way, and Ann's friend Diane also became a mom to both me and Susan. Diane even accompanied me and

Susan to the trial. The people at GCR really did become my family.

I was at work, with a restaurant full of lunch customers, when the process server arrived with my deposition subpoena. I was tired, having been there since before dawn and working the breakfast shift, and was looking forward to the end of the lunch rush. Susan had already had her subpoena delivered there, so I supposed that this was where they would eventually deliver mine, but the timing couldn't have been worse, with a restaurant full of customers, some of whom obviously couldn't wait to finish eating so they could hurry outside and talk about what they had just seen. But that was the least of my worries, being gossip fodder. I was getting used to that.

What was most awful is that I saw that the State of Florida was charging Rickie with first-degree murder. I knew that in Florida, this meant a possible death penalty. This is when harsh reality set in. This wasn't going away, and on April 30, 2004, I would have to speak against my brother. Although Rickie had committed heinous crimes, he was still my big brother, and we had gone through hell together, and while we were all kids—even though there wasn't much we could do to protect one another—we did at least try to stick together and watch one another's backs. Even though he had been found competent to stand trial, it seemed to me that he had to be mentally ill to have done the things he did. I walked outside onto the deck behind the building and sat down on one of the wooden benches, head in hands, crushed.

When I arrived at the state's attorney's office for my

deposition, I was shocked to see Detective Hussey sitting in the lobby. I called Susan, who was still parking the car, and begged her to call my lawyer, Michael Gibson, whom Ann had hired to be a buffer between me and the police as soon as Hussey made his initial threat. I didn't have a clue what that man was doing in the waiting room. He had thrown so many threats at me that his presence made me very uncomfortable. Michael, who was arriving when Susan called him and had just pulled up, walked in with her and told me, "Oh, he's probably here for something else."

When the assistant state's attorney—Linda Drane Burdick, an attractive blonde with a powerful and intimidating personality, who eventually worked the Casey Anthony case—came out to get me, Hussey got up and told both attorneys, "I'm going to sit in on her deposition." Michael said, "No, my client has a right to be there with the state's attorney, myself, and a court reporter and that's all that is required. That's all I'm allowing." Hussey turned to me and said, "You got lucky again," and walked out the door, fortunately, but it set the tone for the day.

I try very hard, as a mature adult, to make excuses for Hussey, that he was just doing his job, and that he must have believed that he was doing the right thing. But I was just as much a victim in this crime as the rest of my family—if not more so, with the way Rickie was dragging me into it—and I was reeling with indescribable fear and pain. Hussey had decided that I was guilty, period, and acted accordingly, with no compassion whatsoever. His lack of objectivity and his sneering, antagonistic pressure on me only made me fear and hate him more.

My stomach was churning as the deposition began. The room, with its nondescript beige walls and conference table that seated eight, was full of lawyers: Gibson, Burdick, and my brother's public defender, Gerod Hooper. I sat next to my attorney on one side of the oblong table, and Burdick and Hooper sat across from us. The court reporter sat, ready to go, at the end of the table.

Hooper began right away by asking whether my father was an abusive drunk, and why no one reported him missing back in 1988. I'd spent so many years not talking about what felt like dirty little secrets that it was uncomfortable talking to these strangers about it, especially in light of the circumstances. I had to tell them what they wanted to know whether I liked it or not. It felt like being abused, all over again, not having any say at all in whether I participated in my current circumstances. It helped that Mr. Hooper was a very kind and gentle man, when he spoke to me. He was very sympathetic about my mother's death.

I knew they were going to ask me about the suicide attempt, and how Rickie was able to bury my mom's body in my own backyard without my noticing anything was amiss. So I braced myself and prepared for the onslaught of questions. I vowed to just tell the truth, no matter how much it hurt to do so. "The truth is the truth is the truth" became my mantra.

I told Hooper that I loved having my big brother back in my life. I loved having a family, after spending an entire childhood without one. What no one could seem to understand—at least that's how it seemed with all of their dubious questions about my knowledge of the intimate details of his life—was that I didn't know every facet of his day-to-day activities. I was at work most of the time and barely saw Susan as much as I would have liked, much less Rickie. Yes, we lived together, but we didn't confide every detail just because we lived under the same roof. I didn't know how much money he made. I didn't pry into his financial life. Those things are personal. I stayed out of his business and he stayed out of mine.

Then Hooper asked about the money that Rickie had given me between my mom's disappearance in September and when they found her body in December. He had given Susan money to make payments on her car, and helped me put a down payment on a new truck, because mine was on its last legs. He said that he had come into some money and wanted to make up for the months he had lived there rent free. Hindsight is twenty-twenty, and I still kick myself for not thinking anything was odd at the time, but it certainly did look suspicious, in retrospect. I told him that I thought the money for my new truck had come out of our landscaping business account, but I could be mistaken. Hooper asked, "Why would there be a possibility that you'd be mistaken about that?"

"That was quite a while ago. I don't . . ."

He interrupted, "Six months, wasn't it? When did you set up these business accounts with Richard?"

"I think we set up one in August and one in the beginning of September. I wanted to go into business with him. I thought it would be a great opportunity. Disney's a nice job but I wanted to go much further." I stammered a reply.

"And you felt that your brother was a reliable business partner?" he asked.

"Yes. I did." Because I did. I was fooled by him, too. I thought my brother wanted me and the family back in his life. I thought he was eager to work and do something creative with his life. While we toiled together in the backyard, and with all the work he did on our house, he proved himself to be a hard and able worker, who didn't mind putting his back into what he was doing.

As difficult as those questions had been to answer, the really difficult ones were about to come my way. Hooper wanted to know about the day I found out that Rickie had killed our parents and what led to our suicide attempt.

"Now, there came a time when you and Richard went to the police station and gave statements and you were separated at that time. After you gave the statements, is that when you and Richard attempted suicide?" Hooper asked, gently.

I confirmed that was true.

"What happened in the police station that led you and Richard to decide to attempt suicide after speaking to the police?"

I recalled that horrible day, shuddering at the memory of Rickie confessing to me that he had killed our parents. I took a deep breath and replied, "When the detectives walked in the room and said, 'We know where your mother's car is,' I pretty much fell apart. And then when we left the police station, he just kept telling me, 'Oh, I did things. Oh, I was horrible. I'm going to ruin your life. You have no purpose. You have no family. You're going to have nothing.' And all I kept thinking was, 'Oh, no, I let you come into my home. I let you come close to the family and what have you done?' It just ripped me apart."

"So was it a joint decision that you and him made?" Hooper asked.

I had to reply that I honestly didn't remember. He wanted to know what we did after we left the police station and I told him that I remembered driving to a store and that I stopped to get gas. As we drove home, Rickie told me that he murdered my mother and that's when he started in with the: I have no purpose. I have no family. I'll have nothing. I'm going to be destroyed. And all I kept thinking was, I let him come in my house and all he did was tear my family apart.

"Did he bring it up or did you bring it up?"

I told him that Rickie brought it up. Hooper now wanted to know where we went, and I told him that Rickie directed me to drive my truck to an industrial storage complex, with large units that some companies actually used as their place of business, like welding and car repair companies. The units had lots of space and a small bathroom inside. I drove my truck into Rickie's unit, and he got out of the truck and closed the large overhead door.

Hooper continued his probing. "Okay. Had you guys discussed how you were going to attempt the suicide, by carbon monoxide, was that discussed at all or . . ."

"I don't remember it being discussed until we actually got inside the storage shed, and by then I was distraught," I replied.

"Okay. So the truck is still running?" he asked. "Other

than the truck running in a confined shed, had you taken any other means to attempt a suicide?"

"He attached some kind of a hose thing from the back of the truck into the window."

"So you are both sitting there with the windows rolled up in the storage shed and the exhaust pipe vented into the passenger compartment?"

"Yeah. I guess that's what was vented. I don't know anything about vehicles," I answered. When he asked if we were talking about anything, I told him, "No. I didn't really say anything to him at all. I wrote a letter to Susan." The next thing I remember after passing out, I told him, was the cops pulling me out of the truck and taking me to the hospital.

Suddenly, he launched into a different line of questions. He barked, "Were you present when your mom got killed?" Surprised, I replied, "No. I was not."

"Okay," he continued. "Did you have any involvement in her being killed or her disappearance?"

"No. I did not."

"And you mentioned you left Susan a note?"

"Yes. I did," I replied.

He continued pressing, "And in the note you say to her, 'We had a part in mom's leaving.' What did you mean by that?"

So again I explained, "We, meaning that I brought him into my house. He was never close to my family until he moved into my house. And then we started having family dinners, pool parties, but until then, he was never close to the family, so I felt, like, God, what did I do?"

Still not getting it, he said, "Okay. So the 'we' you're referring to, you and Susan for bringing him in . . . or just you and Richard or . . ."

"Me and Richard," I explained. "I feel horrible because it wouldn't have happened if he wasn't in my house, or at least that's what I believe. He wouldn't have had access to everybody because he never did before."

Hooper paused and asked, "Well, if he tells you that he killed your mom, so he's going to kill himself, what I'm lost on is how does that get to you having to kill yourself? How does that affect you?"

It was frustrating that I couldn't make him understand. I told him, "He kept saying I have no purpose. I have no family. He put the body in my backyard. I've just as much destroyed my family as he did. I didn't physically do anything, but I brought him back into our family." And that's exactly how I felt. Maybe it's from growing up in such a severely abusive household, but I've always felt hyper-responsible for things going wrong in my life. If anything bad happens, I have a tendency to feel like it's my fault, no matter what. It is what the abuser teaches his victims: "I wouldn't have to hit you if only . . ." This was one of those "if only . . ." moments. If only I had not invited Rickie to live with us, Mom would be alive today.

Hooper changed the subject then and told me that Rickie said, in his note, "'Our father was killed by Stacey.' Did you know he wrote that in his note?"

I replied that I heard that after the fact but didn't know it at the time. I told him that I did not kill our father, and that Rickie had never told me, before that day, that he had killed him, either. All I was ever told was that he was gone.

He pressed on, "Do you know of any reason why he would put in his suicide note that you killed your father?" and I had to reply that I had no idea. I still don't know why he said that. I can guess until I'm blue in the face, but I will probably never know for sure.

Then the subject rolled around to that Christmas check made out in my name. Hooper showed it to me and said, "It seems to be a check made out to you for $2,500 from your mom's account and the back of the check has written on it: Stacey Kananen. Is that your signature?"

I looked and noticed the missing M. "No. It's missing the 'M' and everything I sign has an 'M' in the middle initial."

He dropped that subject without any more questions, and the state's attorney, Linda Drane Burdick, took over from there. She spent a substantial amount of time asking me about what life was like back in 1988, when my father disappeared, just a few weeks before my sister's wedding. "How would you describe your parents' relationship at that point?" I told her it was violent, and left it at that.

"Were you aware of there being any weapons in the home?" she asked.

I explained to the state's attorney that my father had handguns and shotguns and that he pulled them out to threaten my mother almost once a week.

"Would it be reasonable then to assume that within the week prior to his disappearance, you had seen him threaten your mother with a firearm of some sort?"

I probably had. It had been a long time—over fifteen years since that hellish part of my life—so I could not say for sure, but this really was a regular occurrence in our house. It would not surprise me at all if he had. In fact, I was so used to the never-ending death threats and beatings that rarely did I even come out of my room. There was nothing I could do about it but stay out of the way, because if I interfered, it would just be worse for all of us. I would go to my bedroom and hide until it was over. I did, however, call 911 during a particularly heinous attack in the mid-1980s, when we lived in Orlando. I remember it being Saturday afternoon because Mom wasn't working. I don't recall the date, but it was summertime. I hurried outside with the cordless phone, wearing shorts and a tank top. The police came out and rang the doorbell, but she told them everything was fine and they went away.

Then Burdick's questions went in a different direction. "Where were you when your mother rented a concrete saw?"

I didn't know anything about a concrete saw. At this point, I went numb. All I wanted to do was leave. I was torn between being angry because it felt like they were trying to ruin my mom's name, and utter disbelief that what they were implying might be true.

Ms. Burdick asked me to describe my mom's garage. It was a pretty typical two-car garage, with a washer and dryer at the back wall. One side was piled from front to back with boxes, totes, and holiday decorations. The other side had a play table, toys, games, and other kids' activities. Near the roll-up door, a wooden shelf was built in to the wall, and it was covered with tools and odds and ends. The garage was used mostly as a playroom for the kids, with indoor/outdoor carpet on the cement floor.

She asked me, point blank, "Did your mother ever tell you she killed your father?"

"No. She didn't."

"Did you know your father was under the concrete in the garage?"

"No. I did not."

"So who killed your dad?"

"I don't know."

"Who do you suspect?"

"I don't know. I really don't."

The subject then turned to the fact that Mom had been collecting my father's disability checks all those years. This was something that Rickie kept trying to point out the night she disappeared. There was paperwork left on the counter, and he kept referring to it, but at the time neither Cheryl nor I paid much attention. We were too concerned that "the Monster" had shown up after all these years and snatched her away. This is what Rickie had first suggested as to how she had gone missing. We didn't much care about bank accounts and Social Security payments. Cheryl, that night, was terrified that our hideous father would now track down and hurt her kids the way he hurt us. That would be her worst nightmare, and I don't blame her one bit for being concerned, because I, too, believed that he would hurt her kids if he got hold of them.

Burdick asked me about that night, back in September, "How were you made aware of her disappearance?"

"My sister called me Thursday evening, and said, 'She didn't come to work today.' I got my brother and we went over there. I walked in the house, and there were things missing and she wasn't there."

I once had a key to my mom's house. I explained, "I had one at the beginning of the month. My brother told me that when my cousin left, he changed the locks and none of us had keys, except for him and my mother."

Puzzled, she asked, "Did Richard tell you why he changed the locks after she left?"

"Well, it was typical for my mother, whenever she had company in her house, to have her locks changed in case they made copies of her keys, so that's what he said he did. I didn't think anything of it because that was kind of normal."

Changing the locks after a visitor was just par for the course for Mom. We were all used to it and didn't think twice about it. As far as I knew, there were no specific incidents to cause Mom to be suspicious of her own sister, my Aunt Gerri, or even my cousin Laureen. In retrospect, of course—knowing now that there was a body buried under the garage floor, and illegal bank accounts—I can see why Mom didn't want anyone to be able to snoop around in her absence.

"Every year when Laureen came, your mom let her stay in the house and then promptly had the locks changed?" she continued.

"Within a couple days of her leaving, she would have the locks changed. The same thing with my Aunt Gerri, when she would come see my grandfather."

Burdick then asked me, "So at some point while she's missing Richard decides to resurface the garage floor? What did he tell you about that?" After Mom disappeared, Rickie had taken it upon himself to hire a company to install a new, decorative floor in her garage. I didn't think much about it, because he was the one who had taken charge of her house and he thought it was a good idea, to keep the house in good condition. I had no inkling that there was a body buried under the cement for fifteen years, and he was just trying to hide any signs of that in case of any investigation.

"He told me that the garage floor needed to get some work done on it and he wanted to try to get a mortgage on the house to save it. This was after I found out about IRS and Social Security and the checks, and not knowing anything about legalities, I believed him."

She was dubious. "You didn't check into it for yourself? I mean, obviously you're a smart person, graduated in the top ten. So it wouldn't have taken much for you to try to check into what Richard was telling you?"

Honestly, I hadn't given it much thought. His story made sense, after he told me that Mom's house was in jeopardy. I thought he was taking care of business, like it needed to be done, and I never really thought to check up on him. He's my brother. I assumed he would tell me the truth. I was wrong. Very, very wrong. Hindsight is blinding, sometimes.

She continued, "So it's my understanding you were around whenever the floor to the garage was being redone."

"When he had the stone stuff put on it, yes. I was there." Who knew, at the time, that this would be considered suspicious behavior? I didn't know anything about garage floors or how impractical it was to do what Rick was doing. I just helped him pick out a color.

"Were you there when the installer said, 'That's kind of a stupid thing to put on a garage floor? Why would you want to do that?'" she asked.

"I wasn't within earshot. All I had to do with that conversation was, 'Oh, I like this color.' That was it. I didn't have the money to pay for it. He said he was paying for it out of his electrical jobs, so I let them discuss business."

It really did seem to me like my big brother was taking care of our mom's affairs in her absence. He told me and Cheryl that, because of the IRS investigation, we had to protect her assets, lest they get seized. He moved her more valuable things to our garage, and even into a storage unit. When we got letters from the utility companies that her electric and her water bills were not being paid because there was no money in the account, he had me call the bank to question that.

Burdick asked me about the bank account, and I explained that they wouldn't give me any information. They needed to see my mother and obviously she couldn't show up, so I told Richard we needed to pay her bills. We needed to keep her house in order for her, and he said he was going to take care of it.

That's when we found out that the bank accounts had been frozen. My memory of the exact chain of events is somewhat fuzzy, unfortunately, but as a result of my phone call to the bank, red flags went up because she was a "missing person." We were told that we had to call Detective Hussey, so we did. This incident would haunt me years later at my trial as would all of these—individually—small details. Put them all together and they hung a great big suspicious cloud of guilt over my head.

Once again, Burdick led me through the events leading up to the suicide attempt, so I repeated the story for her—again. I was glad that I had already decided to just tell the truth and not try to hide any embarrassing secrets, no matter how painful they might be, because it was obvious that the two attorneys were trying to trip me up. Yes, I know my story of why I so blindly followed my brother sounded lame to them, but they never grew up in a severely dysfunctional, abusive household. They didn't know what I considered strange or "normal" behavior, and why I never questioned what an older, male family member was doing. In my family, you just . . . didn't ask. You did not ask. Period. So I didn't question any decisions, actions, or any of his behavior, even when he was acting a little strange.

Burdick asked, "What does Richard tell you he told them?"

"He doesn't tell me anything until we get back to the house. A little bit of chitter-chatter on the way: 'Are you hungry, blah-blah-blah. We've got to run a couple of errands.' Then we get back to the house and . . ."

"Which house?"

"My house. And he's acting a little strange and he says, 'I killed your mother.' And I just flipped out. I totally just freaked out. I started crying. And then he started saying, 'You don't have a future. You don't have a purpose.'"

"Why would he say that at that point if you had been getting along well and you were having a great time with Richard since he had moved back into your home?"

I wish I knew the answer to that, as well. "I was. I have no idea why he did that. I don't understand it at all."

They insisted I go through the sequence of events. "We drove together. I honestly didn't want to hear what he had to say because in the same interview with the sheriff's department, they brought me in a diagram of my mother's garage and showed me where the other body was also. I, of course, didn't believe it, but came to find out it was very true. I just told him I didn't want to hear anything. I didn't want to hear it. I was trying to figure out what the hell was going on and I didn't want to hear it. I don't remember discussing it in the truck. We may have, but I don't remember it."

"So Richard's basically telling you your life is over at the house? And your response is, 'You're right. My life is over? I didn't do anything. Why is my life over?' Did you say that?"

"I believe I did say that. I don't remember exactly what I said to him. I was pretty hysterical at that point."

Once again, I had to walk her through the story. Yes, we went to Wal-Mart, where I was too afraid and confused to just leave him. I wasn't thinking straight. I had just found out he had murdered our mom and buried her in my yard. Yes, we went to the storage unit where I used the bathroom while he rigged the truck with a hose. Yes, I drank NyQuil because I can't swallow pills. Yes, I wrote that damned, incriminating note.

"Okay," she asked, "did he mention again who he killed or how?"

"He said, 'I killed our mother and put her in your backyard.' That was the final straw. I couldn't handle it anymore."

"Did you ask him anything about your dad at that point?"

"No. I didn't."

"You knew that the police had believed that your dad was under the garage."

"I knew that morning, yeah."

"Okay. But you didn't ask Richard about it when he said he killed your mom?"

"Probably not, but then a part of me said, I hope to God my mother didn't have anything to do with it because she was so beaten all the time."

Burdick asked, "She never said to you that she had anything to do with it?" I told her that she had not.

Finally, after almost an hour and a half, the grueling questions were over. Her last question was about Cheryl, and whether I had been in communication with her.

"I get the impression she doesn't want to speak to me. I could be wrong, but this is very hard on all of us and everybody needs to put it all back together. She's got three kids she has to take care of. And out of anything, that's the most important thing, those three kids."

CHAPTER 9

A Dull Roar

As we settled in, Susan and I took on pretty much all of the day-to-day responsibilities of managing GCR. The buck still stopped with Ann—she made all the decisions—but we did the actual work. By the summer of 2004, we discovered that running a resort was definitely two full-time jobs. I put in seven-day weeks in the kitchen, ordering food and cooking meals. We hosted dances on Saturdays and planned pool parties and special events. The Tiki Bar was open on the weekends, so we held cookouts and served beer and wine coolers in the Florida heat. The customers wanted their money's worth, and we tried our best to give it to them.

The long work hours and social atmosphere helped to take my mind off of where Rickie was, and why, but what helped the most was that I started drinking again. Since I was four years old, my father had gotten me drunk on a regular basis to make me more compliant while he was doing what he did, and as a teenager I started drinking on my own. I was soused pretty regularly until I met Susan at age twenty-two and quit drinking. My father was "gone" by that point, and I didn't feel like I needed to escape in the bottle anymore. But now, living in a tropical paradise vacation resort where the daily "Happy Hour" started before 3:00 P.M. for many of the snowbirds, vodka became my friend again and we spent a lot of time getting reacquainted.

Ann sold the trailer we were living in to some snowbird friends of hers from Canada, so Susan and I moved over that first summer into one of the rental units in the resort. Our address was now "Unit N" instead of "Lot 130." We filed a change of address with the post office so our mail would be forwarded from the homeowners' bank of mailboxes to the resort's general delivery mailbox. The resort and subdivision shared the same address, but the resort office was responsible for sorting and delivering the campers' mail. Anything without a lot number came to the resort office. We all lived within the same small, gated community at 13220 Houston Ave.

I got to be good friends with the staff—most of whom lived at the resort—and many of the residents and snowbirds. Wendell, the maintenance manager, was a gruff Alabama good ol' boy, and he became like sort of a grouchy big brother to me, even though he made it pretty clear that he wasn't sure about my innocence. And then there was Jeff, his assistant, a clown who kept everybody laughing. Jeff—who insisted on working in the nude—was changing a lightbulb in one of the streetlight fixtures, when the ladder fell out from under him. He instinctively leapt forward and clung on to the pole as the ladder fell to the ground. Fortunately, Wendell was nearby to lift the ladder back up, but he took his sweet old time doing it, just to make sure that Jeff realized the full impact of what sort of splinters he would have gathered on the way, if he'd had to slide down. He wore shorts to work from that day forward.

We built quite a team of volunteers, who put together tennis and Petanque tournaments with the other local nudist resorts, and Gulf Coast Resort was beginning to be a player in the local nudist scene. Business grew rapidly as word of mouth let people know that GCR was now a happening place.

I was beginning to think that perhaps life had a chance of being okay again when, in March 2005—right around what would have been my mother's birthday—I received an "anonymous" piece of mail. It was a birthday card that said, in what looked like my sister's handwriting, "I would have been 67 years young this month." I felt like I had been punched in the stomach. The next month I received another one, in time for Rickie's birthday. This one was typed. It said, "I should not be the only one in jail on my birthday. Code of Silence no more. The pact was us together . . . all the way."

I'd had enough. I contacted my lawyer and asked him what to do about this harassment, and assuming that the cards were from Cheryl, he sent a letter telling her that if she wanted to contact me, she should do it through him. I still don't know for a fact whether they were from her, but I never received any more cards like that after that. Up until then, I was saddened and dismayed that my own sister could possibly suspect me. But now I was pissed. If it was her, that kind of behavior was definitely not okay.

I had lost my entire family, for good, and I was resigned to accepting that Susan's family would have to be it for me. I threw myself into working almost nonstop for the resort. Between working and drinking, I didn't have any time to think about how alone I was and how I came to be that way. But then Ann got sick in late 2005. She was getting older and her health was beginning to decline. She was falling out of bed on a regular basis, and it took several men—oftentimes EMTs—to lift her back into bed. Many days, she didn't even have the strength or ability to lift herself out of bed. She was on oxygen by now, because she had been diagnosed with chronic obstructive pulmonary disease (COPD).

For several months, Susan and I spent a great deal of our time taking care of Ann, between 1:00 A.M. phone calls to lift her back into bed and trips to the emergency room. She'd be hospitalized and we'd prepare for the worst, and then she'd rally again and come home. This went on until, finally, she was done in. The doctors said it was congestive heart failure. She had lost circulation in her legs, and they were becoming gangrenous. All of the kids had come to the hospital to say their good-byes, and Susan told her mom it was okay to let go. As far as she could tell, there were no loose ends for Ann to stick around for. Finally, in January 2006, she closed her eyes for the last time and Susan, who was devastated, was now fully in charge of the resort.

We were both exhausted. Too much drama, too much work, and no respite for either of us. And before Susan even had time to plan a memorial service for her mother, Ed and his girlfriend showed up at Ann's house and demanded the keys. They gave Susan and her siblings a few hours to get whatever they wanted out of the house, including all of the business computers and files that Ann kept there, and they moved in. Needless to say, this created more than a little bit of tension between the Kirk kids and their father, not to mention the "Bitch," as she came to be known (she actually had a license plate on her vehicle that said that, so it wasn't like we gave her the title). The two of them came to the restaurant several days a week to get a free breakfast, and we had to serve them. I was used to swallowing abuse, so I was able to just grin and bear it, but poor Susan was beside herself.

She hid it well, however. Well, she didn't so much "hide" it as much as she soldiered on. She still had a resort to run, a Mardi Gras dance to plan, a St. Patrick's Day dinner to buy for, a Casino Night to put together: She had far too much to do to worry about her own personal drama. With Ann gone, she was now free to brighten up the resort a little more, and when some of the residents asked if they could paint the place with Key West colors, if they could get enough volunteers, she told them to have at it. We were hosting AANR Florida conventions regularly and Woodstock weekends with bands and vendors. If Ed and the Bitch wanted to try to pee in her Wheaties, they'd have to stand in line.

Another thing we did, after Ann passed, was patch

things up with a large number of the homeowners, some of whom loathed Ann Kirk with the heat of a thousand blazing suns. In case I haven't made it clear, Ann was a difficult woman, and when she and Ed took over the park from the former owners, it was not a pretty scene and a lot of people held grudges. They refused to buy memberships or use the facilities because not a dime of their money was going to support the Kirk family. But Susan approached them to make amends and invited them all back to the resort that they once loved. Slowly but surely, most of them came back and marveled at what a great job Susan was doing.

She and I made a very special point of bringing the park back together again. We helped to take care of some of the older residents, rewriting some of Ann's former restaurant rules like, "No food deliveries" and "No credit." Some of the residents were elderly or disabled—after all, they came to Gulf Coast Resort to retire—and had trouble cooking. We would have Wayne, one of the other resort employees, deliver dinners to them, on the resort's golf cart, for no extra charge. We made sure that the restaurant building and bathroom were handicap accessible, and even created handicap parking spaces for golf carts, which was the way that most of the residents got around the park.

In spite of the drama with her family and mine, we were building a new life—a bizarre one, to be sure, but it was good. Yes, I was still going to Orlando from time to time to talk to the state's attorney about testifying against Rickie. Yes, he was still putting doubt in our minds as to whether he was truly insane or just malingering. And, yes,

Cheryl and Detective Hussey still apparently thought I had something to do with my mother's death. But they had no case, no evidence, because I was innocent.

Each time I went to Orlando to meet with Robin Wilkinson, the assistant state's attorney who had taken over the case from Linda Drane Burdick, I was never comfortable. I went to Orlando a total of five times—once for deposition, twice for hearings that I can't talk about (they were sealed), once for a pretrial hearing, and once to meet with Robin the week before the trial. Although she had a background in child abuse cases and, therefore, was somewhat compassionate and understanding about the way our lives went, there was something about her that made me very nervous. She was sort of abrasive and had an air about her that just wasn't very friendly. The permanent look of annoyance on her face was intimidating. I always figured, "This is it; they're going to throw something new at me." She and Hussey had me scared.

I was giving depositions on Rickie, going to hearings in order to affirm or disprove things that he was saying, and being asked what I felt about the death penalty for him. I didn't feel he deserved the death penalty. He was destroyed by the abuse we all endured, and someone should have noticed it earlier. Right before Rickie's scheduled trial in 2007, I went for one last meeting with Robin. I felt uneasy and said to Susan, "This is an ambush. I feel like this is an ambush, this trip." Little did I know, it really was.

CHAPTER 10

Rickie Pleads Guilty

I never went to visit Rickie between his arrest in 2003 and his trial date in 2007, but Cheryl did go to see him a few times. This was very hard for me, and I wrestled with whether I was doing the right thing or not. My brother was our protector—he was a human being. But, for me, it would have been so disrespectful to go see him after he murdered our mom—especially burying her in my backyard and then trying to get me to kill myself. I felt betrayed by him, and also physically petrified to go near any type of police area.

I saw him, however, after I was subpoenaed to testify for hearings, on behalf of the State. I honestly don't remember which trip to Orlando this was, but if I had to hazard a guess, I'd say it was in early 2007, as they were preparing for his trial. He was shackled at the ankles and wrists, wearing a blue jail jumpsuit, and he looked horrible, stick-figure horrible, because he had just come off another hunger strike. It made me nauseated to see him. He was as skinny as he had been in high school, when he was so tall and gangly. Then he was slim because he had a teenager's metabolism and was physically strong and active. Now he was emaciated. I couldn't bear to look at him.

Leading up to his trial, I was on pins and needles, waiting to find out if they were going to make me testify, or if he would take a plea. I was hoping for a plea. No one in her right mind would prefer to testify against her brother.

On May 1, 2007, in front of Judge Alicia Latimore and without my knowledge, he withdrew his previously tendered pleas of not guilty of both charges. I had no idea this was going to happen or that it was happening until after the fact. He pleaded no contest to manslaughter in my father's death, and no contest to second-degree murder in my mother's. For the first charge, he was sentenced to fifteen years, and the second charge got him a thirty-year sentence, to run concurrently with the first.

Robin Wilkinson began the proceedings with, "Your Honor, if the State were to go to trial, the State would show that around September of 1988, that Richard Kananen Sr. disappeared from his home . . ." and then she proceeded to tell the story. "The State would show that the defendant before the Court actually called his sister Cheryl, who planned on getting married in two weeks, to tell her that he's gone and you don't have to worry about him, have a nice wedding."

She told the judge, "Based on the family background

and the amount of violence that occurred in the family, along with physical and sexual abuse of those children, Mr. Kananen was not going to be invited to the wedding. The defendant had called her to tell her he had a present, that she didn't have to worry about him coming."

Rickie sat there, in his jail garb and shackles, as the prosecutor told how no one ever reported our father missing, because no one missed him. She then regaled the court with the story of my mother's disappearance, how she didn't show up for work on September 11, 2003, and how a coworker called Cheryl at home to report this extremely unusual situation.

Robin told the judge that Cheryl went to the house to check on our mom, and saw that her car was gone and the locks on the house had been changed. Robin continued that when Rickie arrived at the house, "He would say that he believed that the father had reappeared and taken the mother away. Ms. Bracken felt that was unusual since there had always been the feeling that he was just gone."

The judge was informed that a missing persons report was filed, at first, but that the case eventually was handed over to the homicide detectives who were unable to freeze a particularly large bank account that my mother owned, because it was still in probate. Then came the damning stories about me. She said, "The State would show that Stacey Kananen and Richard Kananen proceeded to have electronic checks sent to different accounts that they had, personal accounts, including their business accounts for Green Acres Services and Emerald Electric.

"The State would show several thousand dollars were

moved from the SunTrust account to accounts of Mr. Kananen, along with his sister. The State would further show that Richard Kananen and Stacey Kananen had a yard sale, which Detective Mark Hussey went by and found they were selling Disney collectibles, which were believed to be the property of Marilyn Kananen."

She paced the courtroom floor, winding up her tempo and launching into how Rickie was seen by Mom's neighbors emptying her house at all hours of the night, taking black trash bags to the curb. "Mr. Kananen went from saying 'The nightmare was back,' and 'Dad must have taken her,' to making statements that Marilyn Kananen had been receiving these Social Security checks of Richard Kananen over a period of fifteen years."

After telling the judge that Rickie told Daniel that he had shot our father, "blow-to-blow," Robin stated that Rickie resented Mom for not doing something more to prevent the abuse. He admitted, she continued, to using Mom's bank account to pay bills, but then he was confronted by police, during questioning, with the fact that it was not bills being paid, not credit cards, the house had been paid off, there was no mortgage, but that it was actually checks to him. She said that he then told police that "His sister actually killed his father, and that he was called over. He's also made a statement his mother actually killed his father, and he's just the one who buried him."

"Once they made statements to the police," Robin explained, "Stacey and Richard were left in a room, and unbeknownst to them, they were being videotaped, in which

Stacey Kananen admitted to making phone calls to banks trying to portray herself as Marilyn Kananen. But the defendant, obviously, aware of SunTrust accounts, started talking about it's all over for them, they know what we've done, and I need you to help me do something." The judge was then told about the suicide attempt in the storage unit, and how we were stopped and "rescued" by the fire department. "At the hospital the defendant confessed to killing his mother, although he continued to state that he only helped bury his father. He told police officers, told the sheriff's office that his father was buried underneath the garage. He also described that his mother was buried in the backyard of the Okaloosa residence, which is a mere block or so away from his mother's house where he and Stacey lived."

After the judge confirmed that my brother's attorney had nothing to add and no objections, his sentence was agreed upon, and the plea deal was complete. Robin then continued, "Your Honor, for purposes of this plea, it's our understanding that Mr. Kananen has agreed to speak to law enforcement." She told the judge that after the plea, he would be talking to Detective Hussey. And that's exactly what he did.

CHAPTER 11

Thrown Under the Bus

Immediately after Rickie was done with the plea hearing and sentencing, while they still had him shackled there in the courthouse building, he met with Detective Hussey, Hussey's partner, Darryl McCaskill, and Deputy Sheriff Wayne Lenihan in another room at the Orange County Courthouse. Officially, there was no deal in the works—nowhere on record is there any sign that he was given leniency in exchange for turning on me—but my defense attorney said to me later, "You can't tell me they didn't do something. I can't prove it, I can't find it, but verbally something was done somewhere." He went to a very good, special facility for serious offenders with mental illness.

The officers, led by Hussey, got Rickie to tell yet another version of the story, but this time he officially implicated me. What bothers me most about the transcript of his interview—aside from his testimony landing me in jail and practically destroying my life—was that so many of the questions were leading and the answers incredible.

They began the conversation with my father's murder in September 1988. Hussey started the ball rolling. "So, tell me about the events of that day."

"The events of that day is that I didn't kill my father," Rickie told Hussey. "My mother and Stacey asked me to come over to the house. When I went over there, he was in the garage. He was laying there rolled up in bedding. I put him in the freezer and a few months later I dug a hole in the garage and buried him. They didn't say anything, I didn't say anything, I didn't ask anything."

Even Hussey thought that was odd. He asked, "That seems unusual that you wouldn't ask, why'd you kill him, how'd you kill him?"

He simply responded, "I didn't," and then told Hussey that it was Mom's idea to put the body in the freezer, which she had apparently purchased for that purpose. The body was in the freezer for months until he rented a concrete saw, cut a hole in the floor, and buried it.

Detective McCaskill asked, "How long before did she buy that freezer?"

Rickie said, "It was there when I got there so, I don't know when she bought it. I never knew she had a freezer. It was just laying on the side right next to the body."

Then it got weird. His responses became very short and terse, and sometimes nonexistent. McCaskill asked, "When you put his body in the freezer, what kind of injuries did you observe he had?"

His response: "I don't know, he was wrapped up."

The detective continued, "So, you never looked at him at all?" Rickie didn't answer. McCaskill pressed on, "And what'd your sister say?"

"She didn't say anything," he said.

"Was she upset?" McCaskill asked.

"Huh?"

He asked again, "Was she upset?"

"I don't think so," Rickie replied.

McCaskill seemed a little nonplussed. "Was she relieved? Were they freaking out because they just killed somebody and the dead body's in the garage?"

Rickie simply stated, "It'd been there for a couple days, I guess."

"Did he stink? Was he bloated? Did he have any . . . fluids or anything like that?"

"He was wrapped up. I didn't see it. I could smell something."

The detective said, "When you put him in the freezer was he stiff? Like a board?"

"Yeah."

"Did anything drip out?" McCaskill asked.

"No."

"Was the bedding wet?" When Rickie replied that he didn't remember, McCaskill asked, "Was it nasty? Did it absorb any fluids or anything like that?"

"No, not that I know of," Rickie said. After McCaskill asked him how he knew who the body was, he said, "I knew it was my father. He wasn't in the house."

That didn't make sense to the officer. "You said you

never undid the wrapping. So, how'd you know it was your father?"

"I just knew," he insisted.

"But how?"

"He wasn't in the house."

"But that doesn't mean it's your father. Why would you believe that your father was there wrapped up in bedding in the garage?"

Rickie didn't answer that question, and Hussey stepped back in. "See, it's just strange that at some point somebody wouldn't ask the questions. I mean, it's just human nature to inquire about things like that. We're talking about a pretty serious event here. I know you hated your father. So, I'm thinking you're going to be pretty happy about this. You know he's not going to mess with you or your sisters . . . or your mother anymore. Every time you came to the house it was a confrontation, right? That's one of the reasons you didn't go to the house."

Rickie's answer was simply, "I wasn't allowed over there unless he called me."

"Okay. So, you get over there and you realize that he's dead in the garage. I mean, that's a good thing, right?"

Rickie admitted that it was. Hussey continued, "I don't know why you wouldn't say, 'What happened?' That seems strange to me."

Both detectives assured him that whatever they talked about that day wasn't going to affect his deal; it was already done. Even so, he wouldn't budge on how he knew the bundle was our father, without asking questions or looking inside.

Frustrated, McCaskill insisted, "If I go home and my dog's not in the house I'm not going to assume my dog's what's wrapped up in the blanket in the garage. How did you know it was your dad? Did you search the whole house? Did you check the bedroom? Did you see if he was in the shower? How did you know that the bundle in the garage was your dad?"

"I don't know how to explain it. I just knew."

"So you didn't feel the need to inquire?"

Rickie didn't answer.

"If my gold fish is dead upside down in the tank, I'm going to say, 'How'd my gold fish die? Did I not feed him enough or did I feed him too much?' And that's a gold fish."

Hussey interjected, "Yeah it's just kind of a human thing we're talking about."

McCaskill continued, "We're talking about a human being. We're talking about a person that breathed air. That lived life. That spawned children. I'm not saying he's a good guy at all, don't misunderstand me. I'm just saying that if a living being is no longer alive, natural instinct for every other human being is to inquire whether it's an accident. Whether it's a heart attack or sickness. Whether somebody put a bullet to his head. You're going to ask. I don't care who you are, you're going to ask. Especially if you're going to pick the body up and put it in the freezer. So, either you asked, or you already knew, how he had died. And what we're here asking you is which is it? Did you . . . how did you already know how he died? Or did you ask and they say he died this way?"

"I didn't ask."

"So, how did you know how he died?"

"I didn't know how he died."

"Then how do you know he was dead?"

"Because he wasn't in the house. I don't how else to explain it."

Hussey, apparently realizing that they were chasing their own tails, switched his line of questioning. "Had you ever discussed with your sister and your mother about doing away with your father?"

"No."

"Then to me this would be a very unusual event for you to come home and find him wrapped up in the garage. I'm trying to put myself in your place. If I had the relationship with my father that you did, and I get to the house and I find that he's dead in the garage, I'd be happy about that. That would be the weight of the world lifted off my shoulders. I don't have to worry about him causing me problems in my life anymore. And while we're on that subject, let's talk about a phone call that you made to Cheryl."

Rickie knew exactly what he was talking about. He interrupted Hussey and said, "No phone call. I went over in person. Told her that she didn't have to worry about . . . he wouldn't be at the wedding, he wasn't around anymore."

Hussey said, "So now you know what has happened and you know he's been killed. He's not coming back. Cheryl's thought was that you did this for her. She said it was almost like you were giving her a gift."

Rickie didn't answer.

"Yes? No?" Hussey persisted.

"Huh?"

"Yes? No? You remember back when you went over and talked to Cheryl?"

"Yes, and I remember what I told her. That he wasn't around anymore. She didn't have to worry about him."

"She asked questions. She said, 'How do you know that? What if he comes back?'"

"I just told her he wouldn't be back."

Then Hussey took Rickie down another path. "Who is the lady that . . . you got arrested for loitering and prowling. Remember when you had a Ryder truck with some duct tape and . . ."

"No, I never got arrested for anything like that."

"Well, I got the police report where they stopped you . . ."

"I wasn't arrested."

I can only imagine how he was exhausting the detective. Hussey persevered, "Okay, you were at this lady's house, somebody you'd been dating. You were near her house with this Ryder truck and the duct tape. You remember that?"

Rickie admitted that he did.

"Okay, what was that about?"

"I don't really remember."

"Okay. Alright. You're not . . . you're not working with me, Richard. You know this stuff where we're not remembering is not helping me. If you want to do this you're going to have to be forthcoming with me."

"I know."

"Or else we're not going to be able to do it. I know you're a smart guy but you're not going to play us. If you're not going to be forthcoming with me, this'll be the end of it. We'll let Stacey slide. It's up to you."

Rickie didn't answer, and Hussey continued, "You understand what I'm saying to you?"

"Yeah."

"I don't think I'm getting the whole story here. Let's move forward to September 11, 2003. Tell me about that day."

"I'm not sure what day it was."

Hussey must have been about ready to tear out his hair by now. "Okay. Alright, well let's . . ."

"I know it was in September, but I don't remember what day it was."

"Alright, tell me about what happened with your mother. Start from the beginning on your mom's murder."

Rickie began, "Well we went to, uh, went out to eat. Went to a movie and we went home to Mother's house. Stacey zapped her with a Taser."

"Okay, what happened to the Taser?"

"Throw it away in the dump."

"What dump?"

"Whatever the trash picks up."

Another dead end, so they began discussing the rest of Rickie's story, which was that he and I supposedly took Mom to dinner and a movie—to Fazoli's and then the early showing of *Charlie's Angels II* at the dollar theater on Colonial Drive—and that Susan stayed home. He told them that I was carrying a Taser that he had purchased at the Spy Store, also on Colonial Drive.

"So," Hussey asked, "where were you in the house when Stacey shot her with a Taser?"

"I was in the dining room area."

"Was anything said? I mean did you say anything to her? Was there an argument prior?"

"They were arguing. Stacey was worried that Mom was going to tell 'em about Dad. And Stacey didn't want to go down for it."

Now it was getting juicy. Hussey pressed on, "Was there some indication that your mother was getting ready to do that?"

"Stacey felt there was. She just felt that 'cause Mom kept on talking to people that, she said he was in Chicago. He was other places and stuff like that."

Hussey was buying it. "So . . . so, the cover story, Stacey was getting concerned that your mother was telling different stories and . . . thought something might be discovered. Okay. I'll go along with that. So, at some point Stacey hits your mom with the Taser. Now, I want you to understand something here. We've collected a lot of physical evidence. We've worked on this case day and night for ages. So, I know exactly how your mother was killed. I was at the autopsy. I was there when they gathered all the evidence. So, I want you to tell me, but I want you to be truthful with me. Because if you don't I'm going to know. After the Taser was deployed, then what happened? Your mother fell down?"

"Yeah, apparently she fell down."

"What do you mean apparently? You were there."

Rickie stated, "I wasn't . . . I was sitting . . . countertop, I was sitting like that. And they were on my side, backside."

"Okay. So, Stacey hits her with the Taser, she falls down, then what?"

"Then what?"

"Then what?"

"Then she got suffocated."

"Okay, tell me about that."

"Put a rag of, uh, what do you call it? Rag of like a bandana thing, like over my mother's head, face."

"Okay."

Detective McCaskill stepped back in. "How long did you hold the rag over her face?"

Rickie responded, "I have no idea."

"Were you pushing down real hard or were you just kind of . . . do you remember?"

"That."

"Okay, so you're squeezing the nose . . ."

"Yeah."

". . . and covering the mouth? What was Stacey doing when you were suffocating her?" McCaskill continued.

"Just standing there."

"Was she over your shoulder or helping hold her down?"

"Yeah."

"Yeah, which one?"

"No, she was just standing there."

"So, she wasn't holding her feet or arms or anything like that? Just standing over top of your shoulder?"

Rickie didn't respond, so Hussey jumped back in. "Were you on top of your mother holding her down? I mean she was obviously struggling some. I mean . . ."

"No, she didn't."

"Okay. Did she make any noise? Was she . . ."

"No."

"How long do you think it took?"

"I have no idea."

McCaskill picked it up. "A minute, two minutes, three minutes?"

"I wouldn't know," Rickie said.

Hussey let it go and asked, "Once you realized she was dead, when did you do the duct tape?"

"Stacey wrapped her legs and her arms in duct tape."

"The arms, behind her back, or in front?"

"They were in the front."

"Okay. How about her face?"

"One, there was one on her mouth."

"Stacey put that on there?"

"Yeah."

Rickie told the officers that we wrapped her in two plastic garbage bags, put her in the trunk of her car, and drove her body to a storage unit, where we supposedly put her in a freezer that he had purchased a couple weeks prior. Then, he said, he went back to Mom's house and changed the locks. Hussey asked him, next, about the house that Susan and I bought.

"You guys bought that house over close to your mom's."

"They bought a house."

"But, by all accounts, you were with 'em when they were looking for the house."

"No."

"Well, that's the information that we got. I don't think it was a coincidence that that house was bought less than a block away. Your mother told the people that she worked with that she didn't want her kids that close to her, right down the block. And she didn't want everybody watching her. She shared that with her coworkers. But she said the only place that Stacey and Susan looked was in the neighborhood. They wanted that house. They wanted a place close. So, that house was bought what eight, nine months before?"

"I think they bought it January, February."

He denied that there were any plans at that time to kill Mom, but said that we started talking about doing it a few months later. "She was worried about Mom going to tell about what was in the garage."

"Worried, obsessed would you say?"

"Yeah."

"Okay. So, at some point a plan was hatched as to how this was going to go down?"

"No," Rickie said, "it wasn't really. It just happened. We didn't sit there and plan this how we're going to do it."

Hussey was confused. "Well, you bought a freezer."

"Yeah."

"You put the freezer in the storage unit. You knew you were going to put her in the freezer because that's how you done dad."

"Yeah."

"Okay. So, there was a plan."

Rickie started backpedaling. "I'm not saying that we didn't, actually what happened . . ."

"You just didn't know it was going to go that specific night, is what you're saying?"

"Right."

Hussey was back on track. "Okay. Alright. But it was talked about. Somebody said, well when we get an opportunity, we're all together, nobody's around. We're going to zap mom with a Taser. That's it?"

It sounded good to Rickie. "Basically, yeah."

"So, that night the opportunity presented itself?"

"Yeah."

Hussey continued, "You moved out some of your mom's clothes to make it look like she left. Tell me what you and Stacey . . . obviously Stacey's with you through all of this stuff."

"Yeah."

"She's helping you move the stuff. When did you move clothes?"

"The next day. That's all I did. Then a couple days later I started packing things up."

Hussey asked, "So the days after the murder. Now the people from work are starting to call because your mom didn't show up at work. Cheryl's getting concerned. What are you telling her?"

"She talked to Stacey, she didn't talk to me."

"Okay. So, after she talked to Stacey then Stacey obviously talks to you." Hussey put more words into his mouth. "You guys are close. You and Stacey are in this. You're talking about things. Tell me what's going on in the days afterwards."

"Just days afterwards, just we're picking up and packing everything up and getting everything situated."

"Were you concerned that Cheryl was going to get the cops onto you guys?"

"Yeah."

"Okay. Tell me about those discussions."

Rickie answered, "Just general conversation."

"Well, did you ever talk about maybe we're going to need to do away with Cheryl?"

"No."

"Maybe we're going to need to shut Cheryl up?"

"No."

"I want to understand what Stacey's involvement in this is. Because the interviews that I've had with Stacey, she doesn't say anything. She's kept her mouth shut. I need to know what she's thinking. The only one that can shed some light on that is you."

"We never talked about getting rid of Cheryl."

Hussey switched his line of questioning again. "At some point you talked to your nephew, Daniel. You shared some things with him, that he eventually came to us with. Did you ever talk to Stacey about things you said to Daniel?"

"No."

"Okay. So, that was just you and him. The day after the murder you went over and you cleaned out some clothes."

"The closet, cleaned up the floor."

"What was on the floor that you had to clean up?"

"Um, when she shot the Taser the little makers fell out."

Rickie told Hussey that he and I sent Susan off on a cruise with her mother, and that the cruise was planned that way so that we would have time to bury our mother in the backyard. He said that it was my decision to bury her there, and that we waited for Susan to call from the ship to make sure she wasn't going to come back.

"How long did it take you to do all that?" Hussey asked.

"Maybe an hour."

"Okay. So, you did all that in one day."

"Yeah it was all . . . all . . . soon as . . . soon as . . . soon as Stacey got the call from Susan we started digging the hole."

"Okay," Hussey continued, "in December of '03, tell me about what Stacey's mood was then and what you talked about when you guys started to realize that maybe we had some idea about what was going on there."

"I said we're going to get caught. Stacey didn't think so."

"Okay."

"I knew we were caught when the sheriffs came by when we were putting the Chattahoochee stone down. I said, after I seen the sheriff came by in the squad car, we're going to get caught. She said, 'We won't get caught.' And that's basically all the conversation."

The rest of the exchange was mostly about how he prepared the floor for the decorative covering of Chatta-hoochee stone, whose purpose was to hide the steel plates. His rambling tale, along with Hussey's hand-fed prompt-ing, were the basis for an arrest warrant being made out in my name. Yes, ladies and gentleman, this half-assed con-versation is the one that landed me in jail and on trial for my life, facing the death penalty.

CHAPTER 12

Hussey Gets His Wish

The state's attorney's office was supposed to contact me and let me know if he took a plea deal, which would mean that I wouldn't have to testify at his trial. When I didn't hear anything one way or the other, Susan e-mailed them several times, asking what happened with the case, what's the status, is it going to trial? We couldn't find any information online or anywhere else for that matter. Finally, I saw a newspaper article that said he took a plea. I looked at Susan and I said, "I think I'm in trouble." The complete lack of communication had me scared.

I was arrested May 9, 2007, at Gulf Coast Resort, in front of a crowd of friends and gawkers. The day the police showed up, Susan and I had gone to Jo-Ann Fabric. We were buying decorations for our yard. Jo-Ann was having a sale on yard accessories, so we were just farting around, having a good time. After shopping, we were going to a birthday party, so we thought we would pick up something to bring as a gift.

We were killing time until the party, enjoying being out of the park. Living where you work can be very difficult, because you're never off the clock. There is always someone with an issue or problem, and if you're outside where they can see you, it's open season. They might not expect you to do anything about their complaint outside of office hours (although many of them do), but it doesn't stop them from tattling on their neighbor while you're trying to relax and grill a couple burgers on the back porch. Once in a while, we just had to get away and leave Wendell in charge.

We finished shopping at Jo-Ann at about 5:00 P.M. Susan had left her cell phone in the car—I rarely carried a phone—so when she saw that she had missed six calls from Wendell, we were both alarmed. Wendell never called just to gab. She checked her voice mail and discovered that he just left a cryptic message: "Call me."

On the edge of panic, Susan called him. He said, "The police are here to arrest Stacey. You have to come back, immediately." Instantly, she was crying, hysterical. Jo-Ann's was about a fifteen-minute drive from the resort and we needed some levelheaded advice.

First, we called my best friend and coworker, Gail, and her husband, Bob. They lived a little north of where we were, and they insisted, "Come to our house! Don't go to the resort under any circumstances until you talk to a lawyer!" I told Susan, "That's Hernando County and I'm not bringing another county in on this." I wasn't going to run. I wanted to do the right thing, but I wanted to do right by me, first and foremost.

Susan understood that, but she was still freaking out. She cried, her voice high and shrill, "Well, we have to talk to somebody to get the same opinion from everybody, because we don't know what to do!" So I asked, "Whose advice would you trust?" The only person she could think of was her mother, and we both agreed that Ann would have trusted one of the City Retreat homeowners, the president of the HOA, Gary.

Once Susan got him on the phone, Gary said, "You have to come back, that's what you have to do." Of course, Susan was still hysterical. She called our other friends, Jim and Alice, and they said the same thing: get back to the resort. We started driving south on U.S. 19, hearts pounding, tears flying, when Susan said, "No, we're not going," and she whipped around back up 19 and parked in the Publix grocery store parking lot.

Meanwhile, back at the park, it was utter mayhem. We heard later that it looked like an entire SWAT team had shown up to arrest me. The police stormed the resort, in black gear and flak jackets, armed to the teeth as though they were there to pick up a cell of terrorists. Upon arrival, they headed straight to Lot 130, the trailer where Susan and I first lived. When we moved, we must have forgotten to change the unit number on record at the Orange County Sheriff's Office, which we had given them three years ago. The address was exactly the same; only the unit number had changed. They certainly had no problem delivering subpoenas.

This scene drew a huge crowd of naked people. Surrounding the trailer, officers approached the front door and pounded, weapons at the ready. The snowbird owners were already back up north, so one of the nudists, trying to be helpful, shouted out, "No one's there. They're in Canada."

From what I've been told by those who were there, the officers' reactions to this news was both frightening and comical, because they apparently thought this meant that Susan and I had fled to Canada. They were panicked, chagrined, and furious at the same time. Fortunately, Wendell pulled up on his golf cart and took charge. He told them that Susan and I now lived just a few doors down, but that we were out of the park. He asked them to calm down and gather their officers, who were spread out all over the resort, by the front gate where we were sure to be coming back any minute. They agreed to do so, as long as Wendell called us to let us know to get back there. And that's what he did, six times, before we got back to the car and heard his voice mail.

What we didn't know was that once Wendell actually spoke to Susan, they took his cell phone and got Susan's phone number in order to track us. By having her phone number, as long as she kept the phone turned on—which she did—they were able to track its signal on the nearby cell towers and keep a general eye on our movements. Fortunately, it never seriously occurred to us to try to run or to pull a Thelma and Louise, even if we did sit in the Publix parking lot for a little while until Susan stopped screaming. Gary had told us that he'd be at the gate waiting for us, so while we were en route, I called Diane, our surrogate mom since Ann died, and told her what was going on. By this time, Susan's brother, Robert, called us, too, because the police were now gathering in his front yard, right by the front gate. I told Diane, "You better go be with Robert because he's going to panic." So Diane was with Robert, Gary was with Wendell, and a whole crowd of nudists were gathered with them, all waiting for us.

Apparently, the resort was swarming with police cars, some marked, some not, but once they were assured we were coming, Gary told them that they should put their weapons away because he thought this was ridiculous. "What are you doing? She weighs a hundred pounds. Who are you coming to get, Bonnie and Clyde?"

On our way down the home stretch, down East Road toward Gulf Coast Resort, we saw squad cars, spaced at intervals, waiting along the road to make sure we were coming because I was now "wanted." There was a warrant for my arrest. They were watching us drive all over on their GPS, but there was no panic because they saw us coming.

The scene in our car was crazy, with the screaming match between me and Susan, trying to decide what to do. I finally said, "We have to go. You're going to get arrested. Then it becomes aiding and abetting. We'll both be in jail and no one could get us out." From the initial phone call, to our actual arrival, was probably about thirty minutes.

To say I was terrified would be a galactic understatement. When we pulled in the gate, the Pasco County Sheriff's car was right in front of Robert's house, and then there was Detective Hussey's car. His wet dream had come true: he was there to arrest me.

We pulled in and parked, as I counted my last moments of freedom, aching for it to be yesterday again. Susan hopped out of the driver's side and started screeching at Hussey, "You fucking asshole!" And even though I agreed, I yelled at her to shut up. I got out of the car and saw Diane and begged, "Get her away." I had my hands on Susan, asking, "Somebody, get her out of here, she can't go to jail."

Robert stared at me, incredulous, as if to say, "I can't believe you're going to surrender." What was I supposed to do? There was a murder warrant out on me. If I didn't do something really calm, I was dead. Both Pasco and Orange County officers were there. I surrendered to Pasco County because if I surrendered to Orange County, I'd be going across the state in a car with Hussey. I wasn't comfortable with that.

I said to the officer, "I understand you need to arrest me." He said, "I do," and looked at me quizzically—he didn't expect this to go so easily. He put the handcuffs on me and sat me in the car. Susan was hysterical, stuttering, "C-c-can I bring her some clothes?" I was wearing shorts and a tank top and she was afraid I would freeze. The officer said it was okay, and Diane said to Susan, "Let's go get her a few things." I think he said yes, just to shut her up and get her away from everybody.

She brought me some sweats, which never left the

trunk of the police car until I actually got to the jail. I never saw them until they checked them in as part of my property, in Orange County. I didn't get to wear them there, either; I got jail scrubs.

Diane was standing by the car door, talking to me, when Hussey came up and said, "I don't want anybody near this car. She's a murderer. Nobody's allowed to talk to her." The Pasco County officer started to say, "Look, man . . ." and Hussey barked, "I'm in charge of this case. I don't want anybody near her." And he slammed the door. As we drove away, I didn't look out the back window. I knew the scene I would see would break my heart: Susan collapsing in tears in Diane's arms and being led to her golf cart to be driven home to our little house that we were still decorating with knickknacks from Jo-Ann's.

CHAPTER 13

Descent into Hell

The long drive to jail, handcuffed and shivering in the back of that squad car, gave me a lot of time to think about my predicament and the bizarre path that my entire life had taken. If it hadn't actually happened to me, I don't think I would have believed that a story line like this could possibly be true. For so many years I had fought to keep my childhood experiences out of my conscious thoughts, but they just kept coming back to slap me as if to say, "It's never going to end." If I'd had any idea, when I was a child, that this is where I would end up, I don't know that I would have fought so hard to stay alive all those years, especially when I was struggling to survive in Arkansas.

When we arrived from Minnesota, to the outskirts of the tiny town of Viola, Arkansas, in the middle of my sixth-grade year, my father found a house to rent. It was way off the beaten path on a dirt road, several miles from the nearest neighbor. I know it seems hard to believe that it could get worse than it was in Minnesota, but it did. Each one of us felt that we would die in Arkansas. The only times we were safe was when my father was at the bar.

I don't know what caused him to snap, but I think the seclusion of where we lived—in Minnesota you could actually see the other farmhouses; in Arkansas, we had fifteen acres of woods—made him believe he could do anything he wanted to and nobody could see him. There was no one around to rein in his madness and nobody could hear us scream. He could do whatever the hell he wanted to. And he did.

Mom worked far away. Oftentimes, my father would force her to walk to work in the morning, then pick her up at night and she would come home bloody. I have vivid memories of constant gunfire in the house.

Cheryl and I only attended classes for a few months that semester. Shortly after we arrived, there was a blizzard and the schools closed down. As the snow melted, the dirt roads were flooded. No school buses would run. That left my sister and me alone, with him, for a long time while my mom and brother were at work. He was drunk every day. He hit us with his fists, pulled hair, slammed us against the wall; sometimes we'd get a dish thrown at us, and if we were lucky we'd see it coming and duck.

One Saturday morning, my father woke us up screaming that he was going to kill us all. He and Mom had apparently already been fighting that day, and Rickie, who was in his early twenties at the time, picked up another loaded shotgun and started yelling back at him. By this time my brother was involved in all the fights. I don't know whether it was because my father dragged him in, or if he chose to take my mother's side.

Rickie and my father went outside and headed toward the woods behind our house. My father hollered to us that only one of them was coming back alive. Three agonizing hours later both men came back. I don't know what happened in the woods, and I don't want to know what happened in the woods. Nothing was ever said about the incident.

One day, after a huge fight with my mother, my father decided that he was leaving and my sister and I should leave with him. He, of course, was drunk and it was early evening when he decided to go. He made us pack our clothes and put them in the trunk, and he drove off with us. First, he decided to stop at the town bar.

Cheryl and I sat in the car for hours, until he came out too drunk to drive far. We returned to the house, and when we got inside he grabbed his gun. He forced me into his bedroom and, with the door locked and a loaded pistol in my mouth, he raped me for the first time. That was the first time he got all the way through the act. Other times he had tried and didn't succeed. Up until then, he was using items, fingers, and tools, which do enough damage, trust me.

He said, "If you make a sound I'll pull the trigger." I *knew* he'd do it. Telling me that he's going to hit me if I move or scream is one thing. Putting a loaded gun in my mouth is a totally different feeling. I was fully aware of the power he had over me then, as well as the changes that were to come regarding my sexual abuse. It was that night I realized my father *would* kill me.

Rape isn't just someone physically violating your body in a cruel and selfish way; it's that they're *getting off* on doing this to you. Imagine being a small child looking up at your father, your rapist, seeing that he is *enjoying* hurting you and forcing you to submit, and treating you like filth. Imagine what that does to your developing psyche.

In the years to come, I never got raped again when anyone was home, except once in a while when my mother was beaten so badly she couldn't get out of bed. He fondled me when other people were home, but that's different from climbing on top of me and penetrating. He fondled Cheryl in front of me and I didn't think anything of it when we lived in Maine and Minnesota. It's just what happened. It's what he did. But that was the first real, hardcore rape, and he didn't want anyone to interrupt him. I think Mom knew what was going on in that room, and Cheryl must have figured it out. He may have already been doing this to her by now. I guess everybody just figured it was my turn.

I believe it was the next day that Mom and Rickie were out in the barn, working with the animals—we had goats back then—and my mother sent me back to the house to fetch something for her. When I got there, my father was in a rampage and he had all of my mother's clothes, everything she owned, piled in the front yard. He said, "You tell her to come to the house or I'm going to set her clothes on fire."

I ran back to the barn and said, "I'm supposed to make you go to the house." She said, "You can't make me do anything," and stayed put. Well, he torched all of her belongings, except for a couple outfits for her to wear to work.

That night, he sat her down in a chair, took a knife, and carved up her forehead, slowly and deliberately. After he passed out for the night, she put a bandage on it and took us kids with her to a pay phone where she called my grandfather. She told him, "I have to leave him and I need money."

My grandfather sent her a thousand dollars, which she handed to my father. She told us kids, "We were going to leave but this will keep him quiet; he'll be nice for a while." Next thing I knew, we were moving to Florida.

CHAPTER 14

A Nightmare Come True

People ask me sometimes why I didn't just take off when I knew they were coming to arrest me. All I can say is that I had a naïve faith in the system and knew that I was innocent. If I was guilty I would have disappeared. Even though I knew Hussey wanted to arrest me, my response was, "Here's my address. That's where I'm going to be. Need me? Come see me."

Well, that's what he did, and I was glad that I had chosen to surrender to the Pasco sheriff, because no one in that department had a personal grudge against me. They were just assisting the Orange County boys. Detective Hussey and his partner took me into an interrogation room at the Pasco Sheriff's Office. I sat there and said absolutely nothing. He asked me, "Do you have anything to say?"

"No." Not only was I angry, but I wasn't stupid. I've seen enough cop shows to know better than to talk to anyone who wants to take you down, not without a lawyer.

He pushed a little bit further. "Your brother tells us you killed your parents. Don't you think you should defend yourself?"

"No."

"What does no mean?"

"I don't have anything to say," I replied. I knew the game by now. I was glaring at Detective Hussey, and he said, "You need to just go ahead and tell me. I have pictures of you in the shop where your brother bought the Taser."

He asked again, "Do you have anything to say?" and I said no. He asked, "No, you weren't there?" and I replied, "No, I have nothing to say."

With that, he stated, "Well then, you're formally under arrest," and I replied, "I'm aware of that." He Mirandized me and left the room. He left with me his partner, who played good cop and said, "Look, it will go easier if you just tell us what happened. Here's my business card, if you want to talk to me."

I said, "I have nothing to say."

He said, "You're making it harder on yourself."

I said, "I have nothing to say."

I cooperated with them back in '03 and '04 and they screwed me in '07. You think I've got something to say? I've got nothing to say. I wanted to see the pictures they had. They got pictures? Bring 'em on, buddy, because they don't exist. You got the man who worked at the store where my brother bought the Taser swearing he saw me there? Bring him to the courtroom.

Bring it on.

For all of my bravado, though, Hussey scared the hell out of me. I sat in that interrogation room and listened to the man lie about all these photographs he's had since 2003. Well, if he had them, I would have been arrested in 2003. He had nothing. He wanted me just to say something to save face and save a murder trial. I don't save face on something I didn't do. And up until nine days ago, I was a witness. It took nine more days for them to transfer me from the Pasco County jail to the Orange County jail. Those days before the transfer were stressful and horrible, as I reluctantly became acclimated to the concept of incarceration. They tell you when to shower and what to eat, drink, and any other normal activities or needs, and I had just been labeled a murder suspect. People look at you funny when you have that label. It wasn't a label that I enjoyed having. The place was so crowded that they didn't even have enough beds, so I had to sleep in what looked like a plastic boat, on the floor. However, the building was relatively new, and the food—such as it was—was edible. I kept to myself, for the most part, and people left me alone. The conditions weren't bad, per se, but the reason I was there was enough to make it unbearable.

Susan came to see me every day, frantic with worry. I didn't have a lawyer because I didn't think I needed Michael Gibson anymore, so I had let him go years ago. Susan was making phone calls, trying to find out how to get some good legal counsel, but the prices were astronomical.

It was looking like the public defender was going to be in my immediate future, and I was mortified. God bless the folks who work as PDs, but we've all heard horror stories about what can happen when you don't have a private practice attorney for serious charges. The public defenders are overloaded and don't have the time it takes to dedicate themselves to each and every case. Chances were good that I would end up having to plea-bargain my way into lesser charges and lighter sentences. I knew I was going to be in jail for a very long time, for crimes I didn't commit. I spent a lot of time wavering between self-pity and sheer terror.

Once I was transferred to Orange County, they dressed me up in the same kind of blue jumpsuit I'd seen Rickie wearing. I was assigned a bunk in a huge dorm room and quickly tried to blend into the scenery. God knows I'd had enough training in invisibility as a child.

The next day, I went before the judge, who told me that I was being charged with murder in the death of my mother, and told me that the death penalty was being considered. The public defender, who was standing next to me, literally had to keep me from collapsing on the floor. I couldn't speak, and I couldn't walk. My knees went weak and it was all I could do to not vomit. The one piece of good news was that, since Rickie had been appointed a public defender, it would be a conflict of interest for them to defend me. Eventually, I was appointed a private attorney, Diana Tennis, who specialized in death penalty cases. The bad news was that she was on a ten-day vacation. I was going to have to stay in jail for a while.

At least in Pasco County I could eat the food. Orange County food was inedible. It took me a long time to acclimate because I was hungry all the time. *All the time.* I couldn't get their food down and I was starving. I wanted to eat; I just couldn't swallow it. I'd force it into my mouth and start to throw it up. It was horrible. I should have been able to eat noodles and rice, because I love those, but the noodles were like glue. All I tasted was salt and slime. The rice was so sticky I just couldn't get it down. I could feel my body deteriorating from not eating.

It's funny what's important when you're locked up. I bought coffee packets at the commissary because they could be used as currency. I saw inmates make jailhouse "cocaine" out of powdered drink mix, sugar, a coffee packet, and a bottle of water. They whip it really fast until they get this frothy foam and then they down it. If they were coming down off of drugs, that's what they'd do for a boost. No one can bring you anything from the outside world. Whenever Susan or Diane came to visit me, it was via video camera, and we weren't even in the same building.

There are some very scary people in jail, but some of the women I met were unfortunate souls who never stood a chance. One had been doing heroin since she was four— her mother taught her how; one was in for prostitution, which she had been involved in since she was a kid; another was just a drug addict. We would sit and play cards until they made us go to bed. And that's how we got through the nights.

We were in a dorm, like an army barracks. I bought a deck of cards at the commissary because sometimes we'd get banished to our bunks and weren't allowed to speak, so the only thing to do was play solitaire. During the day, you either take a class to pass the time, or you watch TV and listen to the guards yell at you all day. You get two hours recreation a day, an hour in the morning and an hour at night. There was a basketball hoop outside, and if everyone was good, we got the basketball.

Everyone had to wake up at 4:00 A.M. in case somebody had to go to court. Breakfast was at 4:30 so they could get to court. Even if nobody had to go to court, we were still up because they do the same process every day.

Every night they came into the dorm with a bag of used disposable razors, which were sanitized and reused until the blades went dull, in case you wanted to shave. And you didn't talk when you were in the shower. Didn't even say "good morning" because they'd throw you out. I saw them cut off the water in all the showers because two people were talking—you were soaped up and had to wait until they got female guards to remove the two who were talking and then they'd turn the water back on. If you had a male guard, you were not allowed to use the restroom until they got a female guard because there were open walls so they could see. So if you had to go, that was just too bad; you had to wait. If you had to go to the bathroom after lights out, too bad. No walking around after hours.

While jail was a horrid experience, I have to give credit

where it's due and say that some of the correctional officers were really good people. When I got a postcard from my aunt saying that I was where I belonged, I went up to the guard, crying—it really hurt—and she said, "You don't want to cry in here." I explained how devastated I was, and she asked, "Do you want to go into solitude just so you can deal with this?" I said no, and she said, "I'm telling you for your own safety, you have to stop crying right now because I won't be able to protect you from all these girls." She explained that they'd think I was weak and bad things could happen. So we talked for a while and she really helped me.

Friday and Saturday nights we got to stay up late because there were no classes and no court on the weekend. The guard on watch those two nights was a really nice lady. We'd have talent contests and she'd give out candy to the winner. She would talk to us like we were human beings. She understood, shit happens, sometimes you're in here for the wrong reasons, sometimes you're not supposed to be here. She said, "I'm not here to know why. I'm here to keep everybody safe."

Finally, after what seemed like an eternity, my court-appointed attorney came to see me. Diana Tennis was a very likable, no-nonsense person, and I grew to be very fond of her over the years. But my first meeting with her wasn't under very good circumstances, so I probably wasn't as nice to her as I could have been. I was innocent and terrified, and I had been waiting for what felt like time without end, in jail, while she was off on some trip. She began our working relationship by shaking my hand and saying, in essence, "I just wanted to stop by and introduce myself. I've been on vacation. I'll be back to see you in four days."

Disappointed that she was leaving so quickly and with not so good news, I shrugged. "Okay, whatever." She asked, "Are you alright? Do you need medication?"

I said, "No, I don't take medication. I'm fine. Whatever."

The thing about Diana that made me trust her so much was her demeanor when she came to me in jail: she didn't look down at me. Some attorneys would come to see their clients, and they were awfully stuck-up. She came at meal-time, so they brought me a tray while we sat and talked, and of course I couldn't eat. She said, "You need to eat something."

I told her, "I can't eat this food. It makes me nauseous." She said, "Well then, we need to get you out on bail."

Next time, when she came back, we met in a private room. She had a huge stack of papers, and as she was flipping through them she said, flat out, "Tell me why you're in here, because this doesn't make any sense to me. I can't believe they're charging you with this when you were their star witness."

I was as baffled as she was. "I don't know why, Diana, other than . . ."

She interrupted, "I can tell you, Detective Hussey is trying to make a name for himself. Your name is on these business bank accounts and that's all they have at this point." She said, ruffling through the papers, "Richard has this story and he has this story and he has this story," pointing them all out to me.

I said, "Exactly."

She said, "We're going for a bond in a couple days. You'll be home that night." I tried not to roll my eyes while I thought, "No I won't, you nutcase. I'm in here for murder!" At that time it was only one count of second degree on my mother. They had not charged me in my father's death yet.

She and Susan had been talking on the phone, and Diana told her that the bond was probably going to be a large amount, and it would help if she could rally some friends or family to show up and sit in the gallery to show the judge that I had a normal life, with normal people who believed in me. Well, the only people I had left were my nudist friends, so that's who Susan turned to. No one else in Florida, not the few friends I made growing up, none of my Disney coworkers, no one would stand by my side and say they believed in my innocence. But the people at Gulf Coast Resort promised to show up, and, to the judge's surprise, they did en masse.

CHAPTER 15

The Sunshine State

We moved to Orlando in late spring of 1977. On the way, our father made Cheryl ride in the moving truck with him to keep Mom from taking off with all of us in the car. When Cheryl got out of the truck when we arrived, she was badly bruised.

Mom got a better job in Florida and his Social Security went up, so for the first time they could live in a decent house, and it even had a pool in the backyard. Our living conditions were definitely better.

Rickie moved out almost immediately. I think he stayed as long as he did because we had always lived in the country and he finally felt comfortable moving out now that we lived someplace we'd at least have neighbors if something went wrong. Little did we know, that didn't make a difference. There was a long period of time when none of us saw him because he was told by my father not to come back.

That's why I can't say anything really horrible about my brother. Yeah, he threw me under the bus. But he also stayed years longer than he had to, just to keep us alive—he even quit college, all those years ago, because our father threatened to kill us if he didn't come back home. We all seemed to have this delusional idea that we could keep one another alive, just by sticking together. I have a dual-edged emotional tug with him, and I think that's why Cheryl wanted to believe his stories, no matter how implausible they were, because he was the one that kept us alive until we got to the city.

Shortly after he moved out that first summer, he met a woman where he worked, a meat-packing plant, and they got married. She was probably a very nice lady, but she was my mother's age, maybe older, with grown kids, and he was only twenty-two. I didn't understand what he was doing, and I never got to know her very well.

I lived in that house from seventh grade until I was twenty-two years old. That's when I met Susan and she and I moved out to Kissimmee in early 1989. In the meantime, we tried to live a normal life, such as it was. There wasn't much music in our home, but my parents used to listen to Johnny Cash, Patsy Cline, and Elvis Presley. I had a radio in my room that I turned on when they were fighting, to drown out the sound.

If I wanted to watch TV, there was one in the kitchen

or in my parents' room. I'd come home from school in the afternoon and he'd be watching *The PTL Club* with Jim and Tammy Faye Bakker, drinking his booze. He was an atheist, but there was something about Jim and Tammy Faye that intrigued him.

Until we moved to Florida, Mom was not allowed to get a driver's license. He drove her everywhere or she walked, so he had total control. Eventually, though, his eyesight faded because intense drinking will kill your vision, so he told her, "You need to get a driver's license if you want to work, because I can't drive you forever."

Well, that was his undoing, because he lost control. He couldn't stop her from going where she wanted. She could make a twenty-five-dollar allowance go pretty far. He would fill her gas tank and hand over her money for the week. She always had money, and he didn't like that.

I don't know the exact year, but Cheryl and I, one Christmas when we were in our midteens, saved up and bought a mother's ring at Kmart for forty dollars. We were so proud that we were able to do that, to show her that we loved her, because she sure didn't get any appreciation from him. That money was just about everything we had saved, and then we realized we forgot to buy something for him. That year, Mom helped us out and got him cigarettes and a bottle of booze and marked it from us kids.

We did try to make our lives feel normal, like the time that Cheryl and I attempted to throw our parents a twenty-fifth anniversary party. Their anniversary was on a Wednesday, and we were planning a party for Saturday, with a few of the neighbors. We hadn't been in that house very long, so they really didn't know any of us—or our family dynamic—that well.

We came home from school on Wednesday, and he said to Cheryl, "Aren't you making a cake?" He had never asked about an anniversary cake the whole time they'd been married, and they've never gone out for their anniversary. Cheryl, disappointed that the surprise was being spoiled, replied, "No, we're planning a party for Saturday," thinking that would calm him down. It didn't. He screamed, "You fucking kids are useless! You don't give a fuck about us. You didn't even make a fucking cake for your mother!" and left to go to the bar.

Cheryl and I made a chocolate mayonnaise cake, and when Mom came home she said, "Oh, how nice! You made a cake!" He came home, and when Cheryl said, "Here's your anniversary cake," he took it out to the backyard and threw it against the fence. He screamed, "You wouldn't make it until I got pissed off and screamed at you, so what's the point of having it now?" We didn't have an anniversary party that weekend. We were grounded for two weeks. No phone or TV. Nothing but homework and sitting in our rooms.

He was big on throwing food, as Cheryl even said during one of her TV interviews after my trial. She told the story about mashed potatoes being flung at every meal if you left a lump in them. The pot would sit on the table and he'd fling it at whoever cooked that day. It was not abnormal. We learned to beat those potatoes until they were almost like soup.

Oddly, having a pot of potatoes thrown at your head was preferable to the alternative, because he usually had a loaded gun at the dinner table. One day, my father was drunk and threatening a neighbor when the police were sent to our house. My father had his pistol on the dining room table, and after many words with the officers he stood up and put his hand near the gun. He was taken down and arrested. My mother stayed home from work the next day and bailed him out of jail. Her three children could have banded together and said enough to put him away for a long time, but she said no. The good news was that he received probation for his actions.

However, one day he was beating my mom so severely that I thought he was going to kill her—he said he was going to. I called the police telling them his name, probation, and his charges. Two officers came out to the house, and my father answered the door and said, "Everything's okay." They said, "Fine, we're just checking on you," and away they went. I got my ass beat for that. That was the last time I called the police.

I watched, helplessly, one night as he tried to drown my mom. He threw her into the sliding glass door and bruised the whole side of her body, and then threw her in the pool. He stood with his foot on her head. She couldn't fight back. She didn't have enough in her to try to stay alive. I don't know what made him stop. There was nothing I could do about it because he'd do the same thing to me. When he came into my room to rape me, I didn't have the physical or mental strength to beat him.

He was drinking a lot more and was allowing my

mother's bruises to be more visible. She'd go to work bruised and limping. One day she called in sick—she really did have the flu. They didn't believe her so they sent two of the guys to the house with a made-up story. When they saw she was "okay," they left.

After such a long time of living like this, it was "normal." We lived our lives, went to work, and had friends. My sister said, in one of her TV interviews, that she didn't realize we weren't normal until somebody in high school said to her, "Where did you get all those bruises?" She said, "My father did it. It's just how it is. It's always been this way."

In high school, I took a psychology class and learned about drinking disorders and abuse. I honestly didn't know what normal was until then. I never talked to anyone about it, though. If any teacher would have asked the question, I'm sure I would have answered it. I would have the marks to prove my stories. But nobody ever asked.

Unfortunately, I think it's up to the person being abused to make the first move. You'd like to think that your teachers notice, but what if they don't? I was afraid that either a) the school would call my father and then, of course, I'd get the shit kicked out of me, or b) they wouldn't believe me and nothing would change. Because nothing did. Nothing ever did change. You could call the cops and nothing would change. I would like to think that things are different now, that teachers pay attention to warning signs. They talk about kids who don't do so well in school, but that's not the only kind of kid to be looking at. They need to be looking at kids that do nothing but bury themselves in books. Because there's a reason they're doing that.

I wish I would have had the courage to tell the stories in a writing assignment in English class. Hypothetical stories, people pay attention to: "Why is she writing about a child getting beaten and a mother getting her head carved? What the hell is going on?" They do that with notebooks of kids who bring a gun to school.

There's a lot of denial, too, such as, "Oh it can't possibly be that bad," and that's why kids in my position don't talk, even to neighbors who hear what's going on. I think when you hear gunshots going off in a house you should be calling the cops. When you hear the same loud voices and tables being thrown several times a week, you should call the cops. I realize that there is a fine line between butting in where you don't belong and stepping in to help, but it's especially hard for kids to ask for help. Many times, they just act out, instead.

My sister's junior and senior years, she became rebellious and defiant. Everything he forbade her from doing, she did anyway. Every time his answer was no, she rebelled against him. This caused her much physical pain and beatings. When Cheryl and my father were fighting, my mom and I couldn't help her. She was doing what she wanted, and he wasn't going to beat her down. To some extent, I was proud of my sister's strength.

Cheryl pulled a fast one when she graduated from high school. She told me earlier in the week that they were going to Daytona for a party after graduation, but she told my parents she was going to Cocoa Beach with a couple of friends. The day they came to pick her up, she said, as she ran out the door, "See ya! I'm going to Daytona for a week," and hauled ass out of the house.

When she returned, she moved out. She left the house at night, telling me that with or without my help she was moving out, never to come back home. While she was gone, I packed her clothes, books, and a few personal items and set them outside my bedroom window. When she came back at midnight, she loaded her stuff in her car and we said our good-byes through the window. She was finally free from the abuse. I was happy for her, but sad that my sister was gone, never to come home again.

My sister was the only one of us who finished college. She was pretty scrappy. She got her RN degree. She got to be head floor nurse at Florida Hospital. She did a lot with her life.

I think my mother accomplished for us children what she wanted to do. She kept everybody alive for us to all graduate high school. Our father got thrown out of my high school graduation because he was drunk and obnoxious. He made it through Cheryl's because it was in the morning, but when I graduated, it was at night, and he was asked to leave. Mom didn't get to see me graduate.

A few days after my high school graduation, my parents were—as usual—fighting. There was blood everywhere— my mother's blood, of course; none of his was ever shed— and my father let me know that Mom was going to die that night. As if he was testing my loyalties, he asked, "What would you do if I killed her and you had to go on the run with me?"

I tried to appear calm as I told him that I would kill myself—I would slit my wrists. His answer was to hand me a knife and tell me, "If I kill your mom, you do it. Otherwise, I will."

Right around then, I went to work for Rickie, moving houses. That didn't last long, about six months, because my father was making his life miserable, calling him around the clock, carrying on. "How many hours did she work? How much money are you paying her?" I was there to help him get his business off the ground and make a few bucks for myself. Finally, Rickie just said, "Ya know . . ." and I knew what was coming. I said, "You want me to quit?" He said, "It'd be nice."

That was the end of that. That short period of time didn't give me much opportunity to get to know who Rickie was. He seemed like a decent enough guy—he was my big brother and protector, after all—but our father was hell-bent against us getting to know each other better.

There was no escape from him, ever, unless he was at the bar. I'd come home from work and think, "Oh thank God, his car isn't there." I'd have a couple hours to get my head together before he came in drunk. Sometimes he'd come in at 2:00 in the morning and literally pass out right by the door. Sometimes he could fight, and other times he was so drunk he couldn't move.

If he was home, drinking all day, it was going to be bad. When he was starting to get too drunk, he'd take an hour nap, get up, and start drinking again. Take another nap, get up, start drinking again. That's when he'd get violent. He was having one of those days when he tried to drown my mother in the pool. He'd been drinking all day, took a nap an hour before she got home, got up, made himself another drink, and started in on her the second she hit the door. There was no hope that day. He drank vodka on the rocks, all day long. Every day we'd have to buy a new bottle, the biggest one you could find. Every day. Cheap brand. Day, after day, after day, after day . . .

CHAPTER 16

Arizona

By 1986, when I was nineteen, my father developed a habit of lighting a barbecue grill in the house, for warmth. One day, he began seeing visions in the smoke. He swore he saw a phoenix bird and that it must be some sort of a message. He'd been watching Jim and Tammy Faye Bakker, and now all of a sudden he had an epiphany and a vision—he had to be wherever this flaming phoenix was.

Just a little north of Orlando is a town of spiritualists called Cassadaga. After his visions began, he started visiting Cassadaga once a week for about two months. I had to drive him. The psychic told him, "You need to go find your people in Arizona." I thought, "You think he's some nice man with a vision, and now I have to drive two thousand miles with him. You better hope I come back alive."

I was terrified that he was whacking out and there was no way I was going to survive this.

His decision was made: he was going and he wasn't coming back. He was going to find his people and lead them, like the psychic told him. He loaded his stuff on a trailer and told me to pack a week's worth of clothes. That was a relief, because at least it sounded like I was going to come home. I hadn't thought about how I was getting back to Florida. I just did what I was told.

I'm lucky I lived through the trip, because brutal rape became a nightly ritual. He drank vodka all day long, and every night when we stopped at a motel I was attacked, some nights multiple times. This went on for days, same routine: drink all day, beat and brutalize me at night. He sat behind me in the backseat and smacked me in the head when he didn't like the way I was driving. I began to wearily think, "Fuck it, whatever. Just drink your bottle of booze, and let's get it over with. I need a couple of hours of sleep and let's go. It's just who you are." It stopped meaning anything after a while, but it never stopped hurting, physically or emotionally. It killed a part of me inside, the part that said there was any point in living.

As we drove through Louisiana bayou country, we stopped to eat. He must have sensed that I couldn't take any more and was on the verge of saying something to someone—anyone—so he told me that if I made one wrong comment in the restaurant I would end up in the alligator swamp, which was across the road, and be their lunch. I was in so much pain and so bruised, with a split lip, that when we checked in to the motel that night, the manager asked me if I needed help. My father pulled out his pistol and told him if he wanted to live, he had better ignore everything he saw or heard. That night he only raped me once, because I was bleeding so badly.

Finally, we got to the Arizona border and I began to feel like there might be a light at the end of this interminably long tunnel. I could drop him off with "his people" and hightail it out of there, and never have to see him again. But once we arrived, he wouldn't even get out of the car. He looked around at the barren landscape, nothing but desert and big, red rocks. He said, "I'm not staying here. Turn around. We're going home."

My heart sank, but I should have known this would happen. There was no way I was ever going to get away from him. We turned around, and the same horrible abuse continued all the way home. He was furious at the psychic who sent him out to "the middle of nowhere," and he took it out on me by smacking me around and making me sleep in the car for the night.

He woke me up, midmorning, to load the car and start driving home. We were only making a snail's pace, on the drive back. He was already drinking and I didn't have much strength left. We only traveled for about six hours because he was out of cigarettes and vodka, so we stopped for the night. I was in so much agony from the previous night's beating that I accidentally screamed in pain while he sexually assaulted me again. I knew better than to do that, from a lifetime of experience—it only fueled his aggression so he was rougher than usual.

The next night he brought some rope from the trailer

into the room and tied me down. I don't know why—I couldn't have possibly tried to get away or even move, for that matter. I was constantly reminded that I was no longer a person—I was just a thing to do what he wanted with. This went on for more hours than I can recall, but because of my treatment the night before, I was certain to make no noise.

That next morning, he untied me and told me to get cleaned up and hurry to the car. I was in pain, looked a mess, and was emotionally empty. We began driving and I was told there was only enough money for gas, cigarettes, and vodka. We had no more motel money and I was going to have to drive the rest of the way home with no sleep. I was exhausted yet so very relieved. For this day, the only physical abuse would be him smacking me in the head from the backseat.

Mom knew we had turned around because he called her to send money but she said, "Tough shit, I'm not sending you any more money. You've got enough for gas." So I drove from Texas to my mother's driveway in Florida without sleeping, almost twenty-four hours.

We arrived at the house at about 6:00 in the morning. I had bruises everywhere. I looked at my mother and said, "I'm going to bed. I don't want to talk to anybody." It was a Saturday. I went to my bedroom and slept for ten hours. When I got up, I heard him taunting my mother, saying, "I taught her how to be a real woman." He said that I was finally grown up and good enough to please a man. I had to fight to keep from throwing up. He made it clear to my mom that from then on I would be his sex slave and there was nothing she could do about it. This changed the dynamics of the house. He was in my room nightly for several months. And we never went back to Cassadaga.

Just thinking about this trip makes me clutch my chest with anxiety pains. It's probably one of my most horrible memories. It's only one of the many reasons why none of us reported that asshole missing, and why I don't blame whoever it was—Rickie or my mom—for shooting that son of a bitch in the back of the head, whether he was asleep at the time or not. As they say in some parts of the country, "He needed killing."

CHAPTER 17

The Wedding Present

It was shortly after this trip that I began having medical problems and Cheryl took me to a doctor. I was having extremely painful, heavy periods and she thought maybe I had cancer. I tried to tell her "never mind." I wasn't comfortable with the idea of some strange man poking around down there, even if he was a doctor, and I really just didn't want to know. But she insisted and finally convinced me that I should go and make sure that she was wrong. The doctor said I probably had several cysts, and then after further examination, he discovered that I don't have much left of my uterus anymore. My father went into me with screwdrivers, and pretty much any tool he could get. Knives, when I was young. We didn't go to doctors. We didn't go to hospitals. We just recovered at home.

The doctor asked, "What happened to you?" I curtly

answered, "I've been raped." No big deal, whatever, you're a male doctor, I ain't going to tell you shit, is how I reacted inside. He told me, "Well, you're never going to carry a child." I should have turned my father in right then, but was too afraid. Even today I kick myself for being so pathetic and chicken. I was no better than my mother, too afraid to do anything.

I honestly believe she kept herself in check until we all graduated. Once I, the last kid, graduated she got antagonistic. She'd grab his pistol and wave it around the house, yelling and carrying on, "You think I can't kill you? You think I won't?" and he'd sit there and laugh. He thought it was hysterical. She'd grab a cigarette—I never knew my mother to smoke—and then she'd pour a drink and say, "I can get drunk like you," and wave the pistol around.

She never got repercussions for it. I found that very odd. I guess he got a kick out of it, because he would chuckle. That was the only time I ever saw him laugh, when she was doing that, like he was kind of goading her on, to see if she had the guts to do anything. Who knows? Maybe he was hoping she'd do it.

Meantime, I got a job at McDonald's and I was pretty good at it. In fact, I opened a restaurant for them at the age of nineteen. When I left them, it was because I had a falling out with the supervisor. Well, it was that and the fact that I was becoming a pretty heavy drinker. My father taught me to drink vodka at a very young age and it just became a way of life. When he would invite me to sit down and have a drink with him, I knew what was coming. It meant that it was my turn that night.

I went to work drunk. I would take a bottle with me and put it in the ice machine and drink out of it all evening long. My teenage staff loved me because we could party. We got our work done, and they watched my back. When supervisors would come in to check on us, they would make sure they buried my vodka, if I didn't catch it in time. They knew if they buried my booze we'd go out for pizza, on me, as long as they didn't turn me in for drinking while I was working. I had the cleanest restaurants, and I had the best reports from my customers. And I was shitfaced drunk.

Cheryl eventually got engaged, and when we could, Mom and I would meet her for lunch to help plan her wedding. We sneaked around for weeks trying on dresses. This was one secret that Mom managed to keep from him. I was to be the maid of honor and, in her heart, Cheryl wanted our grandfather—Mom's dad—to walk her down the aisle. This was her one impossible wish. We all knew there was no way it could happen, not without endangering his life.

It was around this time that the happy couple bought a house and no one told my father. One evening, my brother was at my parents' house—he was invited over every so often by my father, and that was the only time he was allowed to visit. He threw me under the bus and told our father where Cheryl was living. When I got home, my father laughed his wicked laugh and asked, "Where does your sister live?" Rickie said, "Don't bother lying. I already told him about the house."

After the vicious beating that ensued for both me and

Mom when she got home, I went to my bedroom and called Cheryl to tell her that the jig was up—he knew where she lived. She knew then to do whatever she could to stay safe. I was afraid for everyone at that point, because her safe haven was exposed. It became even more important to keep the wedding a secret.

A few months later it was September 1988 and the wedding was scheduled for Saturday, September 24. Cheryl still wanted my grandfather to walk her down the aisle. Somewhere around September 11, my father disappeared. I know, now, that he was shot in the back of the head, possibly while he slept. I'll never know for sure by whom or exactly why.

I don't know where I was when he "left," but I was probably at work. I came home and my mother said he left. No big deal, he'd done it before. I thought, "Good, we can have a wedding without a disaster on our hands." That's what everybody thought.

Cheryl said, when she was interviewed by police after Mom disappeared, that Rickie called her about two weeks before she got married and said, "Have a good wedding. It's taken care of; he won't be there to bother you. Don't worry about it. He's gone." We didn't ask any questions after that. She called Mom and asked, "Is it true? Is he really not there?" Mom said, "No, he's not here." She wasn't jubilant or sorrowful, just matter-of-fact.

For the first couple of days we all wondered if he was going to show up. Our grandfather called Cheryl and asked if it was true, but no one ever asked anything beyond that. We were all just relieved and hoped that he wasn't coming back. People were watching at the back of the church just in case he showed up, but Rickie didn't seem concerned that he was going to be there. Rickie was in the wedding. He was up at the front of the church with everyone else.

Everybody was on edge and refused to stay at the house. They stayed at hotels. We were wary, too, hoping he didn't get wind of it wherever he was and show up while my grandfather was walking my sister down the aisle. It had become apparent, during that crazed Arizona trip, that he had lost his mind, and I had no doubt that he could have walked into the church with his guns blazing. In fact, when we made it to the reception, I said to Cheryl, "Good God, he really didn't come." And she replied, "Yeah, but it's not over yet. We still have a four-hour reception."

After he disappeared, Mom rarely talked about him. None of us did. We pretended the past never happened. We got on with life and tried to find a new normal. We had our own version of "don't ask, don't tell," so we just kept the norm. So many questions we should have had answered. Somebody should have had the guts to ask them.

CHAPTER 18

Freedom from Terror

Cheryl's wedding weekend was the first and last time that I ever saw my mother's mother. I had never met her before and, unfortunately, she went into a coma a few months after the wedding and died the following spring. We all went to the funeral, except for Rickie, who—I learned years later—stayed behind to bury a frozen body under the garage floor. He and Mom told us, at the time, that he stayed home to take care of her dog. I know differently, now.

Following the wedding, we didn't know how to act around one another, because we had never had the opportunity to just be ourselves. It was awkward when we got together for our very first Thanksgiving and Christmas—none of us knew how to talk to one another. Once my grandfather moved in with Mom, after his wife died, his presence seemed to give us a common ground and he somehow broke the ice that had frozen around us.

Grandpa was a wonderful man. He was one of the best things to ever happen to me, and I pride myself in being a lot like him. He grew up during the Depression and had a very matter-of-fact way of looking at life: "You lived through what you lived through. You move on in life and make something of yourself." That was his philosophy. You survive it, you move on, you do what you have to do, and you keep going.

When Grandpa moved in with Mom, he helped her pay off the house, and he also made her get rid of the bullet hole–riddled dresser in her bedroom. She didn't even notice it. It took an outsider to point out how very wrong it was. He did so much to help us find our way back to the way other people live. He couldn't do enough for any of us. He said to me one day, "Do you want me to buy you a restaurant? I have the money. Let me buy you a restaurant. Look how much money you could make! You're good at what you do!" I felt like he was trying to say, "Let me fix what happened in the past." He did that with all of us kids. I told him, "Grandpa, I don't want to own my own business. It's not what I want to do. I'm happy the way I am."

After I got hired at Burger King, I became fast friends with one of my coworkers, a zany woman named Susan. She was funny and happy, with a heart as big as Texas, and we had such a great time together. I don't know when I had ever laughed so much. She was several years older than me, but that didn't mean anything. I had friends of all ages. It wasn't long before we were spending all of our time together.

She and I were best girlfriends, until one evening we went out to dinner at a fancy restaurant and we became actual "girlfriends." As Susan tells the story, "I didn't eat. I had butterflies. I had this weird feeling that I was falling in love with her." It was around Christmastime and the restaurant was so pretty, all white lights, with beautiful music playing. We were sitting there, talking, and I just started pouring it out, telling her my life story. I guess it was just the right moment. Somehow that evening turned very romantic and . . . well, we've been together ever since.

The funny thing was, neither Susan nor I were into girls, and neither of us was looking for a relationship. She had been married to her high school sweetheart, and I was engaged once to a boy in high school. It just sort of happened. Somehow we just knew that we were going to be together—best friends who fell in love with each other.

We moved in together after Christmas, when Grandpa told me Mom didn't need me to watch over her anymore. I was twenty-two years old. It was time to spread my wings and make my own life. "Move out, move on, and get past" is what he said to me.

There is controversy, regarding homosexuality, about whether people choose to be gay or not. I guess I did make a conscious choice, if I'm pressed to declare it one way or the other, but I never thought of it that way. I don't think that from the day I was old enough to perceive thoughts that I said, "I'm going to be with a woman." I think I got to a point in my life, after the intensity of the abuse that I lived through, to say I don't want to be in a sexual relationship with a man. Whether I made a conscious choice to fall in love with a woman, or I made a conscious choice not to be with men, however people want to perceive that, that's their decision. If anyone asks, I'm perfectly at ease with saying I'm a lesbian.

If I hadn't met Susan in my twenties, I don't know if I'd be this okay today. I was a seriously heavy drinker back then. I didn't care if I lived or died. It wasn't until we got together that I stopped pouring the booze down my throat like it was water.

Susan and I had a great relationship. We went to theme parks, movies, and anyplace else we could to have fun. Our families weren't thrilled about us pairing up, however. Even though they got along just fine, Mom never accepted that Susan was more than my best friend. She didn't want to know about our relationship. It was a non-conversation. Yet Grandpa just said, "I knew about those types of boys up north, but we just left them alone." That was his way of saying it didn't matter to him.

Susan's mom hated me at first—not because of any gender issues, but because no one was good enough for her kids. She wanted to know what freebie I was looking for from her daughter. But once Susan told her a little bit about my past, about my father, she calmed down. As the years wore on and it became apparent that I wasn't going away, she finally learned to like me, but it took a long time. She was a hard-nosed woman.

Over the years, we all lightened up. Weekly dinners with Mom and Grandpa were very common. I was learning, because of Susan, that it was okay to have fun and be happy. Once my father was gone, Mom went on trips to Ireland and Hawaii. She and I went to Niagara Falls and California. She went with my aunt to Branson, Missouri, and Graceland. Mom had a job with an airline and got to fly standby for free. Mom didn't date, that I know of. I think once was enough.

If my mother had ever talked to us after my father went missing, we might have understood more, but even after he was gone, nobody brought it up. She just went on as if he never existed, like the elephant in the room—or under the garage floor—that she ignored.

I don't think I could live in a house if I knew that. I don't know how she did it for so many years. Although, it's not like she could ever sell it, for fear of discovery. She was stuck there until the day she died. That was her personal hell. And I wonder what she was thinking when she made the garage into a carpeted playroom for her grandkids. Was that her way of getting the last laugh on him, or was it just a way of lightening up a very dark space? I wish I could ask her. I don't think she had much of a sense of humor. She liked to go places, she liked to experience things, she liked to hang out with the kids. We could have a pool party, everybody would be over, but she didn't laugh. She participated in conversations, more so with the grandkids than with Susan, Cheryl, or me. She rarely spoke to my brother, when he was around. I don't think she knew what to say to us kids. She had a better relationship with my brother-in-law than she did with her own children, because he was an outsider. He didn't live our life, and looking into his eyes didn't haunt her with bad memories.

She ended up being a pretty normal person after "it" was gone. She was happy. She had a good life. Even her neighbor noticed that she came out of her shell after 1988 and was much friendlier. She would chat when she'd see him in the yard, whereas before she would just dart into the house. She was a different person. We called the transformation "Before It and After It."

My sister became pregnant for the first time in 1990. Nine months, and twenty hours of labor, later, in April 1991, my nephew, Daniel, arrived. Susan and I made his first Easter basket four days after he was born, with a rattle and his first Mickey Mouse. He became a huge part of my life and we grew to be best friends. My sister, her husband, and their son were very happy. Holidays and birthdays finally became joyous occasions.

Cheryl was determined to be a great mom, and she really did give it her best shot. It was as if she was declaring to the world, "I'm going to come out of this and I'm going to raise kids and I'm going to show the world how it's supposed to be done." She was going to be the perfect mother of the perfect family with the perfect picket fence.

Susan and I used to take Daniel with us to Disney. We had sleepovers, we watched movies, we hung out and had fun. I loved to play basketball, and he and I would go out and shoot hoops, even in the freezing cold. He wanted to learn how to roller-skate, so I helped teach him. I just adored that boy. He was the son I could never have, and we did everything together. I was Aunt Stacey and Susan was Aunt Susan.

We were learning what a true family was. In 1996, Cheryl had her first baby girl, and in 2000, she had another adorable little girl. Those were good times, and Rickie missed most of them because he wasn't around. I have to say one thing about my brother; he knew he shouldn't have kids. He always had that fear of turning into "it." I similarly wondered, would I have had kids, if I could have? I don't know if I'd have had the temperament for actually raising children. I don't want to ever find out I have my father's temper. It's one thing to be a doting aunt. Having a kid is absolutely different from babysitting one. I always hyped them up on sugar and dropped them off. I could take my sister's kids home and say, "Okay I've had enough. See ya."

At my trial, there was much discussion about Cheryl's relationship with Daniel, but I have to give her credit for doing her best. She probably thought, in comparison to our upbringing, that she was doing an amazing job, and when she heard that he was becoming afraid of her, she was devastated. She took parenting classes and really did try to do the right thing.

Throughout those fifteen years between my parents' deaths, my mom, Susan, and I took lots of trips together—just the three of us. At least once a year, we took a week-long vacation together somewhere. On Susan's side of the family, she and Ann and I went on a Carnival or Disney cruise every September, to celebrate our birthdays, which were all within a week of one another. I was becoming rather well traveled.

Even though she was happier, Mom still never smiled much. It could be that if she was involved in his death, even though it was a good thing, she was probably living with that, the memory of "I'm a murderer. I killed someone." If she did kill him, it was obviously self-defense or because she snapped. Whatever happened, it was justified. But then she would have to live with the feeling of "I've taken a life." So if she'd already been beaten to the point where she was forced to allow the rape of her children, now the only reason she could smile was because she'd murdered her husband or, at the very least, helped hide the body.

The Social Security checks that came every month were a constant reminder. She didn't spend a penny of that money, but every month, there was his ghost saying, "Here's your check. Here's your check." She must have been pretty tortured over those years. That would explain why it was hard for her to smile. She had a heavy load. She had a heavy, heavy load.

There was, however, one thing about my mother that still infuriates me to this day. Ten years after my father was gone, she sat in the living room of my uncle's house and actually said, about my father, "I love him and I miss him." I thought I was going to come out of my chair and start screaming at the top of my lungs, "How can you love and miss that monster?"

I called my uncle later and said, "I've got a problem." He said, "I know. I saw it in your face. There was always something between the two of them. I don't understand it, either. There was something he had, some kind of hold on her."

It drives me nuts that she could think that way. Everything else I can understand, and I can make excuses for her until the cows come home, but saying she still loved him angers me to no end. She must have seen some kind of spark of something worth loving, but whatever was there, it was buried deep. Rickie even said that he was furious because she said she still loved him.

I guess it angered him enough that he just stayed away. Rickie was almost never around. We went years without knowing where he was living or if he was alive. He missed out on so much. He just didn't want anything to do with the family. He never went to visit Mom unless he was going to see Grandpa. He didn't have anything to say to her. If my mother was the only one home, he would not stop. Then he disappeared. I don't know everywhere he went, but I do know he was in Cocoa Beach for a while. He was still married; Mary, his wife, was still in Orlando, and he just took off.

I don't know what finally happened between Rickie and Mary. One minute they were together; the next minute he was living in a shithole trailer and she'd gone to Georgia. There was a really bizarre story that happened during this time frame that I didn't know about until after Mom was murdered and the police started to investigate Rickie's past. In 1999, he met a woman named Catherine Crews, in the Cocoa Beach area, and moved in with her and her husband, as sort of a roommate. He didn't pay rent, but he did odd jobs around the house, which is just like the arrangement he made with me and Susan, years later. He told them that he worked for a company called All Star Electric and was doing renovations on a local hotel. He told us that he owned Emerald Electric and was doing electrical work on a local shopping mall.

Rickie and the husband talked about starting a business together, just like he and I and Cheryl's husband did. Catherine and her husband split up, because Rickie deliberately drove a wedge between them. He became romantically involved with Catherine. In November 1999, her house burned down, due to a strange electrical problem. During the following months, she discovered that Rickie had stolen between ten and fifteen thousand dollars of her fire insurance money and sent money to women named Mary and Marilyn. Catherine had no way of knowing that these women were his wife and mother, because he told her that he had never been married, and never told her Mom's name. After he killed Mom, he started siphoning money from her accounts and giving it to me and Susan. And this was one of the main reasons I was indicted. That's like assuming Mom or Mary were in on his theft of Catherine's money, just because they received it.

Catherine told the investigators about a discovery she made when she and her sister went to his storage unit to get her Christmas decorations. Inside that unit, to which she said he had the only key until that day, she found a trash bag filled with black clothing that smelled like gasoline, a black baseball bat, and a Taser.

She told police, when they interviewed her in February

2004, that he was physically abusive and very controlling. She broke up with him in April 2001, because, she said, "He was like Mr. Crazy, psycho. It was like every move I made I had to give answers to." He forbade her from working, made her account for literally every penny she spent, and demanded to know who she was talking to on the phone. He said he could snap her neck if he felt like it, and that he had killed his father. He said that he would rather kill her children than let them visit their father, because Rickie "knew" that their dad was molesting them— he recognized the signs. He told her that he was writing a book, something along the lines of "The Mind of a Killer."

Finally, she'd had enough. She sent him packing and went back to her husband. They reconciled after comparing stories and realizing that Rickie had split them up with lies that he was telling each of them. The month after they broke up, on May 29, 2001, Rickie was questioned by a patrol officer who spotted him in a U-Haul truck parked next to a wooded area, across the street from where the husband worked. Rickie said that he was looking for a friend's house and he was going to help him move. When the officer asked where his friend lived and what his name was, Rickie said that he had it written on a piece of paper and he lost it. That's when the officer noticed a pair of latex gloves, a change of clothes, and rope lying on the front seat.

When he asked what the latex gloves were for, Rickie responded that he gets cuts on his hands while moving and uses the gloves to avoid getting injured. During that part of the conversation, Rickie got out of the truck and began to vomit and act nervous. When asked why he didn't know his friend's name, and why he was getting sick, Rickie told the officer that he had a stomach virus and avoided answering regarding his friend. But because he wasn't breaking any laws, the officer let him go and simply filed a report. He did, however, let Catherine and her husband know about the incident, as part of his follow-up to filing the report, because Rickie's ID still showed him as living in her house.

We tried to bring Catherine's testimony into my trial, and it wasn't allowed because I didn't need any help discrediting him. I think, however, that the similarities in the story lines are a little too eerie and would have helped tremendously.

That happened in 2001, and we never knew about it. We were living our happy little lives while my brother slowly went batshit crazy. Eventually, he found his way back to Orlando, where he was living when Grandpa died, in November 2002, at the age of ninety-three. He didn't go to the funeral in Massachusetts. He was the only member of the family who wasn't there. Susan and I didn't locate Rickie in time to tell him of the funeral. We left a note on his trailer, but I am pretty sure we were back from the funeral before we heard from him.

Because Mom's name was on Grandpa's bank account before he passed away, she got everything. It was a substantial amount, close to a quarter of a million dollars. There was nothing in his name to his other children. He didn't have a will, but he did express that he wanted his money split up four ways between his kids. Instead of splitting it up like she should have, she kept it.

I don't know why she would do that to her siblings, but I also don't know why she would keep my father's Social Security checks for fifteen years. She never spent them, but she also never touched my grandfather's account. The only withdrawals from it were from my brother's computer, after she died.

She had over $100,000 from my father's Social Security and $250,000 from my grandfather. Plus, she had her own accounts: two money market accounts, about $60,000 apiece, and a bank account worth about $90,000. She was hoarding big-time money, I can only guess because for so many years she didn't have any.

That didn't stop her from spending, though. If a whim caught her, she'd take her car in and trade it in for a brand-new one. If she wanted to go on a trip, she went on a trip. If she wanted to buy a three-hundred-dollar Disney collectible, she wrote a check and bought it. She had it made until she made the mistake of telling Rickie that she was thinking about finally splitting Grandpa's money up for her brother and sisters.

CHAPTER 19

Out on Bond

Finally, the day of my bond hearing arrived. I had been in jail for weeks and looked like hell. I had to appear in court in the grungy blue jail jumpsuit, my cheeks were sunken in, and the circles under my eyes made it obvious that I was unhealthy. I told one of the women in the dorm, "God, I need to do something with my hair," and she said, "I can cut it. They have clippers we can use." It cost me seven coffee packets, at twenty-five cents apiece. She did a surprisingly good job, so at least my hair looked presentable, but I still looked like a criminal on a "Wanted" poster.

That day in court, the gallery was filled to capacity with friends from Gulf Coast Resort. I was touched and grateful to see such an impressive showing, but I was also humiliated by the reason they were there. These people were seeing me at absolute rock bottom. A news camera was set up, pointing right at me, and there was no hiding from it. I knew I was going to be on every channel that night, and now, after all of my previous efforts at keeping some anonymity, everyone in the dorm would know who I was. If I didn't get this bond, I was up Shit Creek without a paddle.

Diana presented her case: Up until very recently, I was considered a witness for the State in the case against my brother, a man who smeared feces on himself and whose competence was questionable; there was no evidence for me to be arrested before Rickie's plea. The only suspicious thing in the prosecutor's arsenal was the banking activity, but even that was only circumstantial.

God bless Judge Marc Lubet. He saw that the State had a pretty thin case and made it clear that he thought so. However, there was enough against me for him to order a bond set at $100,000, and he ordered that I wear an ankle bracelet, at my cost. I was confined to Gulf Coast Resort, and Susan was to put the park up for collateral. I was only allowed to leave the park if and when I had to come back to Orlando for court-related appointments and hearings.

Once he was done talking, the entire gallery burst into cheers and applause. It warmed my heart, but the judge was not amused. He let everyone know that their behavior was inappropriate for a courtroom, and one of them yelled out, "But she didn't do it!" This disgruntled him and embarrassed me, but I was also ecstatic. I got to go home! But then I saw Cheryl, who was there to testify against me—she was livid. That's the sad part about it. Their elation about my release was like a knife in the heart for her.

Before I could allow myself to be too happy, Robin Wilkinson stood up and said, "Your honor, that's okay, she can post this bond because the grand jury is going to indict her next week and she'll be back in jail for good. We're adding a second charge and we're upping the ante." She was so angry that I got a bond, so she was going for everything. She upped the charge in my mother's death to first degree and added my father at first degree. And they were definitely going for the death penalty.

I was back to terrified, again. Diana calmly told me, privately, "This is how it's going to go down. The grand jury is probably going to indict you. You're going to be back in jail. A week or so later you're going to be back home. Don't worry. I'll get you a second bond."

I was taken back to jail to be out-processed, while Diana and Susan met with the bondsman to begin jumping through the legal and financial hoops necessary to get me out of there. I got back to the dorm and fell instantly dead to the world in my bunk. I was asleep when the five o'clock news came on. Now everyone knew what had happened: a murder suspect had been released on bond. Many of the inmates were furious because they were stuck in there for far lesser charges, and here I was, a white girl, walking out with a murder charge. One of the girls that I got along with came by and hit me on the foot and said, "My God, you're on the news and my God, you're in trouble. You need to come down to the dayroom."

Still half asleep, I said, "I'm waiting on my bond," but she insisted, "I'm telling you now, you need to come down to the dayroom and sit with us."

I never came off a bunk so fast in my entire life. We made our way to the dayroom, to the table where the four of us would play cards together. Every badass woman in there walked past me and said something like, "If you're here tonight, you're not going to wake up tomorrow." If they didn't get me out by 8:00, I was there for the night, and it was already after 5:00. I was a wreck, shaking like a leaf. Finally, one of the girls I sat with said to the guard, "What's going on? She's got a bond and they're going to kill her in here."

The guard said, "I don't know. Let me call command and find out." We sat and waited, and all of a sudden the guard returned and ordered, "Pack your stuff. I have to move you and move you now. Your bondsman, the GPS lady, and your attorney are in the lobby wondering why you haven't been moved, so I'm moving you now."

Then the colonel of that shift came in and said to the guard, "We'll both escort her. There's a lot of activity out there tonight." As they escorted me, even the staff was saying things like, "What is this country coming to, letting murderers walk the streets?" It never occurred to any of them that I might not have done it.

Diana wasn't downstairs when I got there. She left as soon as she knew I was finally being released because she didn't want to get caught by the media, who went insane with this story. Imagine the headline: *Sexually abused lesbian, charged with murdering both parents, arrested at nudist resort*. News vans had tried to sneak into the resort when I was arrested, and a news chopper actually flew overhead to get some sort of footage because they weren't allowed inside the gate. My story was now national news, and Diana didn't want my case to turn into a circus like Casey Anthony's eventually did.

I didn't expect to see her; she said she would call me. Susan was sobbing, of course. John Von Achen, my bail bondsman—a former player for the Oakland A's—gave me my jacket, and Jeanice Chevere, the GPS monitoring officer, put my hood up over my head and said, "Put on this jacket and keep your head down. We're going to be on either side of you. Just follow our lead. Don't look up, because they're not getting a face shot of you on these cameras." I did exactly what they told me to do.

We made our way to their office building, directly across from the jail complex, and—just as Jeanice predicted—the reporters were in my face. Susan pushed one of the cameras away. The photographer got huffy and said, "Don't touch my camera," and Jeanice said, "Back up, you're on our property."

Susan and I were blessed to get the right people, because they taught us and forewarned us about what we were facing. They were very protective of us right from the beginning. John Von Achen is Diana's favorite bondsman, and she sends clients to him if she thinks they warrant a bond. Jeanice read my file and said, "This is ridiculous."

They had been following the case to some degree because it was big in Orlando. Those who worked in the law enforcement field knew that in 2003 Hussey tried to get me arrested. So what changed? One crazy man's fabricated fifth or sixth statement was enough to get me arrested, and that's what popped John's cork.

John said to Jeanice, "This is the right thing to do." I was her second high-profile client. Her first was Lisa Nowak, the astronaut who allegedly drove across the country in a diaper to kidnap her boyfriend's new girlfriend. If not for Diana, John, and Jeanice, I would have sat in jail for almost three years, until my trial.

Susan and I drove back to Hudson and, the next morning, tried to live our day-to-day lives. We still had a resort to run, and everyone was stopping in to the restaurant to see me and ask questions. The remarks about my extreme weight loss and sunken cheeks started to get old, even though I knew most of them were just concerned. They just didn't realize that they were not the first, tenth, or even twentieth person to ask me the same questions. And I still had a week of sitting on pins and needles, waiting for the grand jury.

The day that the grand jury convened, I was swamped at work. My stomach felt shredded and my nerves were on edge. I couldn't eat, and even my cherished morning cup of coffee wasn't going down very easily. Just the thought of going back to jail brought me to panicked tears—but I knew that it was inevitable. Susan was watching the Internet for news, between answering the business phone and dealing with customers. She apparently missed it when it hit, because Diane came in and asked, "Have you guys checked what the grand jury did yet?" She and Susan went into the office and got on the computer.

I was out in the restaurant juggling a delivery from the food distributor, running the counter, taking phone calls, and they were locked in the office for an hour. Finally I walked in the office and asked, "Is there something I need to know?"

After a pregnant pause, Susan said, "Well, there's a warrant out for your arrest. I'm waiting on Diana Tennis to call me back. You might as well go back out there and keep working."

What could I do? I went back to work and handled the rush. As soon as it slowed down, I came back to the office and asked, "Okay, what are we doing now?" She replied, "We have to go to Orlando. You're going to turn yourself in." As much as I hated the idea, it was better than having them come and get me. I didn't want Hussey to have that satisfaction. So we drove to Orlando and went straight to John's office.

I begged him, "I don't want to be in with all the people again. After the first bond, they left me sitting there waiting, and it was almost eight at night before they moved me. I got threatened all day long. It's only been a week, so I'm sure some of them are still there. I need to go where I'm okay."

Bless him, he called a friend of his in the jail and said, "Look, I need her in protective custody or I'm not turning her in. We'll go to court tomorrow, whatever it takes." Thank God, they agreed. I said, "Okay let's go." John stopped me and said, "No, it hasn't even hit the sheriff's office yet. We don't want to get there too early." We were in Orlando before the official warrant hit.

Diana already had the paperwork ready, and the judge signed that day that he'd give me an emergency bond hearing in one week, because they didn't have to come find me.

Although I was so grateful to John for keeping me out of the general population, I didn't love my eight days in protective custody, because it was literally eight days in lockup: you don't come out. I got two showers in eight days; I got one phone call to Susan, no visitation. Protective custody is supposed to mean you're not out among the others, that they lock you in your cell every time they go to move somebody else. However, PC in Orange County means you're in that cell all day long and you get forgotten about other than meals thrown through the slot. It was a tiny little room, about the size of the inside of a van, with a cement slab for a bed. The only good thing is you have your own toilet.

Well, now I had two first-degree murder charges on me, was going back for a second bond hearing, and, again, the courtroom was packed with my nudist friends. Before the hearing began, the judge admonished everyone to behave, to remember that they were in a court of law. Diana laid it out for him again, the lack of evidence, the fact that a madman was the only thread tying me to these crimes, and that I was originally slated to testify against him. "Your honor," Robin argued, "she has two first-degree charges against her. She can't get a bond." The judge asked, "Got any other evidence? Got something new for me?"

The only new thing was the grand jury decision to bring me back in, so he re-released me, but upped the bond another $50,000. Susan had to come up with even more money and, thanks to the angels in our circle of friends, was able to raise it. I was going back home again.

It was after that second bond hearing that I thought, I have to listen to Diana Tennis. If I'd had anybody else, I wouldn't have been out on bond—not going from second degree to two first-degree charges with a possible death penalty still on the table. Granted, I had an ankle bracelet that cost a lot of money over the years, and we were out fifteen grand in bond money, but at least I wasn't sitting in a jail cell waiting for my trial.

CHAPTER 20

Life Under House Arrest

Once I was out on bond a second time, it was time to start working on my defense, in between putting out fires at the nudist resort. There was always some emergency—one of the rental units had a leaking ceiling, some naked drunk spilled an ashtray in the hot tub and Wendell couldn't close it down and clean it out because he was off at Home Depot buying what he needed to fix the leaky roof, some-one's feelings were hurt at bingo the night before and the whole place was exploding with gossip—it was always something. And in the meantime, I had to try to find a way to live a normal life and run a restaurant with a GPS bracelet around my ankle.

One thing I had to be careful of, in light of all of the frustrations that daily life was flinging at me, in addition to the tension that was building between me and Susan because I was now unable to run errands and they all fell into her lap, was the fact that I couldn't ever show that I was upset or angry. Anyone who has ever worked in a customer service job can tell you how extremely trying it can be, and I wasn't in a position to react like a normal human being.

I lived those three years under house arrest very quietly because God forbid I piss anybody off. Working in the restaurant, with some of the more obnoxious customers or resort residents—because, while there were many *wonderful* people there, we also had our share of major assholes—sometimes I'd get really angry about something and I'd think, "God, I hope nobody thinks I've got a temper. That's all it would take for someone to say, 'I saw her throwing a fit in the restaurant. She must be capable of murder!'" Some people, who shall remain nameless, used to enjoy poking at me, just because they knew that I couldn't react the way I wanted to. They knew they held a huge amount of power.

On the positive side, my situation really helped me to gain a perspective on life that I probably never would have realized otherwise. Susan and I were out in front of the restaurant when one of the homeowners pulled up on his golf cart to complain about someone in the park, and I could tell that he was just trying to stir up trouble. I asked him, "Where are your facts?"

He said, "Well, it's more of my perception. These are just things I've noticed here and there." So I threw my leg up on his golf cart seat and I said, "You see this ankle bracelet? That's what perception does to people." He couldn't get away from me fast enough. His wife made him come back and apologize to me.

Meantime, Diana introduced me to Toni Maloney, the private investigator she always uses on cases like this. Toni was another angel added to my legal defense team. She was so kind and gentle, with a very motherly energy, and she helped me get through some of the toughest times. I sat with Toni and unraveled my whole life story.

The one thing I always felt that I had on my side was the strong sense of integrity that I learned from my grandfather. I don't go along with his devoted Catholic beliefs, but I do have a lot of respect for his integrity and I try to emulate it whenever I can. I've said from the very beginning, the truth is the truth is the truth, and I've never wavered from that. Susan and I took care of people at Gulf Coast Resort, and we bent over backward. I was always very straightforward and honest with them, and that might be why they supported me during my bond hearings and trial.

That didn't mean that we didn't all drive one another crazy during those years that I was confined to the resort. There were some touchy conversations and sketchy moments because none of us had ever experienced what it's like to have dealings with murder suspects and death penalty trials. People were bound to say things that were either out-of-bounds or downright inappropriate. In the course of a normal conversation, someone would say something as mundane as, "Oh, I could just kill him!" or "I wanted to strangle him!" and obviously not really mean it, because that's just the kind of thing people say when they're frustrated. But then they'd realize who they said it in front of and an uncomfortable silence would follow.

Most of the time, it would happen after people had been drinking, and there was a lot of drinking at GCR. It was, after all, a vacation resort where people came to relax and party. I had to bartend many events at the Tiki Bar and in the clubhouse. I was around a lot of drunks, and some of them would get diarrhea of the mouth after a few frosty beverages. They would crack jokes about coming to visit me in prison or make child abuse jokes. They didn't intend to be mean, they were drunk and making jokes in bad taste, but it was awkward. I had to smile and pretend it didn't bother me, because I was on the clock and the customer is always right.

Then there was a snowbird couple that came back shortly after I got out of jail, and I thought I was good friends with them. I walked over to their camper to welcome them back for the season, and the husband stopped me and said, "You're not welcome over here. We only paid for one month and we'll be leaving." They never came back. It's unfortunate because I thought the world of them.

I think the most glaring example of a foot-in-mouth moment happened about two months after I got out of jail. Behind Gulf Coast Resort is a small housing addition, and between them is a wooded area. A woman named Karen—whom I had never met but with whom Susan had a working relationship because she paid monthly to use

My mom with a very young Rickie.

My third grade elementary school picture. All of my childhood photos were destroyed when Rickie cleared out Mom's house after killing her. I only have this because an old friend e-mailed it to me after my trial.

Me and my mom at a Mother's Day brunch in 1991.

Rickie and me at Daniel's birthday party when he turned four in 1995.

Grandpa, Mom, me, and Susan at Epcot for a show in 2000.

Me, Mom, and Susan at Niagara Falls, New York.

Christmas 2002 at Mom's house, with gifts she gave us. This was our last Christmas with her.

Me and Rickie at Mom's house, Christmas 2002, after not seeing each other for about two years.

My mom's house at 7611 Alachua Street, Orlando, Florida, with Rickie's van in the driveway. This is how the house looked when the CSI unit dug up the garage floor.

ORANGE COUNTY SHERIFF'S OFFICE, ORLANDO, FLORIDA

This photo was taken after the cement had been removed from my father's grave.

ORANGE COUNTY SHERIFF'S OFFICE, ORLANDO, FLORIDA

Crime scene investigators pull my father's body, wrapped in a blue tarp and bedding, from a hole deep beneath the garage floor.

Mom was buried here, beneath the plastic tote. Law enforcement made much of the fact that neither Susan nor I noticed any changes in our backyard after Rickie buried Mom there.

This is the shirt that Mom was buried in, and it was torture everytime the prosecutor displayed it at the trial.

ORANGE COUNTY SHERIFF'S OFFICE, ORLANDO, FLORIDA

This is the notebook that my defense attorney, Diana Tennis, found the week before my trial, which played such a pivotal part in my defense.

ORANGE COUNTY SHERIFF'S OFFICE, ORLANDO, FLORIDA

Me with my wonderful defense attorney, Diana Tennis, about a year after my trial.

Me and Susan celebrating New Year's Eve, 2010/2011.

our Dumpster—owned the property and lived on the far side of the woods.

A bolt of lightning hit the woods adjacent to the resort and started a small fire. The fire was closer to the resort than it was to her house, so there was no way she would know about it. Wendell was over there with the hose, and Susan and I were sitting on the golf cart, sort of "supervising" . . . which is a nice way of saying we were sitting on our asses watching the show.

Susan called Karen from her cell phone as we watched Wendell and said, "Your property is on fire. It's close to us, but it's on your side of the fence. We called the fire department, but I don't know how far onto your land it's burning. You might want to come and check it out."

Karen rode through her property, and then came over to the GCR side, where the fire department was working. Someone had been planting marijuana back there, and there were jugs of water, and big mounds of dirt where they had dug up the ground to grow their plants. She joked, "There's a huge pile of dirt back there! I hope that person who got arrested in your park didn't bury a body back there!"

Wendell didn't know whether to laugh or cry, and I turned to Susan and said, "I'm going in the restaurant to get a drink." Karen didn't know it was me. She assumed that person was in jail. I was mortified.

I could deal with all of that more easily if things were going okay in our household. But the murders and the arrest were starting to damage my home life, as well. Before all of this happened, when Susan and I had a good life, I could wake up and everything was fine. I enjoyed my job, I loved my life, and she felt the same. But Rickie didn't just take my mom from me; he took my life.

Susan said, one day, "We've lost everything. We don't have what we had." She didn't just mean our material things. She meant us. I was afraid we would never get it back. I wasn't supposed to talk to her about my legal issues, because it might damage her testimony, so I had to keep a lot of things to myself. This was my best friend, and I wasn't allowed, legally, to talk to her about the most important issue in my daily life.

This whole thing killed a chunk of who Susan and I were. We weren't able to have date nights or just be us anymore. We tried not to grow apart, and it helped that neither of us was able to leave even if we wanted to—she was stuck running the resort and I was confined to the premises. But the stress of being forced to stay was enough to push us away from each other. We fought almost constantly, and when we weren't fighting, it was because we weren't speaking. It was a long three years between my arrest and my trial.

We got into a particularly vicious argument, one Friday, over nothing, really. We were at our wits' end, and I snapped at Susan, "I can call Diana and change my plea to guilty, and be done with this whole thing!" She screamed back, "Why don't you just do it and get it over with? I can't take this anymore!"

Susan didn't really want me in jail, of course. She was just tired of it, like I was. She'd say, "I'm sick of being tied down to this. I'm sick of your fucking ankle bracelet. I'm sick of driving you to Orlando."

It got so bad that there were times, especially once I found out that Daniel would have to testify, when I talked to Diana about the feasibility of arranging some sort of a plea deal just to get it over with, and I wasn't doing that just to hurt Susan. Sometimes I felt like I didn't have it in me to fight this battle. The closer it got, the more I wondered, "Am I doing the right thing? I'm dragging my favorite boy onto the witness stand. I can't do this to him."

Diana would say, "Do you want to go to prison? Do you want to do the right thing?" and I always said, "I'll get back to you." I'd do some soul searching for a week or so, and decide that I couldn't give up. I didn't do this. I had to keep my eye on the prize, as it were, because I knew I didn't do anything wrong. But on the other hand, I knew I was hurting Daniel.

It was the worst thing I ever had to do in my life, putting him through that, making him testify. They weren't hard on him; it was just the fact that he had to do it. Although, honestly, if Rickie hadn't told him, "I killed my dad," if he hadn't offered to get Daniel's mother out of the way, if he hadn't told him all those stories about killing abusive parents and making it look like they just went away, then our nephew would have had nothing to testify about—heck, if Rickie hadn't killed our mom, none of this would have happened. So I knew it wasn't my fault that Daniel was being put through the ringer, but I still felt horrible about it.

Diana and I talked about the possibility of asking to plead guilty to lesser charges, like misdemeanor check fraud, and things like that, but even to those I said, "The more we talk about it, the more I think about it, I didn't do anything wrong in this whole ordeal. Why am I going to plead to something I didn't have anything to do with?"

Honestly, though, Robin Wilkinson didn't offer any deals. They were going full tilt for the death penalty until May 2009, after Diana pulled off another miracle. She called me up one day and said, "This is really a leap of faith on my part, but I want to put in a Motion to Separate. You'll be charged with first degree on your father, and first degree on your mother, instead of first degree for both."

Alarmed, I asked, "That's double charges. Why do you want to do this?"

She said, "Once I get them severed, I'll demand a speedy trial, which means they have to go to trial on the charges for your father's death within sixty days. They'll have to drop it because they don't have any evidence." By that time, it had been over twenty years since his death, and they didn't have any proof of anything. All they had was a receipt that said my mother rented a concrete saw, and my brother saying I killed him, even though he had been documented in numerous ways confessing to that murder to numerous people.

I talked to Susan about it, and she cried, "No, that's crazy!" I said, "Yeah, but I thought going for a bond on murder charges was crazy, and I thought a second bond was crazy." When I talked to Toni, my private investigator, she said the same thing. "Trust Diana. I'll bet you money they don't go to trial."

I called Diana and said go ahead and do it. That's exactly what she did. She got the separation and then ten days later told the judge, "Your honor, I want a demand for a speedy trial and I have that right—this is a new charge because we just severed it ten days ago." The state's attorney responded, in essence, "Your honor, we need to drop the charges. We have no evidence."

He dropped the charges, with prejudice, meaning they can't ever bring those charges back on me. I finally received a formal letter, notifying me that they were dropping the death penalty, but talk about sweating for two years! Let me tell you, I thought about ending it, myself, many times during those twenty-four months. I didn't want to be subjected to them getting to decide how I died when I knew I was innocent. That may not make sense to some folks, but I'll be damned if I was going to let them kill me when I knew I was innocent. Bullshit, I'll kill myself first, and I'll do it my way.

The whole process was demeaning, starting when Detective Hussey began threatening me, instead of realizing that I was Rickie's victim, just like the rest of the family. Maybe he had stars in his eyes, thinking he'd make a name for himself by catching the next Aileen Wuornos. Maybe he was seeing me as a lesbian serial killer from Pasco County, like her. I do know, however, that he wasn't such a stellar cop. He was reprimanded in 2005 for claiming about one hundred dollars' worth of alcoholic beverages on his expense report, and attributed his bad decision to "laziness" and being too busy to do it right. He also received a written reprimand in 2007 for failure to properly conduct a death investigation, which he chalked up to a "lapse in judgment," just days after being written up for not showing up for another investigation. I get that people make mistakes—I'm not perfect, either—but in light of how my trial ended up, Detective Hussey probably should have dialed it back a notch or two in his overly zealous pursuit of me.

CHAPTER 21

The Year It All Fell Apart

Before Grandpa died, he and Mom were helping us house hunt. We lived on the far south side of the city and wanted to live closer to where the family lived on the far northeast side, especially in light of the problems that Cheryl was having at home. Mom thought it would be good for us to live nearby, instead of a forty-five-minute drive away, in case the kids needed a place to spend some time, and because Cheryl was having issues with Daniel. Cheryl had talked, in the past, of sending him to Cherokee School, which is a school for children with severe emotional and behavioral problems. Mom was extremely unhappy with that idea, and she began to talk about taking Daniel away from her. She told Cheryl, to her face, "I'll take your son and I'll raise him. You're not putting him there. He'll live here."

In my opinion, that wasn't the answer. I thought, "Your daughter needs help. Yanking her kids will only make it worse." My mother could have raised Daniel perfectly well, and they were very close. But I didn't think that was the answer for that family. I thought Mom was overreacting, maybe overcompensating for our childhoods—trying to make up for not being able to protect us.

Mom went with us to look at a house around the corner from her and said, "It's a great buy. You should do it." She was helping me and Susan to figure out how to do a budget. She had our bank account and paycheck info and was doing an overhaul on our finances. So when she advised us that it was a good deal, we decided to go ahead and get the house after we came back to Florida from Grandpa's funeral. Our new house had a big yard and a nice-sized pool. The house was big, too: living room, dining room, kitchen, family room, four bedrooms, two bathrooms, screened-in back porch, two-car garage.

In the meantime, Rickie's life was a mess. His wife left him, and he was living in a horrible little trailer. When Susan and I moved in to our new house, at the end of March 2003, he helped. Susan and I took the week off work, and we all busted our butts and got the job done.

It didn't take long for the subject of the two extra bedrooms to come up—one of the rooms was for Ann when she came to visit, but the other two were empty—and we invited him to move in. It just made sense. He was floating aimlessly, with no anchor, now that Mary had moved back to Georgia.

He was on unemployment and worked occasional free-lance electrician jobs, so we didn't charge him rent—he worked on the house in exchange for a roof over his head. He bought plenty of groceries and definitely held up his end of the bargain. Our new house needed plenty of fixing up. He earned his keep by being the man around the house.

He was very caring, exactly what you would want a brother to be. But sometimes after dinner, when we would be sitting at the table chatting, he would start talking about how things were in the past. We thought he was just talking about our childhood—we didn't pick up that he was still hurting.

We didn't feel that he needed therapy or that instead of dwelling on those things in our company that he should have been telling them to a shrink instead. He didn't seem to have a big emotional reaction; he was just telling stories about stuff that happened, and it became obvious that he wasn't real thrilled with Mom. We all noticed that the two of them had a frosty relationship, in the way that he wouldn't go to visit her when Grandpa was still alive unless he was home, and only went over there if she specifically asked him to.

We went to the movies quite often, and he paid most of the time. If he didn't make dinner, we'd go out to eat. One evening the three of us went to Quiznos and the movies after work, and he said, "See all these lights here?" pointing at the overhead fixtures at the shopping plaza. "That's what I've been working on the past few days." We believed him. We had no reason not to.

Looking back, I can see that there were a few red flags popping up here and there, but they only became noticeable when they were pointed out by the police after he was arrested. I grew up with a father who literally went psycho, and I didn't see the signs of my brother doing the same. Maybe it's because our father was whacked out to the point where nobody even cared if he lived or died. My father's "crazy" was normal to us, and Rickie wasn't anywhere near that. At the time, he wasn't hurting anyone, but he became controlling in a way that I didn't even notice because he was just acting like an extremely mild, nonviolent version of our father. Once he moved into our house, he didn't want to be left out of anything Susan and I were doing. Or, if Susan was gone, he monopolized every spare minute I had, and he used to try to have private conversations, about nothing really, when we were at family gatherings.

I was noticing that, for the first time, Susan and I weren't getting along very well. For fifteen years prior to his moving in, we got along just fine and had an almost perfect relationship. And now we were fighting all the time. I look back on this time in our lives and, knowing now that Rickie split up Catherine and her husband when he moved in with them, have to wonder if he wasn't somehow the cause of our uncharacteristic fighting. It almost seems like he was one of those brood parasites, moving in to a preexisting nest and pushing out one of the rightful residents.

I didn't realize until years later that he was e-mailing various family members and including me in every one of his signatures, as if I were participating in his e-mailing activity. I didn't even use a computer, much less get involved in his e-mail writing. He didn't sign them from himself alone, and many he signed from "Rickie Stacey," as if the names were one. He sent one to my Aunt Nancy, my father's sister, in June 2003, saying that Mother lied to her about our father, and that Rickie knew where our father was. Rickie told her that our father couldn't bother anyone anymore. But he also made sure to tell her the e-mail was from both of us, even going so far as to tell her that he called me "Squirt."

Over the course of the summer, he and our nephew became very close. He used to pick Daniel up and they would hang out and talk. I believe that it was during one of those outings that Rickie told Daniel that he shot our father, "blow-to-blow." He told Daniel a *lot* of inappropriate things—things a boy his age should never have heard.

When Rickie found out that Mom wanted to take Daniel, he did not want that to happen, either. But his reasons were different from mine. He felt that Mom was unfit. I didn't think she was unfit; I thought she did all she could do. To me, unfit means she didn't care. Unfit means she sat back and watched. He remembers her being a part of his abuses, and I do not. I wonder if the fact the he was a boy, being raped, caused him to react differently than Cheryl and I. I don't know much about the psychology of rape and gender, but it seems that a male would have to deal with testosterone-fueled rage, pride, and vengeance issues more than a female would.

Maybe that was why he was particularly concerned

about what was going on between Daniel and Cheryl. Daniel showed us, when we were working on Grandpa's memorial garden, that he had taken his dad's knife and was carrying it for self-defense against his mom. Rickie took it away from him and gave it back to Chris. We had a long talk with Chris and told him that something needed to be done, maybe an intervention, if the boy was stashing weapons to protect himself.

Chris and Cheryl decided to get some counseling from their minister, Pastor Dan, and take some parenting classes. But Cheryl was so upset and humiliated by our interference that she wrote a long letter to me and Rickie, telling us to let her handle it and, basically, butt out. So we did. We stopped going over for family game night, and communication between us ceased.

I won't lie and say my feelings weren't hurt by being given the frozen shoulder, because we really were just trying to help. There was no good way to do this. We didn't want Mom to try to take Daniel, but we certainly didn't want to allow our nieces and nephew to endure a difficult household while we just sat back and did nothing. It sucked that our stepping in caused a wedge to form between us, but I'd do it again if I had to, to help those kids.

I don't know what prompted him to do so, but it was around that time that Rickie bought a chest freezer, in August 2003, under the name John Taylor, and gave a false address. He also borrowed Mom's car, and she wasn't happy about it at all, but he insisted. While he had it, he made her an extra car key, for seemingly no reason at all.

Even though we weren't seeing Cheryl's family anymore, life went on. My cousin Laureen came to visit for a week, and it was a whirlwind of activity: Mom and Laureen went to SeaWorld on Labor Day, Laureen went to Discovery Cove by herself on Tuesday, she and Susan went to Epcot on Wednesday, and then she, Susan, and I went to St. Augustine for a couple of days. After Laureen went home on the fifth of September, Mom, Susan, and I went to Disney on Ice on the sixth. It was a very busy week.

So, when the topic of that year's annual September birthday cruise came up, I was exhausted and begged off. I just couldn't go that year. I had taken off so much time, between moving in March and Laureen's visit, that I didn't have any more vacation time left. But Ann wasn't taking no for an answer from Susan, so the two of them went without me and I was fine with that. She and I were having some relationship issues anyway, so the time apart was welcome. "Go," I told her. "Go with your mother and have a fun birthday."

That decision would haunt us both, in the years to come.

Susan went to Hudson to get Ann and her dog, Sadie, on Wednesday, September 10, and returned to our house the next day in preparation to leave for the cruise on Saturday. I was going to dog-sit.

I found out later, when the evidence in Mom's murder was gathered, that while I was at work on Wednesday, Rickie purchased a Taser from the Spy Store on Colonial Drive.

Mom also went to work on Wednesday, and probably got home at her usual time, about 6:00 P.M. Her routine never varied: in bed by nine-ish, up very early, maybe 4:00 A.M., drink some coffee, read the paper, get a bite to eat, clean the house, take any morning trash—including coffee grounds and the newspaper—out to the can, and head to work. She was planning on going to Boston on Friday, so she would have been particularly meticulous with her schedule.

On Thursday evening, September 11, Cheryl called to ask if I had talked to Mom that day. I told her that I spoke to her on Tuesday, but not since then. She said, "Well, I talked to someone at her work. She didn't come to work today." That was unusual, because Mom *never* just didn't show up. She was extremely reliable. However, because she was going to Boston the next day, I told Cheryl that I would check to see if she left a day early.

Instead, Cheryl called the woman with whom Mom worked at the airline, to check, and called me back to say, "No. She didn't leave a day early." So I got Rickie and we went right over to Mom's house. Her car wasn't in the driveway, and he had to let us into the house. He had the only key, because he had just changed the locks after Laureen's visit.

I walked in the house and noticed that some of Mom's things were missing: some of her clothes, jewelry, her suitcase. Some pictures were gone from the wall, there were papers on the kitchen counter, the coffeepot was left out, and her Oil of Olay was on the bathroom counter. Mom never, ever, *ever* left a mess like that. Never. Not even a coffee cup drying in her sink. You could walk in there any day of the week, with no notice, and showcase that home to sell it. Other than the dents and holes in the wall from my father, it was immaculate.

On the kitchen counter was a letter from Social Security stating that our father's presence was requested, to update their records on him. The counter was covered with all sorts of financial papers, which was also not like my mother at all. She was always extremely private about her finances and personal information. Rickie called Cheryl and said, "The nightmare is back! You have to get over here right away!" She was there within five or ten minutes. It wasn't a very long drive from her house to Mom's.

Cheryl and I went through the house. We were in the kitchen and she was standing by the refrigerator. She had a strange look on her face, and I asked, "What's wrong?" It was so bizarre—she opened the freezer door, looked at the food in it, and said, "I know where Mom is," and closed the freezer.

She recalled the story a little differently, in her deposition. She remembered getting goose bumps, looking at her arms, and saying, "Something has happened. Something is terribly wrong," but I distinctly remember her opening the freezer door and saying, "I know where Mom is." At the time, I thought she was nuts, wondering what the hell she was talking about, but maybe she was having some sort of a psychic vision, because the evidence showed that Mom's body was put in a freezer before she was buried.

The police were called, and Cheryl took charge. She sat down to file the report with the officer, who made it clear that only one of us should do the talking and Cheryl was doing just fine. She told him that Mom's car and personal things were not there. She noted that Mom's work clothes were gone, instead of her leisure clothes, which is what she would have taken with her if she had left on her trip. Cheryl used to borrow Mom's clothes all the time, and she knew which closet held which kinds of clothes. Mom kept her work clothes in her bedroom but the leisure clothes in the spare room closet.

She also put down on the report that, because of the family history of domestic violence, we believed Mom might be in danger and that she may have left, involuntarily, with our father in order to protect her grandchildren because he might try to abduct them or kill them.

The report said, "Ms. Bracken said, fifteen years ago her father told her he promised he would return and he would kill her or hurt her in a way she would never forget. She stated their family suffered from an extreme history of domestic violence, including verbal, physical, and sexual abuse. Ms. Bracken said one incident included their father breaking their mother's arm while she was pregnant at the age of seventeen. She stated they also witnessed their mother being kicked about her head and stomach area several times by their father. Ms. Bracken said their father often used knives or a gun to create fear and rule the home."

Cheryl found Mom's address book and told Rickie she was going to call each and every number in there, but he took it from her and said he'd take care of it because she had a job and kids, and he had more time. Mom's coworkers told Cheryl, later, that Thursday morning when Mom didn't show up, they checked her work voice mail and found a message left by my brother at approximately 7:30 A.M. asking, "Where were you last night? We missed you for Buffy night. Oh yeah, Stacey says hey." They thought it was strange, and so did I, because Mom never watched *Buffy the Vampire Slayer*. She was not a Buffy fan.

Rickie went to the DMV on Friday to change his address from our house to Mom's and drop the "Jr." from his name on his driver's license, so—he said—he could pass as our father and access Mom's bank accounts to track any activity. Susan left on Saturday, with Ann, for the birthday cruise. She asked if I wanted her to stay behind, but Ann was adamant that they go. "She'll be fine." Ann insisted, "The police are doing their job, and those tickets are nonrefundable!" Reluctantly, Susan went with Ann, but she promised to call from the ship before it left the dock. On Sunday, I went back to work and just hoped that something good would happen. There was nothing I could do, and I had to go to work. We had bills to pay, and sitting around the house wasn't finding Mom; it was just giving me more free time to worry.

Monday we met Cheryl at Daniel's football practice, and Rickie brought a legal pad with him. He told us that he had met with the IRS and Social Security that day, and that he had discovered that there were warrants for Mom's arrest for tax evasion. He said that the IRS was going to seize her house, and Social Security was going to prosecute her for all of our father's checks that were in her account, which still had his name on it. He wouldn't let either of us see what he had written on the pad, even though Cheryl kept trying to take it from him and read it. He kept saying, "No, I have it all right here," as if that was an answer. Then he said that Mom had given him power of attorney over her affairs before she disappeared, which Cheryl had a real problem with, because as far as she knew, *she* had power of attorney, and Mom had never advised her otherwise.

When he started taking stuff out of Mom's house, saying that he was removing her things before the IRS could seize it, we believed him. He told Cheryl that he didn't want either of us involved because he would be the only one with his hands dirty.

While Susan was away on her cruise, Rickie was emptying Mom's house by the van load. Mom's neighbor Steven saw him carrying out countless black plastic trash bags, some of them for the weekly trash pickup, but many more were put in his van and driven away. We found out later that he only kept things with a monetary value. Everything else, he just pitched: all of our family photos, yearbooks, memorabilia—gone. He made a point of taking a few things out of her house and bringing them to my house. He took her fridge and some DVDs for the kids.

My birthday was a few days later, on September 19, and I didn't feel like celebrating. To be honest, I didn't expect any sort of celebration. Cheryl was still mad at me because of the Daniel incident, and now everyone was upset about Mom. I thought my birthday would just sort of come and go without notice. But I was surprised when Cheryl, Chris, and their three kids dropped by to bring me a gift.

I had to hurriedly lock Ann's dog in her room because Sadie didn't like kids and I was afraid she would bite someone. Daniel needed to use the restroom, and started heading to that room, but because the dog was in there, I directed him to the other bathroom.

At the time, I didn't give these mundane events much thought, but Daniel told me something about the way Rickie acted that day, years later after the trial was over, "I looked in his eyes and knew he did something. I didn't know what, I couldn't put it together, but I knew because he was looking to see how much I hurt." I can understand how a twelve-year-old wouldn't know what to do with that, but I wish he had said something to me about it then. He just held on to that feeling; he just knew Rickie had done something.

Daniel knew, at the time, what Rickie had said about killing our father, and didn't say a word. It wasn't until Mom was missing for over a month or so that he told Cheryl. He didn't say a word to me, eight days later when he walked in my house and he sensed that Rickie knew more than he was telling.

I also didn't find out until years later that Rickie sent an e-mail to Senator Bob Graham, on September 20, demanding an investigation into Mom's accounts because he believed that she was defrauding the government. *He* started the investigation nine days after she died. He was going to need letters to show to me and Cheryl.

No one but Rickie knows for sure when exactly he moved Mom's body from the house to the storage unit freezer, and then from there to the grave he dug in our backyard. I've checked Susan's meticulous calendar for clues, and the only time that looks likely is two weeks after Mom disappeared. Susan finally got home from the cruise on September 20, and Rickie took us out to dinner and a movie on September 24, 25, and 26. That was the only time that entire year—before or after Mom's death—that the three of us went to dinner and a movie three nights in a row. This would have given him three full days to dig that hole in the backyard during the day, and a way to distract us away from using the pool in the evening. Hindsight surely is twenty-twenty.

CHAPTER 22

A Family Divided

It seemed like, after Mom's "leaving," there was always something odd going on. One day Susan was coming out of the bank and, to her frustration, noticed that her license plate was missing. If it wasn't one thing, it was another! She reported the plate stolen and had to go get a new one. We were wondering if our weird luck would ever change.

The month of October was pretty much a blur. Susan and I kept busy at work, Cheryl and I still weren't speaking, and Rickie kept emptying Mom's house and reporting his "progress" to us. Every couple of days he'd tell us about an appointment or phone call he had with this official or that, and we were grateful to have him taking charge. I assumed, because he had updated Cheryl about the IRS and Social Security at Daniel's game, that he was keeping her in the loop. Once again, hindsight was to show me later that he did not. But since she and I weren't talking, I didn't know that at the time.

More hindsight showed, in the form of trial evidence, that Rickie was in and out of his rented storage units an awful lot during October. In the meantime, he also started playing around online with Mom's bank accounts. He left a voice mail for Cheryl saying that he had come into some extra money and wanted to put it toward payments on her car. He set up online banking privileges so he could "bill-pay" out of Mom's account to four recipients: himself, me, his business—Emerald Electric, and our new landscaping business—Green Acres. In early November, he began sending out checks, much like he did with Catherine Crews's fire insurance money when he sent funds to Mom and Mary.

The $2,500 Christmas check, written to me, is the one that would come back to bite me later. I don't recall ever seeing that check, and the endorsement on the back said, "Stacey Kananen." I always, *always* sign my name Stacey M. Kananen. I don't know why; I just do, and always have. When Toni dug up ten years' worth of paycheck endorsements from Disney, she was able to prove that. Yes, the handwriting looked rather like mine, but I will go to my grave not remembering ever seeing that check.

In early November, Daniel finally told Cheryl about his conversation with Rickie about his killing our father. Cheryl, of course, immediately contacted law enforcement (she neglected to tell me and Susan), and they turned the case over to the Homicide Division, who assigned it to their newest rookie detective, Mark Hussey, as "busy work." Hussey, who became a cop because of his admiration for the TV show *Dragnet*, took the ball and became so gung ho that he was unable to tell when he ran it out-of-bounds.

Hussey and Cheryl began communicating on a regular basis, tossing ideas off of each other, and their suspicion of me began to grow—again, without my being aware of any of this. I didn't even know that the case had been turned over to the Homicide Division until late December. The detective told my sister to invite us all over for my niece's birthday that November, to see if she could discover anything—he put her in the position of being his sleuthing sidekick—but told her to make sure that she had someone armed in the house. She invited a friend of the family, who attended the event, armed with a gun. When I found out about this, much later, I was devastated that they knew Rickie had told Daniel that he was a murderer but didn't do anything to warn either me or Susan about the fact that we might be living with a killer.

I thought we were invited over because Cheryl was maybe trying to patch things up. They did, after all, come over on my birthday, and we did have our missing mom in common. Now was not the time to be mad at each other over the whole August incident. I had been leaving the occasional voice mail to check in, but we really didn't talk other than that.

It was a week later, in mid-November, that Susan and I had our garage sale. It's become such a point of contention that there is no way to talk about it without sounding guilty or like I'm making excuses. But people have garage sales all the time and there is nothing wrong with that. We had a garage sale, and in addition to a lot of other excess household items, yes, we were selling some of our Disney collectibles. We had *hundreds* of them, many of them duplicates. Detective Hussey, on his day off from his first days on the case, decided to mosey by that day. We didn't know him at the time, and he recognized me from my driver's license picture. He saw that we were selling Disney items and called Cheryl, telling her that we were selling Mom's things.

Before I knew it, the phone was ringing. It was Cheryl, absolutely unhinged, saying, "Who the hell do you think you are and what have you done with Mom?" I was more than a little pissed by her accusation and said, "If you bothered to come over and check for yourself, I'd prove that I'm not selling Mom's stuff." She hung up on me and never came over. That was pretty much the end of all communication with my sister. I don't think we've spoken since that day.

So now it was just me, Susan, and Rickie, who kept saying that he was on top of things, that he was taking care of business. He was getting Mom's affairs in order, clearing the house of her stuff, and talking to the IRS and Social Security, taking care of the charges and warrants against her so she could come back home. I was on my way home from work one day when I saw him at Mom's house, with the garage door open, and he was talking to a man inside the garage. I stopped to see what was going on.

He introduced me to the gentleman and told me that he planned to take the carpet up from the garage floor and put a nice, clean covering of river rock down, the kind they use for pool decks and patios. He told me that if the IRS and Social Security forced us to sell the house, we'd get more money for it, because the cement under the carpet was cracked and damaged.

Once again with blinding hindsight, I now realize that he needed to make sure there was a new finish on the floor because if somebody bought the house and decided that they didn't want carpet in the garage, they'd take the carpet up and see the steel plate that covered my father's concrete grave. Silly, naïve me, I just said, "Sounds good. Go ahead." And he did.

In late November, Rickie came home with good news: he had won the Fantasy 5! He played the lottery frequently and was happy to report that he won a large chunk of money. Neither Susan nor I asked the exact amount, because you don't ask other people about their money if they don't volunteer the information. When he offered to make a couple mortgage payments or pay off Susan's car—our choice—in exchange for free rent since we were running out of renovations for him to do, we gladly took him up on it. He also helped me with a down payment on a new truck, which I badly needed. I traded in my old truck and got a gorgeous new one. I loved my new electric blue Nissan pickup. The payments were affordable enough, even if it would be tight with the house payments, and I was content. Rickie apparently had enough lotto winnings left over, because he bought himself a new Dodge Ram and paid it off in full.

There were a lot of things going on under the surface

that I didn't find out about until years later, while preparing my legal defense with Diana. For example, by early December, Detective Hussey had started looking into my mom's bank accounts. The account was frozen, and if anyone called about it they were to be given instructions to call Hussey.

About a week later, Detective Hussey brought Cheryl and Daniel into his office for an interview, and Daniel told him some fascinating things. Even though he had previously told Cheryl that Rickie admitted to killing our father—which I also did not know about—that day Daniel told Hussey, "Uncle Rickie told me another way to kill somebody. You Taser them. He told me he had a Taser." The boy added, "A whole week before my Grandma's disappearance she was talking about dividing all my grandfather's stuff up and giving it away. The money, the stuff and everything. [Uncle Rickie] also mentioned that he was gonna write a book when everything was coming to an end."

Hussey asked him, "What do you mean, everything was coming to an end?"

Daniel replied, "He said that 'Soon enough everybody's gonna know my story when everything's coming to an end.' I asked, 'What do you mean? Like, when your life's over?' He said, 'When everything gets so bad I just give up.'"

I also found out, years later, that the same day Hussey was interviewing Daniel, Rickie received an e-mail from our Aunt Gerri, who lived in Ireland at the time. She was very concerned that some of Grandpa's heirlooms might come up missing and she wanted them. She kept e-mailing Cheryl to ask where they were. When Cheryl told her that Mom's house was being emptied, Gerri sent an e-mail to Rickie on December 16, asking why he was cleaning out the house and whether he had the legal right to alter the home of a runaway. She also asked if there were warrants out for Mom's arrest on charges from Social Security and the IRS.

His response to her on December 17 told her what he was telling everyone else—at the beginning, we thought that our father was involved, but after looking at the paperwork that she had supposedly left out, he discovered that Mom had been collecting Social Security all those years, and that she filed joint returns with the IRS, with our father's name attached.

He told her that Mom's bank accounts were frozen and none of her bills were being paid as a result, and that our cousin Laureen had advised him to get Mom's stuff out of her house before it was seized. His intention, he told Gerri, was to save Mother's things so when she returned all of her irreplaceable collectibles would be waiting for her.

He signed it, "Love, Rickie Stacey."

Christmas was just around the corner, and that year was going to be hard. Susan and I were torn over whether we should decorate or not, but we were trying to live a relatively normal life. Susan loves the holidays and festivities—she's just like a little kid; it's one of the things I love about her—so we went ahead and tried to merry the place up a bit. But Rickie wanted none of it. His attitude was, "Don't put this shit up in my room."

I told him, "It's not going in your room, but you need to respect Susan's wishes." I put lights and decorations up around mid-December, because I was trying to give Susan some Christmas joy.

We were also trying to maintain a modicum of normalcy at Mom's house, even if he had placed her belongings in storage—so I thought. Rickie mentioned to me that the utility bills over there were not being paid by the automatic online system that he had set up. So he asked me to call the bank and find out what was going on.

This is where it gets dicey, because I honestly don't know whether I called saying I was Marilyn Kananen or if I used my own name.

I can, realistically, see either scenario playing out. We all know that banks will only talk to the account holder, so it's feasible that I did say I was her, because that was the only way I could get the information I needed. On the other hand, the way I *remember* it is that I said I was Stacey Kananen, Marilyn's daughter.

In any case, I do not deny making the call and never have. Mom's utilities were in danger of being shut off, and we were trying to keep her house up and running. Rickie asked me to help out by making the call, so I did. But the bank employee who took my call and reported it to the police said that I pretended to be my mom.

Because it was already a suspicious situation, it looked pretty bad for me. However, after the bank employee told me the account was frozen and gave me instructions to call Detective Hussey, I did so immediately. He didn't answer, so I left a voice mail telling him why I was calling, and left our home phone number for him to call back.

Detective Hussey called back later and Rickie answered the phone. He told Rickie that he had some information about Mom's bank accounts, and he wanted him to come down. Even though Hussey did not specify that he wanted to talk to me, Rickie told him I'd be there with him. That night, Rickie was up, shredding papers. Call me stupid and naïve, but I didn't think anything of it. I guess I should have. It's no big deal, usually. Shredding papers doesn't mean you're guilty of murder.

CHAPTER 23

The Rug Gets Pulled . . .

Sometimes, when I look back on my life and the story that I've lived, I think about the weekend of December 20, 2003, and realize that it marked the end of my innocence. Yes, I had been viciously molested and raped in every way possible, I was raised and tortured by a criminal psychopath, I had witnessed and survived things that no person should ever have to experience. But that weekend was the last one where I believed that my parents were both still alive and my brother was not a murderer.

When I went to the Orange County Sheriff's Office that Monday morning, December 22, I was told that they had information about my mother and I was both hopeful and fearful about what I was about to hear. But Rickie assured me that all was well; we'd just go in and see what they had to say. Once we got inside, however, they took us into separate rooms and the life-changing conversations began.

I sat down at the table in what was a pretty typical police interview room, the kind you see on TV shows, and was joined by Detectives McCann and Ruggiero. They started out with some fairly innocuous fact-gathering questions about my parents and their relationship. I didn't think much of it until their questions started to veer toward me, like what kind of vehicle I drove and how much I paid for it. That seemed sort of irrelevant to me.

Then came the question, "Has anything belonging to your mom been sold since her disappearance?" Oh great, I thought. That damned garage sale. "No, it has not," I told them.

To my relief, they dropped it and asked what Rickie was saying about Mom. I told them, "He thinks she's afraid of the IRS, and she'll be back whenever things settle down with them."

I was surprised to hear, "According to what we know she had no problems with the IRS."

I responded, "He has a letter, something about she didn't put his income into the income tax. She had to send them a payment."

McCann said, "I mean the fact that she's missing has nothing to do with the IRS," and I replied, "Okay. I was just hoping . . ."

He interrupted, "Is that what you have been led to believe by Richard?"

This wasn't going the way I expected. Led to believe? What? I said, "Well, I was hoping that's why she left and maybe she'll be back when whatever's screwed up is taken care of."

Then began a barrage of questions about changes that Rickie had been making to Mom's house. What about all of her personal items? What about the new garage floor? Why were these things being done? All I could do was tell them what he had told me. I gave them as much information as I had, but it wasn't helping much.

"Did your brother represent himself as his grandfather, to do internet banking in his name to withdraw money? Has any money been provided to you by your brother?"

I didn't know anything about him using Grandpa's name, but I was sick when I had to admit that, yes, he had given me and Susan some money recently, almost seven thousand dollars, between paying off the car, helping me with my truck down payment, and things like that. I could have kicked myself when I had to own up to being naïve and trusting, and not asking him exactly where he got the money from. I told them, "Well, he's been doing a lot of electrical work so I just assumed. I don't ask a lot of questions. I grew up in a household where you just didn't ask those kinds of questions."

"Now," one of the detectives said, "the Nissan that you have, we understand was paid for in cash. That you don't owe anything on it."

Immediately, I corrected him. "Yes, I do. I have a payment book coming. My truck was not paid for in cash."

This was turning ugly. He continued, "Since your

mom's disappearance, upwards of a hundred thousand dollars has been taken from the trust fund."

All I could say was, "Holy smokes!"

He pressed on. "Now, how did that happen?"

I was flabbergasted. "I have no idea. I have absolutely no idea."

"Did some of that money go for the purchase of your pickup truck?"

"No! No!" I insisted.

"Did your brother go with you when you purchased the pickup truck?" he asked.

"Yeah, he was with me because my truck was dying every couple of blocks. I had to have somebody with me to help me drive it."

He wasn't letting up. "Well, why does Nissan say that it's paid for?"

I insisted again, "My truck is not paid for. I have the paperwork at the house. I have a payment book coming of $227 a month!"

When he asked how I came up with the six thousand dollars for the down payment, I explained, "My brother helped put it together. A little bit of electrical work he's been doing, some money I've been saving. Not six thousand. He gave me a couple and then I had some in my bank account. I believe it was maybe twenty-five hundred and I had the rest in my account."

One of the detectives asked, "So, the reason he's living in the house with you and not still at the mobile home is what?"

"He moved in to help me do some work on my house. I bought it in March 2003. He asked, when we were working on the house, 'Well, this is really nice. Can I move in with you guys?' and we said sure. We'd love to have you. I'd like to think it's because he wants to be closer to me. I haven't seen him much in a lot of years."

"Does he pay you rent?"

"He hasn't," I said, "but he's been helping me with home repairs I guess in lieu of rent. So, I assume when he gave me some money it was to help pay for the bills."

Detective McCann asked, "How did you learn that the bank accounts were frozen?"

"McCoy Bank sent a letter and it said, nonsufficient funds, accounts frozen."

He asked, "So, who called the bank?"

I told them, "I called to ask a question and of course they won't give me any information because I'm not Marilyn. I asked them if they could tell me why the accounts were frozen."

"So, they told you that because you weren't Marilyn they weren't going to give you any information on the accounts?"

"Uh huh. That is correct."

"Why did you call the bank about the frozen accounts?"

"Because I was curious and I was concerned."

"Did Richard tell you to call?"

I told McCann, "He might've mentioned it, but not in a way that he made me call."

"Is your mom's car in one of those storage units?"

I was beginning to get sick to my stomach, because it

was becoming apparent that they knew something sinister was going on. "No, I don't believe so," I said. "I only know about one storage unit."

"When we go to your house and dig up the garage floor, are we going to find anything?"

I was confused. "No. You're going to dig up my house?"

"We're going to dig up the garage floor where the metal plates are."

More confusion. "Are you talking about my mother's house? Not to my knowledge. No, I wouldn't expect you to find anything."

"What if she's there?"

My heart lurched in my chest. "I . . . why did you say that?"

"Because we think she may be."

I couldn't answer that. The implication was sinking in.

Detective Ruggiero said, "You've lived in that house, correct? And your mother's lived there for quite some time? And after her disappearance these metal plates appeared in the garage floor. Did you find that strange?"

"Yeah, a little."

"Little bit. We do, too. We get paid to ask questions. We work in Homicide. If you know something about what happened to your mother . . ."

I interrupted, "I have no . . ."

"Listen, hear me out. If you know something about what happened to your mother, you need to be completely honest with us. Did Richard tell you how to answer us?"

"No, he didn't."

He persisted, "You guys are coming in to talk to

Homicide detectives and you don't talk about questions you may be asked? I find that very strange. If I was going to talk to a Homicide detective with somebody, I would be talking about questions that may be asked."

"I honestly didn't know you guys were Homicide detectives. He told me that we had to talk to Mark Hussey about Mother's leaving."

"You didn't answer my question about the plates. You would find that strange?"

"Yeah, I guess so," I said.

"Who put them there?"

"My brother did."

"Why?"

I stammered, "I don't know. I didn't ask. I don't ask questions. When I grew up as a kid you just didn't ask questions." That comment led into a long conversation about what it was like when I was growing up. I explained that our father was a dangerous man, and we were all lucky to have survived. When they asked if Rickie was like him, I had to say that I didn't think he was. I really didn't. I couldn't see him being violent.

Ruggiero was dubious. "Even to protect all three of you and the mother?"

"I can't see my brother being that kind of a person."

McCann said, "It's happened before. Where to protect the family something is done like that and then the family isn't hurt anymore. I think that's probably what happened in this case with respect to your father."

I had no response to that. He asked, "Your brother has a take-control type personality, would you say? He seems to have taken charge after your mother's disappearance pretty quickly. I mean what with moving stuff out, with getting a storage unit, redoing the garage, taking care of all kinds of things. I don't know him. I've never met the man. But it would seem to me that would be his personality. Do you understand where we're coming from?"

"I'm having a hard time with what you're thinking, but I think so."

McCann continued, "Now we're talking about your mother, who has been working solidly every day for eight years or more. Every day. She never disappeared once. She was very conscientious. All of a sudden she doesn't show up anymore and her car doesn't show up? Now that tells us that whoever did this is pretty secure that we're not going to find her or the car. That's why I asked you if we're going to find the car in one of those storage units. And then we have the issue of the hundred thousand dollars. Where is the money?"

I felt stupid, but had to say, "I don't know."

Detective Ruggiero said, "What we're getting at is people like your mother don't tend to disappear. Then we have the hundred thousand dollars coming out of accounts, which have been accessed in all likelihood via the computer. It would seem that whoever's doing this would have information that she isn't going to come back. And then we have the whole scenario with the garage and the residence itself."

McCann asked me again about making that phone call to the bank. He said, "You know what that situation would put you in. If we're talking about a homicide here. Alright? So, we want you to be absolutely up front with us, Stacey, right now. Because from now on it's a downhill slide, alright? If there's something you know, we need to hear it right now."

I was beginning to get a little panicky. They wouldn't believe anything that I was telling them. I said, "I don't know anything. I'm just a little taken aback by what's been said and . . ."

He asked, "Why didn't you report your mom missing?"

"We all three were in the house at the time the report was made!"

"Your sister reported your mom missing. And she's been in regular contact with us. I don't recall any information about you coming in and talking to anybody. That didn't happen, Stacey. Didn't you love your mother?"

I was practically in tears. "I love my mother very much. I miss my mother very much. This is probably the worst thing that could ever happen to me, is to not have her here."

"Right. Are you and Richard in cahoots?"

Why wouldn't he believe me? "No. Goodness, no!" I cried.

"This is over something as simple as money. Simple greed, money! Did he take money out of the trust to go buy a truck?"

"I don't know."

"Did he kill his mother because he wanted to go buy a truck? Because I bet that his business is worth crap. I bet that he doesn't make crap day-to-day in his business. And

I bet that he's home more then he's somewhere else, and he's how old?"

"He's forty six."

"And he doesn't have his own place, he's got to live with you?"

I didn't answer. He had a good point.

"Huh?" he jabbed at me. I had nothing to say in response.

"If he had such a great business, he'd be living on his own; he'd be living with his wife. But apparently, she's had enough."

The truth was crashing down on me. "I don't know. I don't know!"

"Is Richard dragging you into something, Stacey?" Mc-Cann asked.

Detective Ruggiero took over. "Stacey, I think that you need to maybe open your eyes a little bit regarding your brother. Because I think he's manipulating you, and I think he's taking advantage of you. Because maybe you are a little too trusting. But now is the time where if you know something or you've heard something, now is not the time to protect your brother. Because I'm here to tell you, we're going to find your mother. We're going to dig up that garage and I'm here to tell you people don't put steel plates down on a garage for no reason."

I could barely speak. All I could say was, "Okay."

"It's going to be over today. Your life is not going to be the same after today, ever."

That statement shook me to my core. I whispered out a quiet, "Uh huh."

His voice got a little kinder. "So, you need to get some strength, inner strength right now. Not from anybody else, but from you, okay? Because your life has changed—is going to change right here, right now, today. You need to tell us exactly what you know. I think that you've been manipulated. But I can tell you that with the scenario as we have it, your brother's been living with you for six months, this thing appears pre-planned and appears to have been carried out. And like Detective McCann says, the motive is simple, it's greed. It's the oldest one in the world."

Even though I could hear his soothing voice, and began to comprehend what he was saying, he sounded very far away as I retreated to my safe, inner world. He kept going. "Now, it doesn't appear to be your greed, but you need to help us out with that, okay? Because as it appears right now, you're not looking very good as things lay right now. I think your brother's been in your life for the last seven months and manipulating you. You're not the mastermind here, you're not the strong one, you're not the take-charge one. I believe he is. And I believe he may be leading you down. He's giving you seven thousand dollars, helping pay for your truck. He's doing all these things. I don't think any of this is by coincidence. Personally I don't believe in coincidence. This is money that's been obtained through those accounts because he knew that your mother wasn't coming back."

McCann's voice jarred me back into the room when he said, "And once the accounts were frozen it's like, oh my God!"

Ruggiero continued, "Sometime this afternoon when we dig that garage up, his world is going to be coming to an end. And lying is going to come to an end, it's going to stop. Now, usually people sense somewhat of a relief at that time because the lie is finally over. It's kind of like the world's come off your shoulders. I'm hoping to get that sense of relief from you."

I was briefly wounded that he seemed to be so caring for a few short moments, but then came back to his implication that I had been involved in murder. I stammered, "I haven't lied at all. I . . . I don't know what's going on with the money. I . . . dear God . . . I hope you don't find anything in the garage. I . . ."

McCann sneered, "What do you mean you don't know what's going on with the money?"

"I don't know . . . I don't know who took it. I . . ."

"So, you're saying that he took a hundred grand out and hasn't given you a dime?"

"I don't know that's where the money came from."

He shot back, "Well, what does this sound like, Stacey? Let's have a reality check here. He's buying you off to shut you up. What else is he giving you other than that six, seven thousand dollars? Is he going to tell us that, oh yeah, she knows, Stacey knows? She wanted half of it or else she was going to come to the police and tell the police what she knew. So, yeah, I had to give her thirty or forty thousand dollars. But, that's all she wanted and she told me that she wouldn't say anything. Is that what happened, Stacey?"

"No! No!" I shouted.

"You wouldn't cheapen your mother's memory by just wanting some money?" he taunted.

His words brought back a heartbreaking image of spending time with Mom, all the good times we had together, all those years, and tears came to my eyes. "God no! I loved my mother. I was with my mother all the time!"

"Yet you didn't report her missing."

Why didn't they get this? I was there, and Cheryl gave the report! "I was in the house the night that my sister did!"

Ruggiero asked, "What's going to be your reaction when we do go dig up the garage?"

McCann said, "What if we find your dad there, too?"

I said, "What do you mean? I . . . I'm . . . I'm just freaked out by what he said. What do you mean by what's going to be my reaction?"

"Well, what's going to be your reaction? Are you going to be surprised?"

"Yeah! I'm . . . I'm . . ."

"That would surprise you? Funny, it wouldn't surprise me. It wouldn't surprise me knowing what I know. What other explanation is there for these big metal sheets to be placed down on a garage floor? And then the garage floor redone in river rock? Go ahead. I'm more than game to listen."

"I don't know. I . . . I . . . I don't know."

Ruggiero continued, "I don't, either, but I got a pretty good guess."

McCann added, "Maybe you don't want to know. Maybe you just say, 'If I don't think about it, it'll go away.

And I won't have to think about my mother and my dad being under concrete in their driveway in the garage.'"

I started sobbing. "I think about my mother every day. I think about my mother every day."

Ruggiero asked, "What's going to be your reaction then if we find her? You going to think that we planted her there?"

"No."

"What would you think happened?" I couldn't answer, so he asked again, "I'm asking you what would you think happened?"

I finally said, "I . . . I . . . I would guess he would've done something."

"You don't find that unfathomable?"

"I have a real hard time with it."

Detective Ruggiero said, "What Detective McCann has in his hand right now is a search warrant that's been signed by a judge. We are going to go to the house later today. I'm not telling you anything that's not going to happen. But let's say, hypothetically, that after we do dig it out, that we find her there. I'm asking you, what would be the explanation?"

I stammered, "I . . . I don't know. Well, I guess, I . . . I don't know. I guess . . . he would've had to have something to do with it."

"What would've been your brother's motive for doing something like that? Why is the motive being money or simply greed, why is that not believable to you? It's believable to me, but why is it not believable to you?"

He didn't know Rickie the way I did, at least the way

I thought I did. I tried to explain, "Because he's always told me money's not important to him, being happy is important!"

"But he's driving a 2004 Dodge truck that he just paid for in cash."

"I didn't know he paid for it. I thought he had payments to make."

"People who don't think that money is important to them usually don't drive around in their net worth. Somebody living with their sister usually doesn't go and buy a twenty-five-thousand-dollar automobile and pay cash."

McCann took over. "The logical inference is that if your parents are underneath the concrete in the garage that your brother killed them. Maybe he killed your dad because he was a bad guy, and he was protecting you and your sister. But he killed your mom simply so that he could buy stuff!"

Ruggiero agreed, "That's what it appears."

McCann said, "Now that is a low denominator. And he felt the need to provide you with the proceeds from the trust until the account was frozen by us. Because we knew that eventually somebody was going to make the call to the bank. And the call was made by you."

"Yes, I did," I said.

Detective Ruggiero said, mildly, "Money makes people do strange things. How would you account for your role in this incident?"

"I don't have a role. I just want my mother to come home."

His cruel words struck me like a blow. "Your mother is

not going to come home. I think we're going to have some answers by the end of today and you may not like them. But we're going to have them nonetheless. There's a good chance that your brother isn't going to be coming home with you."

I couldn't answer, so he continued, "What do you think he's going to say regarding your role? What would you say if I told you that he's already told somebody he's killed your father?"

McCann said, "That's why he's absolutely sure that he's not coming back to hurt you or him or anybody else. Because he's already dead."

My head was starting to hurt. I just wanted this to be over, to not think anymore, to not hear anymore. I said, "I'm having a hard time with this. I'm having a real hard time with this."

McCann taunted, "You're not having a hard time yet. This is the beginning. If he tells us that you profited, if you got money from the trust . . ."

Ruggiero added, "That you knew . . ."

McCann finished his thought. "That makes you a principal to murder. But we want to make sure while we're talking that we get one hundred percent truth. Because if there's a variation from the truth, later on, that gives you a problem. So, I want you to be absolutely, positively accurate and truthful with us. Because we're going to find out whatever it is that you're trying to hold back."

I started to say, "I'm not . . ." but he interrupted, "Alright, we found out a whole hell of a lot up to now. That's why you're here! That's why you're here! We don't bring you in and start thinking of stuff to ask you. We got pages and pages of information. We have technicians waiting to go to the house, alright? We're going to dig that garage up until we find her and him, too. That's what we want, very simply: the truth. The truth rings true and it always prevails."

I cried, "I've given you the truth!"

Ruggiero said, "Okay, these are the facts that we have. Do you see how, even if you're naïve as the day is long, how that's a little suspicious?"

I had to admit that it looked pretty bad. "When you put it all together, yeah."

McCann said, "Do you kind of get the impression, from the conversation we're having, that you're a doormat for him? That whatever he needs to do, he can use you. He can tell you to call the bank and find out why the bank accounts are frozen. What did Richard tell you over the weekend about this pending interview? What did he tell you about coming down here then?"

I told him, "He just said we were coming to talk to Mark Hussey about Mom being missing."

There was a knock on the door, and two detectives came in. One said, "Stacey, we just got finished talking to Richard. These are the keys to the house. He's admitted to those steel plates, that your parents are there. He's put the blame on you. You guys are working together."

I lost my breath for a second. "No, we're not!"

The new detective continued, "This is the diagram of the garage with the steel plates. And he specifically pointed to this area right here. That's his drawing. We're on our way to the house. And he's saying that you, because of the abuse, killed your father."

The other officer said, "Listen, we understand there's two sides to every story. We want to hear your side. But what you do by continuing to lie, is make yourself look guilty. You're at a crossroads right now and you got to make a decision. You're gonna either continue to lie, or you're going to tell the truth."

The first detective said, "How do you think we got the key?"

"Your brother is playing you, okay?" the second officer said. "Your brother doesn't care about anybody but himself. We don't want to believe him, but we've got nothing from you."

I insisted, "I don't know what's under those plates," and he said, "You know a lot more than what you're telling us."

"No, I don't."

"Yeah, you do."

"No, I don't!"

"And we can sit here and play, 'no, I don't, yeah, you do,' all day long. We're not going to play that anymore."

Ruggiero asked, "So, he's saying she had a more active role?"

"Right," the first detective said, "and he drew a diagram of the garage with the metal plates and specifically said right here. And that because of abuse that your father was doing to you, you killed your father."

I couldn't even speak above a whisper, I was so horrified. How was this happening? "No, I did not kill my father. No way."

"But I wouldn't take all this blame on myself . . ." he said.

"I didn't do it!" I insisted. "I . . . I . . ."

The detective continued, "The bottom line is you know your parents are there. You know that they're in the house."

"I . . . I don't! I . . . I . . . I don't. I swear to God I don't!"

McCann asked, "But were you a victim of sexual abuse by your dad? That made you angry, didn't it?"

"Yeah," I said, "but it made me more scared of him than anything."

"Are you scared of your brother?"

"No, I'm not scared of my brother."

"You love your brother?"

"I do love my brother."

"Is that why you're trying to cover for him?" McCann asked.

"I . . . I don't want to believe . . ."

McCann said, "He's not covering for you. Sounds like he would give you up in a New York second. He gets all the money and he puts the blame on you. Now how does that happen? Unless you're the mastermind. Maybe that's it. Maybe you've just been conning us the whole time, Stacey. Maybe you're the one that put Richard up to this stuff."

I could barely keep from crying. This was a nightmare. I gasped, "No. All I want is my mother to come home."

"You know," McCann continued, "if I was being accused of involvement in a murder of my parents, I would be outraged. I would be pounding the table. You haven't showed one iota of anger that we are accusing you of something so heinous as the murder of your own parents."

Was that what they wanted? Histrionics? I never learned how to do that. I only learned to stay extremely calm and quiet when under attack. All I could say was, "I'm just baffled by this whole thing."

Ruggiero asked, "But what have we said that's a surprise to you?"

"I just can't believe he would do that." I was about to fall apart. I couldn't take any more of this. "I . . . I can't. I just can't. I just want my mom."

"Well," he said, "you're going to fall under the category of state's witness or co-defendant, as well as your significant other. Which one do you want to be?"

Jesus, what a choice. I said, "Well, I . . . I don't want to be either, but I prefer to be a state's witness because I didn't know anything about any of this."

And that was the end of that. Once they were done with me, they took me into another interview room. Rickie was sitting there, and they left me with him. Alone.

CHAPTER 24

Rickie's "Confession"

While I was with Detectives McCann and Ruggiero, Rickie was having a disjointed conversation with Detectives Hussey and Russell. He brought the letter from Social Security and various tax documents with him.

Hussey asked Rickie when he last saw Mom, and the answer was Sunday, September 7. He said that Mom dropped in because we were getting in the habit of eating together several times a week.

That was a lie, but the officers didn't know that. He told Hussey, "She said she was real busy and she had to go." Hussey asked if that was unusual behavior on her part, and Rickie said, "No, sometimes our . . . our mother, she . . . I know she was getting depressed because she didn't like September 11th."

Hussey asked, "What was up with September 11th?"

Rickie babbled, "Well when it first happened she wanted everybody ready when we . . . gonna walk the Appalachian Trail. I mean, um . . . she . . . the *Sentinel* came out with a report, you know, what to do for emergencies. She wanted to have a big family meeting and that. She just didn't like September 11th."

Hussey said, "Okay. Because of the World Trade . . ."

"So I didn't really think anything of it and that's the last time I heard from her."

He told them that since she disappeared, no one had called to find out where she was. "See," he explained, "that's not unusual, the way we used to live. But no one has called her. Her two friends here in Orlando, one is—I don't know her name: I call her the cookie monster lady—and Ginger. They haven't heard anything from her, either."

Hussey brought up the bank account that we called him about. He said, "What bills were you paying out of that?"

"Well," Rickie said, "she used to have everything direct deposit from McCoy. McCoy kicked the bills back and I called them up so it's on hold now, Social Security. And just her everyday bills and fixing up her house."

Hussey was already confused. "Why is it on hold for Social Security?"

Rickie responded, "When we went in the house, when we decided to call the police, this is what my mother left on the table. That's the Social Security benefits from my father. We have never heard or seen him since '88 and I mean to leave something like that on . . . she knows what . . . you . . . you know what I'm saying."

"The checks were continuing to be mailed to . . ." Hussey was having difficulty following.

"No, direct deposited to this bank."

Detective Russell took a shot at it. "Even after he disappeared or moved he didn't get his check forwarded? Didn't you guys find that unusual?"

Rickie said, "Well that's what we're telling everybody, ev . . . all . . . all along that, you know, something's wrong here. Yeah. Cause she left all this for me to go through and it's from '88 on. All of her returns have got him on there. And I know he was not living in the house 'cause my grandfather would not have moved in that house and none of us would have had anything to do with her with him being around."

Russell asked, "Was he ever physically abusive to her?"

"Oh yeah. Yeah."

Russell replied, "Those are all her income tax forms?"

"From '88 on up," Rickie explained.

"How do you know she left them for you?"

Rickie said, "About, sometime, August maybe we were just sitting there and she just . . . she said it out of the blue, what was it, exactly what . . . You all aren't gonna be happy with what's gonna happen but, you know, you are gonna have to accept it. I'm thinking she's got a boyfriend or something. We asked her and she wouldn't say anything. And with our mother she would say something, we'd drop it, that's the end of the discussion. And then this comes up. And I told you, you can get very little information from Social Security or IRS."

They spent a large amount of time talking about Rickie's frustrations with getting any information from the IRS or Social Security, until he finally said, "I guess when my mother forgot to report his income, Social Security lets IRS know and then I guess this wasn't the first time and I guess they wanna know why he hasn't collected his Medicare. All the lady would tell me is that they had no record that he was going to the doctors. And he was going to the doctor in '87 . . . '88 about every other two or three days and they'd put him in the hospital to dry him out and say it was a heart condition."

Hussey didn't seem to know what to make of that, so he asked, "How were you accessing her account?"

"She left the thing online."

"She did?" Hussey asked. "Okay."

Russell said, "I don't understand what you meant she left the thing online."

"Well," Rickie explained, "she set it up where you can do it online. It was all with all this other stuff in September."

Hussey asked, "She did it in writing?"

"No. When I was younger we always lived in code. Because of my father. She would just, you know, leave things like this and then I would know what to do with it because we couldn't let my father know what was going on. And then I thought all that garbage was gone but . . . I guess not. It was just like laying . . . just like . . . just lay there. Just . . . and then you just infer what she wants. I mean she just . . ."

"Yeah, but"—Hussey must have been scratching his head—"I'm confused about the online banking thing. You must have had some specific information about how to do . . ."

Rickie interrupted, "Well yeah. Well she just . . . she just left her thing . . . her code and all that on there. You know what I mean?"

"Left it where?"

"Just in a bunch of papers."

"So have you got those papers?" Hussey asked.

"No, I don't have it anymore. I'm sorry, I don't."

Detective Russell asked, "How do you remember the codes and everything?"

Rickie said, "When I was five my father just reiter . . . I gotta remember everything . . . everything . . ."—he startled mumbling—"certain times that I just (mumble mumble) remember."

Rickie then told them that Mom always asked him to take care of her things when she was gone, but paying her bills was outside of the norm. He rambled, "But, well I mean . . . I mean when . . . when . . . when . . . when you go (mumble) table and . . . not a table but it's like a . . . like a little counter. And you haven't heard, thought . . . think about this person since, you know, '88 and that's laying there on top. And then you look through things and try to find out and then you find all this other stuff here and then you find this stuff here and then you call . . . no, it is out of line."

Detective Russell, perhaps to change the subject and get Rickie back on track, asked, "Can Detective Hussey makes copies? Those might be important to the investigation." Rickie handed over the papers that he had brought with him.

They talked a little bit about his relationship with me and Cheryl and asked if I had ever been abused physically or sexually. "Both," he replied. "Physically I knew when I was living in the house, sexually she just told me recently. The mental . . . the physical abuse was when we were born all the way up."

"The sexual abuse?"

He said, "I hope it didn't happen until after I left but I don't know."

They kept Rickie gabbing for a long time about his business, and seemingly inconsequential stuff, until Detective Russell asked him about buying his truck with cash. "Where'd you get the $21,000 cash if you don't mind me asking?"

Rickie said, "I've been saving it for a long time. Where we used to live with my wife my bills had been nothing. I made $60,000 and our bills weren't even $800 a month. I paid cash for my wife's car a couple of years ago."

"Will you give us consent to go search your mother's house for any clues that might lead to her or your dad's whereabouts? We may have to dig up the yard, we may have to dig up plants, we may have to look anywhere in that house, okay?" Rickie gave his consent.

Russell asked him, "Anything else you think that we need to know about your mother being missing? Anything to help us try to locate her."

Rickie said, cryptically, "We used to do this all the time when we was younger."

"What's that?"

"It'd get in trouble and then we'd leave. And her family (mumble) wouldn't even know where we were for sometimes six months, a year or two years."

Russell said, "But she hasn't done that since your dad's been gone."

"Nothing . . . nothing . . . when we moved to Florida and . . . and it left and my grandfather moved in I . . . you know . . . I thought everything was gone . . . it was over with. It was, you know . . ."

"Right. And you said since 'it' left." Russell caught that. "You didn't think much of your father, did you?"

"No."

"I mean he abused you, he treated you and your family like shit."

"Yeah."

"Supposed to go to your sister's wedding, never showed up."

"No, he didn't," Rickie confirmed.

The detective was finally onto something. "Did you notify her that he wasn't coming to the wedding?"

Rickie said, "My mother told me to go tell Cheryl have a good wedding because he was gone. He wasn't coming back."

Russell abruptly asked, "Did you kill your dad?"

"Excuse me?"

"Did you kill your dad?"

Rickie said, "No, sir. No, sir."

Russell pressed on. "If you killed your dad, you did it to protect your family."

"I didn't kill my dad."

"You did it to protect your sisters."

Rickie said, "There was nobody living there anymore."

"Doesn't matter," Detective Russell stated. "He abused everybody for years."

"No, I didn't kill my dad. That doesn't say I didn't want to many times, but I didn't."

"You kill your mom?"

"No," Rickie told him, "I loved my mother. My mother was my savior a lot of times."

"Did your mom kill your dad?" Russell asked.

"No, I don't believe so, no."

Detective Russell pushed it harder. "If your mom killed your dad and asked you to help get rid of his body would you have done that?"

"Yes, I would," Rickie admitted.

"If your mom became afraid of your dad and killed him, and you came over there and buried him, that's one thing. If you cold-bloodedly killed your dad that's a different story. I don't think you killed your dad. I think something happened between them back in '88. If your mom gets scared and kills your dad and she doesn't know who else to call and you help her to dispose of his body, that's a misdemeanor, okay?"

Rickie listened, possibly taking mental notes for future versions of his story. "Uh huh."

Russell continued, "It's a minor charge. I can understand that you would do that for your mom. Now your mom's been living her whole life collecting your dad's check."

"I know."

"She leaves this file out, she thinks Social Security's freezing her account, coming at her and she's gonna go to jail for the rest of her life."

"Uh huh."

"And now your mom takes her own life and you get scared. You come over there and find your mom and now they're both dead, and now you dispose of your mom's body. That's a misdemeanor. If you killed your mom that's first degree murder."

"Uh huh."

Russell continued to feed Rickie various versions of the stories he could tell. "If you killed your dad that's first degree murder. I asked if your dad was sexually abusive and you said yeah. Was he physically abusive? Yeah. I think you're being honest with us but I think that your dad is dead. Whether she was defending herself or not, I think she killed him. And I think your mom took her own life at your house. I think that maybe you, not wanting to shame your mother, buried your mom or killed your mom . . . I don't think you killed her, I think you buried her . . . probably with your dad. I would rather go there with you saying here's what you're gonna find, than for us to work up a first degree murder investigation on you for two counts. I don't think you need to go to prison for the rest of your life. I think something happened. Your dad was an evil, evil man and you covered for your mom because you loved your mom."

Rickie agreed, "Uh huh."

"I think that your mom felt that she had no other choice. All this was coming down, they were freezing her account, she was going to jail and I think she might have taken her own life. And instead of putting your sisters through that I think you buried your mom. But here's your chance. If that's what happened take us there. Give closure to your mom. Let us tell your sisters what happened."

Rickie wasn't falling for it. "I don't know where my mother is. I wish I did."

"You know where your father is?"

"I don't really know where he is," Rickie said.

Russell was winding it up. "If we go there and find bodies and we gave you a chance to tell us the truth up front . . . you understand what the difference is gonna look like?"

Rickie said, "I know that. I don't know where my father is. I don't know where my mother is."

Just then, there was a knock on the door, and a voice asking Detective Russell to come out of the room. He said to Rickie, "Alright. Sit here and think about what we talked about." He got up and, just as he was about to leave, Rickie stopped him.

He said, "I don't know where my father is, but this is a piece of paper my mother left."

It was the receipt for the concrete saw, in my mother's name.

CHAPTER 25

"We Had a Part in Mother's Leaving . . ."

There Rickie sat, calmly watching me being pushed into the lion's den. I was face-to-face with the man who, at least according to the police, murdered my mom—our mom—and I didn't want to believe that. I didn't know what to say or do. How do I even respond to that? How do I even wrap my head around the reality of murder, in my own family, committed by my own brother? They told me that she hadn't run away, she hadn't been kidnapped, she was murdered by *him*.

That news was enough to lay me flat. But then, our father was dead—not that I cared; really, I didn't—and I was being accused, by my brother, of killing them both! It was all I could do to maintain my composure. The police stuck us together assuming we were both murderers, so they didn't have much concern about my safety. In their eyes, I was his coconspirator. But I'd just been put into a closed room with a murderer, and I was one of his pawns! I hoped that the police were watching us on video or something.

Rickie said to me, "It's over, it's over."

I didn't want to talk to him, to hear him, to have anything to do with him. He said it again, "It's over. What did you say?"

I told him, "I know nothing, I know nothing, I know nothing."

He was acting like everything between us was normal, as if he didn't just throw me under a bus. I began to wonder, did he really say those things, or were the police playing games with me? I've seen enough cop shows to know that they do that sometimes, but I had never experienced it myself. In any case, here was Rickie, acting like nothing was wrong, and I had no reason to be upset with him. He asked, "Are you okay? You don't look too good."

I told him, "I'm just tired . . ." and he started right in again, saying, "It's over, they got all the checks from Sun-Trust."

I just wanted him to stop talking to me! I said, "I know, I know. We're going to jail."

"Are you sad?" he asked.

I couldn't believe he was asking me that. Mom was dead, and we—yes, we—were going to jail. I said, "That we're going to jail? Yeah." At that point I just shut him off and stopped listening to him, as he rambled on about the garage floor. Finally I said, "They told me you said I killed our dad."

He continued, "They know about the car and the storage units. They're going to get a warrant." He sighed and said, "You're going to have to help me do something you won't want to do. I'll tell you later, after we leave. You okay?"

I just wanted to get out of there. I had to go to the bathroom. I wanted to go home. The walls in that room seemed very tight around me. "I had to tell them we paid off Susan's car," I said. "They asked me about the garage sale and what kind of things of Mother's I sold. I said I didn't sell any of Mother's collectibles."

He replied, "That's dumb, if they think we stole any of Mother's collectibles. You're going to have to help me do something."

"What are you talking about?" I asked. I couldn't imagine what he would be asking me to help him with, after all of this.

"Take my life," he said.

No way I was going to help him do that! I said, "No, you can't!" and he just said, "No, we have to be in control, and I'm going to write a letter." I started crying, and he said, "Stacey, come on. Baby . . ."

He extended his hands out to me, and although I was loath to do so, I took them. I said, "They think I'm guilty, too. They think I masterminded this."

"No, they told me I did," he replied. "They're just trying to break you, don't worry. I'm at peace. It's the gas chamber, anyways for me. I had a rough . . ." I began sobbing. "Shh, don't cry," he said. "No . . . no . . . no . . . Stacey, no. Concentrate . . . no . . . be strong, okay?"

He changed the subject, talking about trucks, storage units, and bank accounts. I was losing track of what he was saying. I wasn't sure what was real and what was a story he was telling. I told him that I had to go to the bathroom, and he got up to get someone. Hussey came in and took me to the restroom. When I got back, he asked, "What are you going to tell Susan?" and I told him, "I don't know."

He kept rambling and said, "They talked to the Chattahoochee guy. This is where we are supposed to talk, and you know . . . and reveal shit and tell the story. You didn't say anything, did you?"

I told him, "I played stupid about all the things. I played stupid about everything. That's how come I know we are both going to jail. We both are going to jail."

"I don't know about you, but I am," he said. "This isn't going to go well with anybody. Right at Christmastime, too. I didn't even get to see the *Lord of the Rings*. Well, I don't have to worry about the storage unit anymore."

I said, "They started to say Susan could be mixed up in this."

"That's what they said?" he asked. "I'm ready to end it, are you?"

At that moment, I was. There didn't seem to be any hope for any sort of future. I told him, "I wish I could swallow pills."

"I'm going to write a note," he said, "then do it."

"What are you going to say in your note?" I asked. "They still may come after me. It doesn't matter." I thought, just because he wrote a note admitting to killing our parents, that doesn't mean they won't still arrest me.

He explained, "It's a dying declaration. There are no witnesses, no evidence."

He was wrong. I told him, "They talked to the IRS. The IRS said she was not in trouble."

Just then, an officer came to the door and let us walk away, with no charges and no explanation. They just let us go.

We left the sheriff's office in silence. I didn't want to be alone with him, but we came in my truck and he expected a ride home. I certainly didn't feel safe but thought that as long as he didn't know that, I'd be fine. I needed time to think. I felt like I was dealing with a caged animal—if I stayed calm, so would he. We didn't talk during the short ride home.

As we drove by Mom's house, I could see the CSI unit in the garage, busting up the concrete, and I asked him, "What in the fuck is going on at Mom's house?"

He said, calmly, "Well, they told you something was there," and I cried, "Yeah, but I didn't believe them! I truly didn't believe them."

"No," he said, "there's a body there. It's Father's." I shrieked, "His body's under that floor? They were telling me the truth?" That's when it hit me, like that scene from *Rosemary's Baby*, when she realizes she isn't dreaming about being raped by Satan, and says, "This is no dream! This is really happening!" because then I *knew* he would have killed me if I had said, "You need to turn yourself in," or "We need to not do this." I firmly believe that.

It was the first time in my life I was ever scared of my brother. He was never any threat at all, until this very moment, and then I knew he was capable of doing this and therefore he could easily turn on me. When he changed his name from Richard Jr., to be more like my father, I had no idea that the transformation was deeper than just a couple of letters.

We got home and went inside. He headed straight to his computer, and I went into the kitchen, still dazed. That's when he came out and started talking to me about suicide. He said, "I had Mom's car in my storage unit." I didn't want to hear any more of this. I didn't want to talk anymore, but he continued, "You and Susan are going to be guilty with me. You know you're both going to go down."

Once he threw Susan in there, I went into protective mode. You don't fuck with Susan. I said, "So, what's the answer to this dilemma I'm in?" I looked right at him and he said, "You need to die so we can leave Susan free of all this mess."

I had to think about that for a minute. The police were already talking about bringing Susan in, and it wasn't helping that Rickie was telling them that I was involved. I saw no way out. He said, "By the way, I need to go to Wal-Mart."

I said, "Fine, we'll go to the store." I picked my keys up and we went back out to the driveway to get in my truck. I was trying to think while I drove, but he kept talking, saying things like, "You know, Susan's going to be involved in this, if we don't kill ourselves. They're going to come and get Susan."

He went on and on and on, and all I could think was,

"God, what has he done? There's a body in Mom's garage, and obviously it's not her, or he would have told me." I asked, "Why are they going to come after Susan if the body's in that garage?" I still wasn't putting pieces together. He ignored my question, because we had just arrived at Wal-Mart.

He went inside while I waited in the truck, feeling my entire life collapse down on top of me. It felt like all those years of hell were finally coming to a head and it was finally time to end it. There was nothing left to do but die. There was no escape. The police let him loose. He lived in my house. If I didn't do this with him, who's to say he wouldn't kill me or Susan in our sleep? He had already killed two people. What's two more?

I had no one to turn to. The police surely wouldn't help, and Cheryl had turned against me. If I left him there at Wal-Mart, what was he going to do when he had to find his own way home—kick my ass, or worse? I literally had no options. I couldn't stop a shopper there in the parking lot and ask for help. How do you approach someone walking by with their shopping cart full of Diet Pepsi and Cheese Nips, and say, "Excuse me, but my brother killed our parents and now wants me to commit suicide with him. Will you help me?" I wasn't a kidnapped child who could run for help; I was a grown woman and this wasn't a sudden, urgent emergency situation that the police could help with. In fact, the police had helped to *cause* it.

So I did what I always did, growing up. You just go with the flow, take the abuse, and move on. It hurts a lot less if you just allow it to happen and it ends more quickly.

Frankly, with all of this in my head, I was sort of looking forward to it ending. I just couldn't take one more iota of pain.

Rickie finally came out of the store with a couple of bags, threw them in the back of the truck, and said, "Let's go for a drive." He directed me to turn here and there, and we got to a large, industrial storage unit that he had rented. Then he turned to me and said, "By the way, I drew them a picture where to find Mom's body, in your backyard."

That took my breath away, like a sledgehammer to the chest. I said, "You know what? Let's just go ahead and die. You're right. You've drug Susan into some fucking mess she's got no business being in, you asshole. You son of a bitch."

I don't think I said much to him after that. I just thought, "Fine, we're gonna do this." I couldn't let Susan be guilty of something she didn't even know was going on. It wasn't her fault my family was so fucked up. I finally gave up. That was the first time in my whole life that I wanted to stop trying. All those years ago, when Cheryl and I struggled to make it to shore at Lake Hebron, what was that even for? I didn't want to swim anymore. Just didn't want to.

He opened the big garage door to the storage unit, and I drove the truck inside. It was a very large unit, with a little bathroom at the back; the kind that some companies actually run businesses out of. My truck fit inside easily. I got out to use the bathroom, and when I came back, Rickie had already closed the overhead door and rigged the truck with a dryer vent hose attached to the exhaust pipe and run it into the truck window. He handed me a bottle of NyQuil, and I understood what he had in mind. Drink this to fall asleep, and never wake up.

We got settled in, in the truck cab, and after starting the engine I downed more than half a bottle of NyQuil, while he took some sleeping pills, washing them down with a Diet Pepsi. I told him, "I have to call Susan to tell her there's gonna be police officers all over our house, because you put a body there."

I knew I'd get her voice mail because she was at work, and I said, very calmly, "When the police get there please be calm and let them do what they need to do, and they will explain everything." I hung up then because I couldn't figure out how to tell her on a cell phone that they're going to find a body in our backyard. I thought, no, I'll let them deal with that.

I was starting to get a little woozy, when Rickie suggested that we write suicide notes. I took the notepad that he handed me and wrote a letter to Susan:

I love you with all my heart. You are very precious to me. Please know that I did this because of everything in my life. I want you to have a chance at a future and me being with you will not allow that. Please know that when I called you about the cops that Rick and I knew it was over for us. We had a part in Mother's leaving. Please let the police do whatever they must at the house. I have sold off my Disney stocks to have a check sent to the house. They would only send it in my name. Maybe you could deposit it. It will give you an extra fifteen hundred dollars to live on. The next mortgage payment is due March first. Please give the bag of sweatshirts in the car back to Angela. They were hers when we were carpooling. Please make sure that I am cremated and that you have no service for me. I am certain because of the events that the Brackens will not want to see you for Christmas.

I Love You,
Stacey

Rickie took the pad and wrote notes of his own, which I didn't see at the time. I was becoming very sleepy and it was hard to stay awake. He wrote, on another page in that notebook:

In September 88 my Mother came over to my house and asked me to come over. I did. Our Father was killed by Stacey, I begged my Mother to call the police, she refused. She had bought a freezer and later decided to bury him in the garage. In September 03 Mother told Stacey and me that she was going to use Grandpa's money and take Cheryl's kids away. She helped destroy three lives she could not destroy more. She is in the ground by the shed. Please read Grandpa's will it needs to be done right.

Richard Kananen

I found out later that he wrote to Cheryl on another notebook page:

I have always loved you I am sorry for this, please get help for you and the kids and Chris. There is nothing I can say. She was going to use Grandpa's money.

That notebook page, with the note to Cheryl, also had a note that had my signature, but I don't recall writing it:

Cheryl—I love you and the kids with all my heart. Please believe me when I say we couldn't let Mother take the kids away from you. I have always loved you and the kids.

Stacey

I felt a sense of peace as I started to drift off—knowing it was finally going to be over—mixed with brief spurts of terror because it was getting hard to breathe. The air reeked of thick exhaust fumes, and I could feel my body panicking, rebelling against inhaling. I heard Rickie say, "Here, drink some more," but I waved him off. Then another wave of sleep would hit me and I'd drift deeper, and it would be okay. Back and forth it went like that, peace and terror, and I wished that it would just end already. Just as I was about to go down for the last time, I rested my head against the steering wheel and a voice told me to turn on the air conditioner, so I flipped the switch on. I gratefully gasped in some cool, fresh air and closed my eyes . . .

. . . and woke up to someone pounding on the window, shouting, "Unlock the door! Now!" I was way too groggy to have any idea what was going on, or even where I was, but the urgency in that voice shook me into action. I fumbled around, trying to figure out how to unlock the thing they were calling a door. The world spun as I turned my head and saw the same scenario taking place on the other side of the truck.

Rickie had his door open, and an officer flipped the unlock switch on that side, so my door was now open. I felt myself being dragged from the truck and laid down on something flat. I looked up and saw a giant camera lens in my face, and heard a voice saying, "Get that camera out of here!" I was being wheeled into an ambulance, handcuffed to the gurney.

As they were carrying me out I saw Detective Ruggiero, and he was saying, "Stay with us, stay with us, we need to talk to you, stay with us." I went out several times, as he was talking to me. I'd be in midsentence and . . . zonk. I was on advanced life support in the ambulance. I realized that it was Detective Ruggiero's voice, telling the news photographer to leave me alone. He didn't have to do that, but he had enough respect for me to treat me like a human being that day. I've always appreciated that. He was a good man.

He told me, in the ambulance, that the reason I lived was because the AC was on, that's what saved my life. This might sound weird, but I've always had a feeling that it was my grandpa's voice telling me to turn it on. I wasn't supposed to die in that truck that day.

CHAPTER 26

Led Away in Cuffs

I woke up in the emergency room, with Detectives Russell and Ruggiero standing over me. A nurse was trying to work around them. Detective Russell dove right in. "We want to talk to you about what happened. Let's go back eighteen years ago. Your dad was a pretty violent guy, huh?"

I felt enough strength to answer, "Yes."

He was encouraged by the spark of life and asked, "What happened to your dad that put an end to the violence?"

"He left."

"No, he didn't leave," he argued, "your brother's saying that you put an end to him hurting the rest of the family."

"No."

"Well, that's what we're trying to get straightened out. He says that you were the one that hurt your dad."

It was too hard to talk. All I could say was, "No."

He kept asking me questions about the night my father disappeared. Was he drunk? Was he violent that night? I didn't remember. He said, "We're at your mom's house now with a search warrant. We know that your dad's buried there. We know your mom's buried there."

I felt a jolt of heartache and groaned, "Oh God."

"Your brother has admitted killing your mom."

"Oh God."

"And burying her in the backyard. But he says that you killed your dad."

"No, I didn't."

I didn't have it in me to argue this again, but he kept pushing, "We don't think so, either, but you have to tell us what happened that night."

It was so long ago, and I wasn't there when he was killed. And, honestly, I didn't care who killed him. Good riddance! I told the officers, "I remember Rickie telling me he knew that he wouldn't hurt anybody anymore."

Russell said, "He's dumping everything on you and you're saying he's not telling you anything."

"When he told me to drive to the storage unit . . ." I began.

"There we go," Russell encouraged.

". . . he told me that he killed my mother. I . . . I freaked out. He told me something about she was gonna take my sister's kids. He didn't want my mother to do anything to the kids. I guess he thought my mother was the reason things happened to us. She was a good mother."

"He blamed her?"

"I guess he did," I said. "I didn't know any of this until today."

"Where did he tell you that he buried your mother?" Russell asked.

". . . something about my backyard . . ."

"We have the note to your girlfriend," he insisted. "And you put in there that the cops are onto us."

I tried again to explain. "When he directed me to the storage unit he told me that because he put Mother in the yard, you would never believe that I didn't have anything to do with it. I didn't want to die. All I wanted was my mother to come home."

Russell said, "You're not gonna die, but here's your chance to show some remorse for what happened. I know you were scared. Did he tell you how he killed her?"

"No, he did not."

"Did he tell you how your dad died?"

"No, he did not."

Detective Ruggiero asked, "Did you read the note he left?"

"No, I did not." I had no idea that he wrote that I killed our father, but Ruggiero knew that's what the note said. Detective Russell just went on and on, trying to trip me up, but I told the truth, just like I had that morning. I said, "All I wanted was my mother to come home."

"Well, that's not gonna happen," he taunted, "but you know what? I want to be able to lay her to rest. I want to be able to sit down with your sister and your girlfriend and say, when the time came for her to tell us everything she knew, she told us the truth."

I started crying. I just wanted him to leave me alone. "I'm telling you everything I know."

He kept at it. "Well, I don't think you're telling me everything. I think you're telling a little bit, but I don't think you're telling everything. If you want to be remorseful and you want to help us recover her body you have to tell us everything. So, after he killed your mother, how did he take her over to where he took her? Did he put her in the truck?"

"I don't know!"

On and on it went, more accusations, more denials. He just wouldn't believe me. Finally Detective Ruggiero said, "You know that we recorded your conversation with your brother this morning, right? You kept telling him to be quiet. You knew we were listening."

I said, "He kept trying to tell me that it was over and I didn't know what he was saying and I just kept telling him be quiet. I didn't want to know. And then he kept saying something about SunTrust. I didn't know what he was talking about."

Russell asked, "If you could say anything to your sister right now, what would you tell her? What would you have us tell her?"

I replied, "I love my mother with all my heart. And I love my sister and her kids. I never dreamed he would do this and I'm very sorry he did this."

"How come you didn't come forward before today, before we called you in and tell us?"

God, this man was dense! "I didn't know," I insisted.

He insisted back, "You did know!"

"I swear to God I didn't know he did anything to my mother or my father. I was just happy my father wasn't there beating my mother anymore."

Russell kept hammering away, until finally Ruggiero said, "We've been over this."

Russell asked, "Anything else you want to say to us before we go?"

"I can't think of anything," I said. "I'm just really sorry for my mother. I loved her so much. I moved so close to her so we could have time together."

My heart was breaking and all he could do was say, "Alright. Go off tape at this time," and he walked away.

I don't know if they were playing good cop, bad cop, but again I have to say that Detective Ruggiero was kindhearted, at least as much as he was allowed to be. When Hussey showed up, his demeanor changed. While Hussey was talking to my brother, Ruggiero came to me and said, "Look, I don't have a dog in this fight. I don't think you need to be involved in this, but you are in over your head and I can't help you. But I'm telling you, keep telling the truth."

I told him, "That's all I've been doing." He said, "I know, but you need to keep telling the truth. Don't let them twist you up when you're screwed up right now." A doctor heard him say that, and when Hussey came out to talk to me, the doctor said, "I just Baker Acted her. I've signed the papers. You can't talk to her for three days."

In another section of the ER, when the two detectives interviewed Rickie, he told them where Mom's body was. It was the first question they asked him, and he said, "By the shed." He told them she was wrapped in plastic and five feet down. But he still kept insisting that I killed our father. He told them, "I didn't do it. All I know is him laying on the concrete floor. He was already dead. My sister and my mother were there."

"Why would she tell us that she didn't know anything about it until today?" Russell asked. "I mean if she's not involved, Rick, now's the time to tell the truth and there's no use her taking the fall for this if she wasn't involved in it."

He was groggy, but he managed to say, "She signed a note. It's in the car."

"Well, we've got the note, but I'm just telling you, if she's got involvement in this, then you need to tell us. But if she doesn't then you need to tell us." At least he was being fair, even if it wasn't in my presence.

"Already dead when I got over there," Rickie said.

"What happened with you and your mom?"

"She was gonna take my sister's kids away from her."

They talked for a few minutes about the whole Cheryl situation, and Russell asked, "How'd your mom die?"

"I don't even know."

"Is there gonna be gunshot wounds in her? Stab wounds? Were you guys physically fighting? Were you choking her?"

"No," Rickie said.

Detective Ruggiero asked, "Well, how did she die?"

"I don't really remember."

Russell said, "I read the note and if you weren't remorseful you wouldn't do what you tried to do. You just would've taken off on the run."

Rickie responded, "No, I don't run away no more. I run away all those years."

"Tell us," Russell said, "what happened with your dad."

"I have no idea. I wasn't there."

"Well, I mean you show up, your dad is dead, and your mother goes and rents the saw for you to dig a hole in the garage and bury him. At any time did you say, 'Mom, what happened?' You just said, 'Okay Mom, I'm gonna go get a saw and bury dad in the garage'?"

"I didn't get the saw." Rickie said, "She did. I wanted to take him somewhere else, but she wanted him there."

"Rick," Russell continued, "I don't think you meant to kill your mom. Because when we sat in that room today and I asked you did you kill your mom, you got teary eyed, man, and you told me you loved your mom. Well, I want to tell your sister what happened that night. And I don't believe that you don't know what happened that night. I think you know what happened."

"I really don't remember," Rickie said. "I'm sorry, but I don't remember."

Russell asked, "What do you want me to tell your sister when she asks me what happened?"

"I killed her mother."

They talked for a while about where exactly in the garage they would find our father's body, and Russell asked him, "When did you tell your sister that you buried your mom back there?"

Rickie was curt. "Don't want to say."

"Did she help you?"

"Don't want to say."

"What do you want me to say to your sister when I talk to her and tell her what happened?"

"Just tell her Mom was gonna take the kids, 'cause Mom had the money."

"You told your nephew that you shot and killed and your father."

"No, I did not."

"Well, he gave Detective Hussey a statement saying that you told him that," Russell insisted.

"No, I didn't," Rickie insisted back.

Detective Russell asked, "If you had a chance to do it all again would you do it the same?"

"No," Rickie said. "I mean I wouldn't do it. I would've called the police in the first . . ."

Russell interrupted, "I just don't understand, Rick. You cared so much about your mom and loved her so much. I understand maybe she was gonna take the kids, but I can't see you intentionally killing her. I mean, if you got in an argument with her or you all got to fighting or something and it was an accident, I need to know that! I just need to know that for the investigation. Your sister, for closure, needs to know that."

Rickie was having trouble talking. "I can't remember. I remember . . . she started screaming she's gonna take Cheryl's kids."

They went around and around in circles, and finally realized they weren't going to get any more information out of him. They ended the interview and placed him under arrest. He was taken to jail straight from the ER. He stood up from the stretcher. They handcuffed and shackled him and walked him right past where I was still lying on a stretcher, wearing an oxygen mask and having my blood gases checked. He looked at me and I looked at him, and nothing was said. He just had a blank stare.

I don't know what happened when he got to jail, but I know when he went to his arraignment the next morning he was in what they call a turtle suit. The turtle suit means you acted up and went crazy, so he had already started his crazy routine that night.

They locked me up in a psych ward with an attendant sitting right there because they were afraid I was still suicidal. The next day was Christmas Eve, and I was allowed to call Susan and say, "Hey, I'm still alive." I was in there three days. I talked her into going to Hudson to visit her mother, because I was going to be locked up over Christmas, and she needed to be with family.

When they finally released me and I went home, all the neighbors were staring at me. No sooner did I get inside than the doorbell rang. It was a reporter. I didn't answer the door; Susan did. She said, "No comment." I walked around the house, and as soon as I entered the family room, I looked out the sliding glass door, and there was the hole in the backyard. They left the fucking hole. I fell right down on my knees and started bawling. I sobbed to Susan, "I wish I had died. I don't want to deal with this, I don't want to see this, I wish I had died."

I was done. I said to Susan, "I can't fill it. You can't move the dirt and the rocks. What are we supposed to do?" So we called our neighbor Betty, who eventually testified against me. She had said, "Anything you need, call me," so Susan called and said, "The police left a hole in the backyard." Betty brought some friends over and they covered the hole and fixed the yard.

I found out years later that when they discovered my father's remains, they found remnants of a zipper, a belt buckle, and a pocket, and a pillow and mattress cover. He was wrapped in bedding. They found rope wrapped around his legs. He got a bullet in the back of the left side of his head. It stopped right above his right eye. Since it passed through both sides of his brain, it did extensive damage, so even if his body had recovered, he would have been a vegetable.

Rickie vehemently claimed in all of his questioning that he didn't shoot him, but he tells non–law enforcement people that he did. I don't know if we'll ever know what really happened, but I do know that there were lots of suggestions from his interrogators on how the crimes might have gone down, many of which he used as his stories later.

CHAPTER 27

Pretrial Prep

During the three years between my arrest and my trial, there were a lot of delays. The trial would be scheduled and I'd be ready to go—albeit scared shitless—and then it would be put off for another six months. Some of the delays were in my favor, because new information would be discovered by Diana, but other times they were just red tape.

Detective Hussey remained gung ho. One facet of the trial was going to be handwriting analysis to see if it could be proven who wrote which notes, because I didn't remember writing the note to Cheryl and barely remembered writing the one to Susan. Plus, there was still that check for $2,500 that I supposedly signed. I had to supply a huge amount of sample handwriting, and Hussey showed up that day. He gave me a dirty look, and Diana said, "My God, he looks like a boyfriend scorned, like he's out to get you." It was a very uncomfortable moment, and Diana thought it was very unusual for him to even be there, like he was really out to get me.

Diana was sure that Hussey had a lot to do with why Cheryl turned against me. She believed that Hussey was feeding Cheryl half-baked theories about his investigation that made me look suspicious. He was the one who convinced her that we were selling off Mom's things. Diana thinks he worked on her to get her more firmly in their camp, and it was effective. I don't know, now, if we could have undone that brainwashing.

In the meantime, Rickie wavered back and forth over his willingness to testify against me. He would make it known that he didn't want to do this anymore, and then Robin Wilkinson and Cheryl would go visit him in jail and apparently talk him back into it. In fact, Rickie said that right before his guilty plea, Cheryl visited him and asked him to not put the family through his trial—she begged him to "do the right thing" and turn me in.

In 2008, in preparation for my trial, Diana set up a deposition with Rickie, which was attended by Robin Wilkinson, and he wove an entirely new story. According to this version, he never told Daniel, Catherine, or her husband that he killed our father. He also said that when Aunt Nancy, my father's sister, came to visit us the month before Mom's death, Mom was telling her that our father was in Chicago and that I became alarmed that she was talking too much and needed to die. He denied having told anyone that he was a vigilante, hired by a cartel, to "get rid of" abusive fathers.

He told Diana that he decided to take the plea because it would be better for the family to not have a trial, as he was worried about Cheryl and Daniel. He said that he told them that I killed our father, and that I killed Mom.

Diana asked him, "Did you tell them the full truth about things?" And when Rickie said that he had *not* told them the full truth, she asked, "What is it that you had told them about what happened with your dad?"

He replied, "I told them Stacey killed my dad."

Then she asked, "What did you tell them happened with your mom?"

"Stacey killed my mom."

She then asked, "So what is it that you told them that was not the full truth?"

"That Stacey killed my mom," he replied, in front of God and everybody, including Robin Wilkinson.

Diana asked, "You said that Stacey killed your mom when you had killed your mom?"

"Correct."

"And why would you say that about Stacey if that wasn't true?" she pressed.

"I don't know. It just seemed like . . ."

"Were you upset that Stacey had been listed as a state's witness against you? Did you know that Ms. Wilkinson had talked to her about being a witness and that she was going to be called at your trial? Did that upset you?"

"Yeah, a little bit. Yeah." He told Diana that he thought I was just saving myself, and that he made the decision to tell them that I had helped kill Mom because of the conversation he'd had with Cheryl. "It was just seeing her and hearing her talking. It was just better for the family not to have a trial. Cheryl said I should let out the whole truth and say everything that was going on so she could have closure."

I can't say this for a fact, but it wouldn't shock me if he said what Cheryl wanted him to say—she and Hussey both wanted me to go to jail for Mom's death—just because she was the only one who came to visit him during those years. Diana asked if he was surprised that I didn't come to see him, and he said, "No, I didn't think she would visit me."

"Because she would be embarrassed, too afraid to face you?"

"I really would have no idea," he replied.

"Okay. But you didn't expect it?" Diana asked.

"No."

"And you didn't feel badly about the fact that she didn't?"

"A little bit."

I can't help thinking that if I had gone to see him, this whole thing might not have happened. If only . . .

Diana disagrees. She thinks Rickie turned on me because he got to be the star of his own show and this was sort of his last hurrah. He had the audience of the family, people were paying attention to him and his manuscript, and then he spent three years of sitting in prison while nobody gave a shit about his stories anymore. She thinks he did it to make his life exciting, to have something to do. He got to take a car ride, everybody poured over his every word, and maybe he thought this would somehow make Cheryl think better of him, as if to say, "I can't take back what I did, but if I can make Stacey involved that somehow makes me a hero."

Diana did everything she could to keep me calm and to prepare me for what was to come. There were a few things that we argued about, though. Some of my explanations would sound fishy to the jury. She would say things like, "This doesn't make any sense to me. Are you sure there isn't some other explanation? If the explanation were like 'this' I would totally understand. That would make total sense." I would say, "No, that's not how it was." She wanted me to remember signing a check I don't remember signing, and to say I must have just left the M off. But I don't remember signing the thing. I'm not gonna say I did.

I also don't remember writing that letter to Cheryl. If I was half drugged out of my mind and he dictated, maybe I did. Yes, I always sign things to Daniel and Cheryl "I love you with all my heart," or whatever. It's something I've always done. I didn't know my own name that day. And if "I don't know" isn't a good enough answer, then I don't know what to tell you.

It was those little things that drove Diana crazy. She was able to work around them because she hoped that they would improve the overall impression of credibility, and Diana tried to point out later, "Hey, how easy would it have been for my client to make up a story?" She realized that it's very easy to lie on the stand, but it's harder to say, "Wow, you're asking me a good question and, ouch, I don't have a good answer." She assumed that the jury would have known that I would have had a lot of time and a really good lawyer who would have helped me come up with a more believable story, if that was the goal.

Leading up to the trial, we had a screaming match in her office, and I thought, "God, she really thinks we're going to lose this thing." But then I realized she was just getting me ready for Robin to rip me apart to see if she could get me to change my story. I told her, "Diana, I'm gonna tell it like it was. It's who I am. I can't make up stories and try to follow them. When your life's on the line, you better know what's real in your head." That's one thing my brother never knew. There were too many stories in his head. He never knew what was real.

Diana told me one day, "I have to have some childhood stories from you. We have to prepare for you to tell one of them on the stand." She sent me away and said, "I'll see you in a week, and I want a list."

I wrote down ten or twelve. There were so many to choose from. She also had to prepare me for forensics testimony. She knew they would be showing pictures of my mom's body being excavated and using words like "mummified remains." There would be autopsy photos and graphic descriptions of the conditions of Mom's body. It was going to be absolutely horrific and there was no avoiding it.

She never coached me, and I was surprised about that. I always thought that's what lawyers did. We had the conversation about how to act: they're watching you, they're watching you, they're watching you. Look like you care, and keep in mind that they're watching you at every moment. Don't fake emotion; be genuine. There is no way you're going to convince people who don't want to be convinced, so you might as well just be real and not do anything that's distracting to what you're trying to get people to pay attention to.

Toni briefly interviewed Rickie, twice. He was very receptive, very guarded, but at the same time courteous and respectful. He was very noncommittal when she spoke with him about whether he was going to be a part of the trial. He wasn't sure what his testimony would be. She told me that he looked like a chronic mental health patient. He was on medication at the time, but he was oriented as to time, place, person, purpose of the visit. He wasn't very forthcoming with information, however. When she went to see him, he said, "I don't think I really want to do this anymore. I don't think I want to testify."

The whole entourage went to see him—Robin, Hussey, Cheryl—and all of a sudden he was gung ho again. They were apparently saying something to him to make him keep going, because a week earlier he didn't want to testify. Up until he got on the stand we weren't sure what he was going to do.

Catherine Crews's testimony wasn't going to be included in the trial. Although telling that story may have helped my case, I made it very clear to Diana that I did not want any attacks against anyone in my family, if at all possible. We had suffered enough, and if it wasn't going to help, then I didn't want to go there. She said, even if we did, it wouldn't do too much to help, so I said, "Then don't do that. I don't play that way. You need to respect my family. It's still my family."

I love her for respecting my wishes, especially when it came to Daniel. I told her that if Daniel was forced to testify, I wanted him protected. She had a few interviews with him over the years, and she would wait until his parents left the room for a minute, and told him that she had a message for him from me, that I loved him and missed him terribly. I'm very grateful for her doing that, because it let him know that I wished we could communicate. That was one bright spot buried in three years of shit.

CHAPTER 28

The Last Delay

We finally had a court date, and this one was definite, after all the false alarms over the years. No more delays—February 22, 2010, was the day I had to be in Orlando to face a jury of my peers. Susan and I booked a hotel for two weeks and arranged for Wendell and the staff to take care of the resort in our absence. This couldn't have been worse timing, because February and March were always the busiest snowbird months of the year and the park was booked solid. But, unfortunately, I had no say in it, so I just did what I was told.

Susan sent out an e-mail to all of our friends and supporters, letting them know the date and location, so we could pack the gallery again. Diana had told me to get as many people as we could, because she knew, from the bond hearing, that we had a lot of support. She explained, "I have clients who are very likely innocent and everybody around them scurries away. Jurors know that. You've got people coming from far away, they're putting themselves out, getting hotel rooms and paying for gas, and they obviously believe in your innocence. The jury may figure, if this whole room believes in you that strongly, maybe we should, too."

I realized that some of the people who went to the bond hearing only attended because they had a business agenda—they wanted to keep the resort up and running. There were also people who wrote letters to the judge on my behalf and were there because it mattered to them what happened to me, personally. I knew the difference. Either way, they wouldn't be there if they didn't believe I was innocent. Their presence there, on my side of the courtroom, implied that. They wouldn't have supported me if they thought I was a murderer.

The first day was supposed to be jury selection, so no one from Hudson came, but as soon as I arrived in the morning, Diana told me that there was a one-week postponement. I was about to get upset, but Diana said, "I'm not going to waste this time off. I'm going to go back through the whole file again. I booked three weeks for the trial and I have nothing to do. I might as well use it."

So off I went back to Hudson, and off Diana went to what she called "the stinky underworld of the sheriff's office" to go through mountains of papers and scraps of mostly meaningless garbage. Diana is usually impeccably groomed, but I could just imagine her in jeans and a T-shirt, hair up in a ponytail, sorting through this grungy heap of papers and trash.

She told me that, in any case like this, you're going to have trash bags filled with endless pieces of paper. We had a cash receipt for the Taser and a receipt for the freezer with a false name on it, and records from the storage units, which were in Rickie's name. In addition to all of that, she wanted to take a look at the evidence that they hadn't given to us because either they didn't plan to use it or didn't think it was going to be helpful. She said there were TONS of little pieces of paper that no one paid much attention to.

So while I was back home, spending most of my time fighting off the waves of panic that constantly threatened to overtake me, she rolled up her sleeves and started rummaging. She spent countless hours examining scraps of nothing until she found that the actual spiral notebook from the truck—the notebook that held the suicide notes—was in one of the trash bags. Those notes were seemingly insurmountable evidence for the prosecution, and Diana had been given photocopies. This was the first time she had seen their origin. She looked at the notebook and thought, "That's interesting!" and took it with her.

CHAPTER 29

State of Florida v. Kananen

I couldn't believe it, after all the delays, but the trial was finally starting, albeit a week late, due to the latest postponement. The jury of seven women and five men was chosen, and the courtroom was packed to the rafters with spectators. Outside, it was a media circus, not just because of my trial, but because the Casey Anthony trial was also building up there in Orlando, so there were reporters from all of the TV stations.

My trial was going to be taped and later televised on CNN's *In Session*, so there was a camera next to the judge's bench trained on my face at all times. Another camera pointed, from the back of the courtroom, at the witness stand. I sat between Diana and Toni, and behind me the wooden bench seats were filled with people from the nudist resort—so many, in fact, that they spilled over onto the prosecution's side of the courtroom, where Cheryl sat with her estranged husband and her victim's advocate. Susan had to wait in the hallway because she was going to be called as a witness for my defense. She wasn't going to be able to watch the trial until then.

I had knots in my stomach and felt a mixture of terror and relief. This must be what soldiers about to go into combat feel—fear that they are about to die, but a profound wish to just get it over with.

Robin Wilkinson got up and began her opening arguments. "Ladies and gentlemen of the jury, September 10, 2003, Marilyn Kananen, a mother of three children, a grandmother of three, left her work at the Delta Connection Academy, drove home to never be seen again."

She laid it out, the whole story—no holds barred, with a tone in her voice that deliberately implied that Cheryl was the only one in this tale who was telling the truth, and that Rickie and I were both sneaky and vicious. I had to just sit there and listen, showing no emotion.

She told the jury that Rickie and I sold Mom's collectibles at a garage sale, and still Cheryl struggled on, working with police tirelessly to find Mom. They were told about the bank accounts, the checks, the trucks, and the police interviews. Finally, they were told about the suicide attempt and the note that said, "We had a part in Mother's leaving," and that a handwriting expert would testify that I wrote two notes in that truck. She closed by saying, "I am quite confident that you will find that Stacey Kananen, back in September of 2003, decided that her mother's life should end. The State is quite confident that you will find that Stacey Kananen is guilty of first-degree murder."

Then it was Diana's turn, and the difference between the two attorneys was palpable. Robin was tense and seething with hostility, and Diana was like a breath of fresh air, very likable and friendly. I was relieved when she got up to speak.

She stood up and started her opening statement by saying, "Good morning, everybody. My name is Diana Tennis." She put her hand firmly on my shoulder, with a clear implication that she liked me, trusted me, and had no problem touching me like I was a good person, and said, "And this is my client, Stacey Kananen. As you would probably expect, I disagree with a lot of what I believe the evidence is going to be in this case."

Diana continued, "I want you to pay attention to what evidence existed and when. Pretty much all the prosecutor's evidence that points toward Stacey existed and was known by law enforcement on December 22, 2003. All of it."

She was just warming up. She told the jury, "On December 22, 2003, Richard Kananen went from the hospital to jail. He was charged with first-degree murder. When Stacey got out of the hospital, she didn't go to jail and was not charged. She went home to the house where she discovered her brother buried her mother. She moved with Susan to Hudson and has lived there ever since. She doesn't flee. She doesn't try again with a suicide attempt. She goes about her business.

"She becomes a witness," Diana continued, "for the State of Florida against her brother. She is listed as a witness that the prosecution," she said, pointing at Robin, "*this* prosecution, is going to put on the stand, swear under oath, and tell everybody about what little she knows about her brother having killed their mother.

"The only thing that changed between them only having a case against Richard in December of 2003 and Stacey being arrested for murder in May of 2007 is that her brother decided to weave his fifth version of what happened.

"He is facing first-degree murder. At the bare minimum, he faces life in prison, possibly the death penalty. His sister is standing by, ready to testify against him. At the last minute he said, 'I have things to tell you.' He enters his plea and within minutes he gives his fifth version of what happened."

Diana wrapped up her opening statement by saying, "Only Richard Kananen was arrested in December of 2003. He was the one charged with the cover up and he was the one with the motivation. He was the one who bought the Taser and the freezer. He was the one who had the strength and ability to carry out the act. I believe when all is said and done, you will not find that Richard Kananen is a credible witness. If he is not a credible witness, you will not find near enough evidence to convict Stacey Kananen of murder. I appreciate your time. Thank you."

She sat down next to me and gave my hand a reassuring squeeze as the State began its case. Their first witness was my sister, Cheryl. I knew how it would look to a jury, both of my siblings testifying against me, but that wasn't even what bothered me at that point. What bothered me was that Cheryl, a churchgoer, was prepared to swear before God that she believed I could commit murder.

Cheryl was sworn in, and Robin started asking her about her own experience with being abused by our father. She told the jury, "I remember being in fifth grade living in Minnesota. My father became very upset that I lost a razor blade and I couldn't find it. My punishment was that he took a metal broom and beat me up and down one side of my body."

She told them that our mom saw the bruises and did not take her to the police. She said, "When I decided I was going to show her, that was the day I decided that my mom needed to know what was going on. I decided to put on a tank top and shorts and I went downstairs and she said 'What happened to you?' I looked at my father and I said, 'Why don't you ask him?' He said, 'I don't know what happened to you,' and she told me not to tell lies." That, she said, was the last time she ever told our mom what he had been doing to her.

Diana had supplied me with a yellow legal pad to write notes on just in case I noticed something in testimony that she needed to know about, or to write out anything that I needed to vent about. That way, I didn't have to sit there and silently try not to scream about whatever was going on up there on the witness stand. I wrote a note to Toni, "*The abuse conversations are going to bother me. How do I get through that?*" She wrote back, "*Deep breaths. Totally tense muscles, then exhale and totally relax. Squeeze chair arms, then relax or squeeze hands together.*"

When Robin asked if she had been sexually abused,

Cheryl stated, "When we lived in Minnesota, my father would routinely lock my mother out of the house and make me go to his room. I remember going to the room. I don't remember past that. When we lived here in Florida, I moved here in ninth grade and graduated here. I would go out at night and come home and find him hiding in my room." She said that continued until she moved out, and she finally moved out after her nineteenth birthday because, she said, "My father kicked me in the head and stomach and said, 'By the way, happy birthday.' I told my sister, that's it. I'm not coming back."

Robin asked her, "Do you see your sister Stacey in the courtroom here today?"

"I do," Cheryl replied.

"Can you point out and describe what she is wearing, please?"

Cheryl looked me right in the eye and said, "She's wearing a black suit and a white shirt and glasses and blond hair. She's sitting next to Diana Tennis and Toni Maloney."

I could feel the tears coming to my eyes, but I bit my lip to keep from crying. Robin Wilkinson said, "May the record reflect the witness has identified the defendant."

"Did you ever see your brother Richard abused in your house growing up?"

"All the time." she said, "My father choked my brother for not passing the salt when we lived in Minnesota and rendered him unconscious. He would routinely put my brother behind a closet door and shoot through it to see if he could hit him or not. He would take my brother out all hours and tell us that was the last time we would see him alive. He used to put chains on him and make him work in the field for many hours at a time. Make him stay outside and wouldn't let him eat or drink."

She testified at length about the abuse that all of us suffered, and that our father had his mistress living in the house with us. I remembered that. The woman came to stay with us for a visit while we lived in Arkansas. She and my father had met in Minnesota, and we thought, at the time, she was his girlfriend, but I was a young kid so I really didn't know what that meant.

Cheryl told the story of our move from Arkansas to Florida, which is what I remembered as happening right after Grandpa sent Mom a thousand dollars to get away from him. She told how we were taking two separate vehicles, Mom and us kids in the car and our father driving the truck. "As we were getting ready to leave, my father came home and took me by gunpoint and put me in the U-Haul because he knew my mother wouldn't leave without me."

Robin then asked about the house fire in Maine, when Rickie climbed a ladder and broke our bedroom window to save us. "When he brought us down, my mother was in the car, crying, and my father was out with the firemen in the yard, somewhere. Two weeks after we moved from Minnesota, our house there was burned to the ground."

Robin asked Cheryl if she ever saw me being abused by our father, and she said that she had not. This blew me away, because I saw abuse of all kinds in that household, against every one of them, so how she could have possibly missed seeing me get my turn was beyond me.

She fast-forwarded the conversation to 1988, right before Cheryl's wedding. She told the jury that a lot of relatives were afraid to come to the wedding, because of our violent father. Robin and Cheryl both had to be very careful to not mention why my father was "missing," because his murder was not a part of the trial, so there was no mention made of why he was gone, just that he wasn't there anymore. That had to be confusing to the jury.

Robin asked, "As you had your children, how was your mother as a grandmother?" and Cheryl replied, "I used to say that she was the mom that she never got the chance to be. She was great with my kids." I completely agree with that statement. I wish we'd had the chance to have that mom as our mom.

The questioning led to the fact that Rickie was gone a lot over the years, and we rarely saw him. Robin slowly meandered her way up to September 2003, when Mom went missing. Cheryl told the story of that night. She said that while Rickie was ranting, "The nightmare is back! The nightmare is back!" I was sitting there, rocking and wringing my hands. She then told the story of getting goose bumps when she stood next to the refrigerator and said that something terrible had happened, and told the jury I said, "I have to go talk to Rickie," and ran out of the house.

She told the jury, at Robin's prompting, that when they came by my house nine days later, on my birthday, I wouldn't let them into my house even though Daniel needed to use the restroom. She said that I told her that we had to put the dogs away and that he knew all of our dogs so that should not have been a concern. She said I prevented him from using the bathroom, without any explanation. Robin asked, "Is there a window in that bathroom?" implying that I was preventing Daniel from seeing our backyard through the window.

This didn't come up at the trial, because I didn't notice it on Susan's calendar until years later, but if Rickie didn't bury Mom in the yard until those three days that he took us to the movies, September 24, 25, and 26, then that event was the week prior. If that's the case, then there wasn't even anything yet to hide on my birthday, when I didn't allow Daniel to use Ann's bathroom because of her dog's presence.

Then she showed Cheryl a photo, and she immediately started crying and said, "That's the mother's ring that I had bought for her. Rickie and Stacey gave me money. It's got two sapphires and a diamond." Cheryl sat there chewing her lip as I tried to not hyperventilate. Dear God, this was hard, and it was just the first day.

Finally, Robin was done with her and Diana took over with her cross-examination. She asked Cheryl, again, if she had ever seen our father abuse me, and she said no. Diana said, "If he was abusing your sister, he was doing it in a way that you did not see?" and Cheryl said, "Correct." Diana continued, "If he was able to abuse Stacey in a way that you did not see, he would also have been able to do things to your brother that you did not see?" Cheryl agreed. "Did you ever see your father sexually abuse your brother?" Diana asked, and Cheryl said that she had not. "And yet that's what your brother has said happened to him," she said, and Cheryl replied, "That's what I had heard."

"Your father, in fact, as far as your perception was concerned, seemed to treat Stacey better than you and your brother," Diana stated. Cheryl thought for a moment and said, "If you're asking me from an abusive standpoint, I guess I would say yes." She testified that he often called me his only biological child and, because of that, I was treated better.

She also questioned Cheryl about how things were tense between the three of us because of issues about her parenting, and how the three of us stopped communicating after she wrote us a letter telling us to butt out. Diana asked her about Mom taking the kids away from her, and Cheryl testified that Mom never told her she'd try to take the kids.

Diana finished up with her, and then Robin got back up for redirect examination and asked her what she wanted to have happen to Rickie. Cheryl said, "I thought that twenty years and telling everything he knew was what I needed."

When she was finally done testifying, Diana tried to explain to me so it wouldn't hurt so badly, "She's not hurting you; she's not helping you. She's stating her facts the way she sees them. She's not going to damage you." And, yes, in retrospect I can see that she didn't really say anything *legally* damaging against me, but the fact was, she was not a hostile witness for the prosecution.

CHAPTER 30

Father and Son

The next day of the trial began much the same as the first, with the room packed with people from Gulf Coast Resort, many of whom drove there that morning, others who were paying for hotel rooms to avoid the four-hour round-trip drive. Robin called to the witness stand an employee of the bank that I called in December, the one who told me that I would have to call Detective Hussey because the account was frozen. She testified that I said I was Marilyn Kananen.

Next up was Cheryl's husband, who testified about the conversation that we had with him regarding Daniel having a knife to protect himself from his mother. He said that Rickie and I wanted Cheryl removed from their home, which was not true. I wanted Cheryl to get help without their family being disrupted.

He also told the jury that during game nights at their home, Rickie and I would go off together and talk quietly. "When approached," Chris said, "they would stop, turn toward whoever approached them, and talk about something else." It's true that Rickie tried to monopolize my every moment. But cast in this sinister light, it looked to Chris like we were plotting murder.

They talked about my niece's birthday party in November. Chris told Robin that he had invited an armed friend over to act as sort of a bodyguard, because he was afraid of me and Rickie. After telling the jury that he had visited Rickie in jail and that he and I hadn't spoken since Rickie was arrested, Robin said that she had no further questions and Diana took over.

Diana started out by asking Chris to confirm that, as an outsider, he was able to see that our family dynamic, due to the violent abuse, was unusual and dysfunctional, that we didn't respond to one another in the way that an average family would. He did agree to that assessment.

He also confirmed that Mom would have her locks changed whenever an out-of-town visitor, like Aunt Gerri, would go back home, and that Rickie would be the one to do that. He confirmed that Rickie was very upset and animated that Daniel had a knife for self-defense, and that Rickie said he knew of a way to make Cheryl leave the home. Chris said, "His words were, he could 'break her.'"

Diana asked Chris if he was aware that Rickie was writing a book about his life, and Chris said he was. He testified that Rickie said that he sold his moving company so he could devote his time to rescuing abused kids. "He was hired by cartels to plan the perfect crimes," Diana continued, "and was paid well to do so when they were successful, correct?" Robin popped up out of her chair. "Objection. Hearsay."

Diana looked at the judge with exasperation and said, "Not offered for the truth." When the judge asked, "What is it offered for?" Diana responded, "Offered to show the mental health, state, intent, motive, and devolving mental health of the witness that's in this case. I'll rephrase."

"In your presence," Diana said, "he told you about how the vigilante justice was funded. And he told you that he was hired by cartels to plan the perfect crimes and was paid well when they were successful, correct?" Again, Robin said, "Objection. Hearsay. Relevance."

Judge Lubet sighed and said, "Overruled," and Chris replied, "Yes, ma'am." Chris confirmed that Rickie said that one of the cases he worked on involved law enforcement.

He was excused and the State called their next witness: Daniel.

I hadn't seen him since 2003, and I was overjoyed to see that he had grown into a handsome young man in those seven years. He reminded me of Rickie as a teenager, tall, lean, and strong. He had become a martial arts instructor, and I was so proud, even though my heart was breaking over the reason we were once again in the same room, after all those years.

Robin started out asking him how close he was with Mom, and Daniel testified that he was very close to her and to me and Rickie. He said that he and I went to Disney and played basketball together, and that he and Rickie would just talk.

As he testified about having a knife to protect himself from Cheryl, and about Rickie sharing stories of abuse, I wrote on my legal pad to Toni, "*It hurts to know that Daniel and I were best friends and may never be able to build that friendship.*"

Robin asked him about their visit to the house on my birthday, and he testified that I prevented him from using the bathroom in Ann's room. I wrote on my pad, "*He went into the other bathroom because of Susan's mother's dog.*" He testified that he didn't remember if I told him why he couldn't use that bathroom and directed him to the other one.

The prosecution didn't have very many questions for him, once Robin laid out a foundation that Daniel had told me and Rickie about his abuse and that we weren't happy with his mom. He testified that he had been forbidden to talk to me since 2003 and that he had visited Rickie in jail a few times.

When Diana got up, his demeanor changed. I wrote to Toni, "*Now he smiles when Diana gets up.*" She started out asking him about all of our trips to Disney together, and all the family outings that we all took, Mom included. She took him down a meandering path, talking about how he and I had a different relationship than the one he had with Rickie, that he told Rickie things he didn't tell me and Rickie told him secrets, too.

"He acted out for you," Diana stated, "how violent and

angry his father had gotten at him, one time using a ladder and throwing it around. Is that right?" Daniel said, "Yes, one time." Diana continued, "And he told you, one time, that his father had sodomized him. Raped him." Daniel nodded and said, "Yes."

After a long pause, Diana asked, "You and Rickie had kind of a pact between you, that you would tell each other secrets, correct?" Daniel agreed. "When you would tell him that his mother loved him, he told you to quit talking like that. Correct?"

"I don't know if he used those words, but he didn't like that," Daniel replied.

She asked, and he answered, that Rickie had told him tales of traveling the country, helping abused kids, and that he knew how to rob banks and commit other crimes, like hacking into bank accounts. He told Daniel that he knew how to kill people and make it look accidental, or like suicide. Daniel confirmed all of those things.

Diana's final question was, "If you were going to get help on the computer from anyone in the house, would it be Stacey?" and Daniel responded, "No."

With that, he was done and gone, sent back out of the courtroom and back out of my life.

CHAPTER 31

My Brother, My Protector

It was day three of the trial, and I wasn't any less terrified, even though many of my friends were assuring me that there was nothing being said that was actual evidence that I was guilty of anything. "There's plenty of reasonable doubt!" they would say, but it wasn't enough to make me feel better.

It was odd, during lunch, to go downstairs to the little courthouse diner and eat with the jurors sitting at tables nearby. I felt like I stuck out like a sore thumb, but Diana assured me that it was probably good for them to see me out in public, like a normal person, surrounded by my friends from GCR, who obviously liked me and didn't treat me like a murderer. As long as no one discussed the trial in their presence, there was no issue.

So while my initial tension was starting to alleviate, the

overall tension in the courtroom that day was palpable because everyone knew that Rickie, himself, was going to testify. When Robin called him to the stand, we could hear his shackles first, as he was brought in, wearing blue prison scrubs, unshaven, his hair disheveled. He was sworn in and sat down heavily, looking around the room nervously. Robin started, "Can you tell us your name please," and he said, "Richard Kananen."

Robin continued, "Mr. Kananen, do you have somewhat of a hearing loss?"

"Excuse me?" he asked, his face bursting into an impish grin. Robin was having none of it. "Do you have a hearing loss?" and he replied, "Yes, left ear."

Robin led him through statements about his sentence, that he pleaded guilty to second-degree and got thirty years. His replies were rushed, so Robin asked him to slow down. "Mr. Kananen," she asked, "did you kill your mother?"

"Yes, I did."

"And was someone there to assist you?" she asked.

"Yes. Stacey, my sister."

Robin asked, "Do you see Stacey in the courtroom?" and he looked at me. "Yes, she's sitting over there at the table." I couldn't even look up at him.

They talked about our abusive upbringing, with Rickie using as few words as possible, his responses rapid-fire. He told about beatings he received for no infraction, depending on our father's mood. Robin asked if our father drank alcohol, and Rickie said yes. "How would that affect him?" she asked.

He shot back, "It didn't matter. It made him worse

sometimes, it made him better sometimes." I scribbled, "*Not true. He was much, much worse when he was drunk— sober he was almost human.*"

When asked about our mom, he said, "Sometimes she would intercede, sometimes she wouldn't." As he testified, Cheryl sat in the gallery, sobbing. I wrote, "*I can't look at him. Is that bad? Bothers me. I have feelings.*" Toni patted my hand, as if to say, "It's okay."

He told the jury that he witnessed verbal and physical abuse between our parents, beatings, thrashings, whippings. He testified that he was sexually abused by our father, behind closed doors, starting at age six, until he was about ten or eleven.

Rickie testified that our father beat both me and Cheryl, as well. He said that we moved around a lot, because our father would get in trouble. She asked how his hearing loss occurred and he rapidly stated, "Took a double barrel shotgun blew it off in my ear when I was sleeping."

She asked him about the fires in our homes, and he said that the first one occurred in Maine. He said he was in high school. "Who got your sisters out of the house?" she asked.

"I did."

"What did you do?"

"Broke a window. Got 'em out of the window."

"Where were your parents?"

"Outside."

"Did your father make any effort to rescue his daughters?"

"No."

"What was his reaction when you got your sisters out?"

"Wasn't too happy."

"What was your mom's reaction?"

"Wasn't too happy."

There was more testimony about the abuse, about our father putting him in chains and locking him in the closet. Robin led him into testimony about when he moved in with me and Susan because "it seemed like a good idea," and that he became aware of how much money Grandpa had left to Mom. So far, there was nothing new being said on the stand. I was just concerned that he look drugged and rehearsed, answering too quickly, in too pat a way, with creepy, weird facial expressions.

Robin asked him, "Did you ever discuss with Stacey killing your mother?"

"Yes," he said, without hesitation.

"Did you two plan to do this?"

"Yes."

"When you were planning to kill your mother, what did Stacey say about how she wanted to do this?"

"She just wanted her dead."

"Did you discuss with her ways to kill your mother?"

Rickie replied, "No, we decided on suffocation."

He told Robin that we decided to use a Taser to incapacitate Mom, so we could suffocate her. He said we talked about it quite a few times.

She abruptly changed the subject. "Did you tell Daniel about your sexual abuse?"

"No."

"Did you and Stacey approach Chris that Cheryl should move out?"

"No."

"What," Robin asked, "was your mother's reaction to what was going on with Cheryl?"

"She was gonna take the kids away from my sister." He said that he didn't want Mom to take her kids because most of the time she wasn't a good mother. She didn't protect us children.

Robin asked, "Was your mother, herself, physically abusive to you?" and Rickie, surprisingly, said, "I won't answer that," and grinned. "Mr. Kananen, you're under oath and you have to." He started laughing and shook his head, no.

"Your Honor, may we approach?" she asked Judge Lubet, and she and Diana went up to the bench for a private conversation with the judge. After they returned to their places, the judge told Rickie, "Mr. Kananen, sir, you're under oath here. And you're in this courtroom as a witness and it's not a matter of a Fifth Amendment right not to testify because this can't incriminate you any further. You've already admitted to what you've done. Therefore, the question I have for you is, are you going to answer the question?"

"Yes," Rickie answered, quickly.

"Thank you. Let's continue."

Rickie's demeanor changed. Suddenly he looked dark and sullen. Robin asked again, "Mr. Kananen, did your mother ever physically abuse you?"

"Yes." He told her it happened about once a month, and he never saw her abuse either me or Cheryl. I wrote on my pad, *"He is lying. My mother never hit or abused any of us."*

Immediately, Robin brought him back to questions about our plotting to kill Mom. He said we had talked about it for several months, over ten or twelve discussions. He told Robin that he went to the Spy Store to buy a Taser. He told her that after Susan went to Hudson to pick up Ann for the cruise, he and I took Mom to Fazoli's and a movie, *Charlie's Angels II*. I wrote, "*I saw that movie prior to that.*"

He testified that when we went out, I had the Taser behind my back, underneath my clothes. I scribbled, furiously, "*How could I go to dinner and a movie with a Taser under my clothes? That is large to supposed to have hidden under my clothes and no one to have noticed.*"

He said that we met Mom at her house and went to Fazoli's, and then the movie, then back to Mom's house. He said we went into the house, and he went into the dining room area. I wrote, "*That is quite a story he's weaving. We would not have been asked inside after dinner and a movie because she would have had to get ready for work the next day.*"

He said, "I sat down, at the dining room counter, Stacey and my mother were standing over there talking. And a few minutes later Stacey Tasered her and said, 'Rickie help me,' and Mom was on the ground. Then I took my bandana out and suffocated her."

"Did you know Stacey was going to use the Taser?"

"Yes."

"How?"

"Because," Rickie said, "she had it with her and the opportunity was there."

"Had you had a plan of what would happen after your mother was Tased?"

"Not really, just ca . . . cam . . . came that way," he stuttered. "Tasered, she fell down, suffocated her. Took a bandana, put it over her mouth and nose."

"How long did you keep that bandana on her?"

"I have no idea," he said.

By this time, I was trying to maintain my composure, but not doing very well, just picturing what he was describing, my mom's murder. I wrote, *"He has quite a story. I am very upset by all of this. How are people ever going to believe that I had nothing to do with this?"*

"Were there things that came out from the Taser into your mother?" Robin asked, and I bit my lip. I couldn't let myself cry. Not now, not with Rickie watching me.

"Yeah, things came out. Came out," he said.

"What was your sister doing as you were suffocating your mother?"

"She was standing over there, over me."

"Was she saying anything to you?"

"No."

"When did you pull the bandana off?"

"After a while."

"Why?"

"There was no more breathing."

"When you did that, what happened?"

"Told Stacey to go in the garage and get some duct tape. She duct-taped her hands and her feet."

"Why did Stacey duct-tape her hands and feet?"

"For when we carried her in the . . . car . . . hands wouldn't fall over," he slurred. He said that we took Mom to the storage unit in the trunk of her car and that I drove. He said we put her body in a freezer, parked the car in the storage unit, and went back to the house. I wrote, *"I hate the 'we'—I didn't have a part in this. How do I prove this?"*

"About what time of night was this that you were driving to your storage unit?"

"About 8:00, 9:00."

The two of them went on and on, Rickie telling the jury that he and I gathered up Mom's clothes and some family photos in some trash bags and took them to the dump. The reason "we" put the papers on the counter, in spite of everyone knowing that Mom was a neat freak, was to give the appearance that she had left. He also said that the weekend that Susan went on her cruise, he and I dug the hole in my backyard and buried Mom's body, and that I chose the location.

Robin asked, "You take any appliances out of your mother's home?"

"The refrigerator."

"Stacey ever ask you why you're having an extra refrigerator in the house?"

"No," he said, and I scribbled on my notepad, *"I did ask him why he moved the refrig. He chose not to answer me. I grew up not asking questions twice. It got you in trouble."*

Robin brought the conversation up to December 22, the day we attempted to commit suicide. Hearing him tell his version of that day brought back all of those horrible memories of how desperate I felt that day, just wanting to not know what he had done. I wrote, "*This is harder to go through than I thought.*"

"Any discussions between the two of you on the method of suicide?" Robin asked.

"Through exhaust pipe from the vehicle."

"When you went in Wal-Mart, did both of you go in the store? Were you together the entire time?"

"Yes."

"Ever hold a weapon to your sister? As you're walking in Wal-Mart, are you holding onto her?"

"No."

That was a lie. I scribbled, "*I didn't go in Wal-mart. I waited in the truck very upset, confused and depressed.*"

Robin took him down the path of that day, leading him into telling about what we did when we got into the storage unit. I could tell it was difficult for him, too, because he was shaking, practically vibrating, as he talked. She asked him to identify the notes that he wrote and read them aloud.

She showed him lots of pictures to identify, the truck in the storage unit, the bottle of NyQuil, my backyard, and the steel plate that he used to cover the hole he said I dug. My head was reeling with all of the visual evidence of my mother's horrible demise. I wrote on my legal pad and showed it to Diana, "*The pictures of the backyard, the holes in the ground and steel plate and the visual that is in my head about duct tape is just overwhelming. Can we disprove any of this that he is saying?*" Diana just nodded. It was her turn to question Rickie.

She dove right in with the tough questions. "Your mother was physically and sexually abusive to you as well as your father, correct? And your mother quit abusing you about the time you were a teenager, correct?"

"Yes."

"The fact that your mother stood by while your father burned down two of your homes with you and your siblings in it is something you never forgave her for, correct?"

He answered very quietly, "Correct."

Diana continued, "When you left home at twenty two and your father told you that you couldn't have contact with anybody remaining in the household, that was not a surprise to you, right? And he told you that if you tried to have contact with your sisters he would coerce them into saying that you had sexually abused them?"

"Yes."

"And you believed that he could do that?"

"Yes."

She talked to him about how he became close with Daniel. She asked, "You told him about how abusive your father was to you? You told him about how your father raped you?"

"No."

"You told Daniel that you traveled around the country helping children who were abused."

"No."

"You told Daniel that you know how to rob a bank."

"No."

"You told Daniel that you knew how to plant drugs on abusive fathers so that the police would arrest them instead of you."

"No."

"You told Daniel that you were learning how to hack into computers and into bank accounts."

"No."

"You told Daniel that you knew how to kidnap people."

"No."

"You told Daniel you knew how to kill people and make it look accidental."

"No."

"You told Daniel you knew how to kill people and make it look like suicide."

"No."

"At family gatherings you would tell your sisters and your brother-in-law and your nephew that you traveled around saving children from abusive parents."

"No."

"At family gatherings, you would tell your family that you were hired by a cartel to go commit crimes and paid very well when you succeeded."

"No."

"You would tell your family at gatherings that your business had been sold so that you would have the time and money to travel the country taking abusive parents out of their children's homes."

"No."

Watching her was dazzling, and I was hoping that the jury was paying attention to all of the lies she was catching him in. She changed the subject. "At some point according to Daniel after he talked about his mom going to classes, he indicated to you things were getting better."

"Yes."

"And he indicated to you that things were improving in the late summer of 2003, that his mom was being nicer to him and she seemed to be dealing with her anger in a better way. He had confidence that this was going to be a long-term improvement and you believe that your mother, Marilyn, also saw this improvement over at that household."

"Yes."

"During a family get-together at their home, you indicated to Chris that you needed some help in the backyard at Marilyn's house in order to get him there so that you could confront him with this knife situation. During that conversation you offered to get Cheryl out of the home, that you could get her out of the house because you knew how to break her."

"No."

"When Daniel told you about problems he was having with his mother, you offered to take her out of the way for him."

"No."

She, like Robin, took him down the long path from September 11 through December 22, talking about the story he told everyone about Mom and the IRS, the money he took from the bank account, our interviews at the police station, and the eventual suicide attempt, oftentimes trying to trip him up into saying that he acted alone, but he was on his toes, on that account. He never missed a beat and continued to implicate me as his accomplice.

She asked him about the suicide attempt, "You walked

away from the storage unit. You were never unconscious for any period of time. You were not admitted to the hospital. In fact, you went from the hospital to jail later the same day, correct?"

"Correct."

"And then sometime later, you tell law enforcement that you and your mom got in an argument over her taking Cheryl's kids. You told them that part of this argument was that your mother was worried that if Cheryl didn't do the classes she would lose the kids."

"Correct."

"And then you told police, Mom started screaming, she's going to take Cheryl's kids, correct?"

"Correct."

"And then you told law enforcement that as you and your mother were having an escalating argument, you don't really remember what else happens."

"Correct."

"And then you admit to killing your mother. At that point, you were arrested for first-degree murder. Now you are in the Orange County jail with a first-degree murder charge pending, you go on a hunger strike, you lose one hundred and eighty pounds, and you start talking about having hallucinations. What kind of hallucinations have you had?"

Rickie testified that he heard our father's angry voice, ever since he was a child, yelling at him. He admitted that he stopped taking care of himself in jail because he wanted to go to the state hospital. Diana asked, "You go so far at some point to put your own feces on your body?"

That, he would not admit to. "No, I did not do that."

Although she was surprised by his denial, she pushed on. They discussed his being found incompetent, and that the voices stopped after he was put on medication. He testified that he was sent back to jail, and he tried again to fake symptoms so he would be sent back to the hospital, but this time it didn't work.

"And so finally in the early part of 2007, you got a court date coming up, and it doesn't appear that there's going to be anymore stalling this event. At that point, you were still facing first-degree murder which, if convicted, and you had admitted to killing your mother, you would receive a life in prison sentence without any possibility of parole. And you knew that your sister Stacey was a state witness against you and she had been listed as a state witness against you from way back in the early part of 2004?"

"Correct."

"You knew that your sister Cheryl was listed as a state witness against you and she would come out and see you on occasion with your nephew, and you told your sister and nephew that Stacey killed your mother? And Cheryl encouraged you to take a plea, correct?"

"I thought it was best for the family not to have a trial."

I wrote on my legal pad, "*I guess he picked me because I never went to see him. How can I go see someone who buried a body in my backyard and involved me in all the stealing of money?*"

Diana continued, "But she encouraged you to do that, correct?"

"Yeah."

"And when you accepted the thirty-year offer, you went in front of the court and there was a discussion, and a part of that discussion on the record is that you were going to talk to law enforcement that very day?"

"There was no discussion about that."

"There was something on the record that said you were going to talk to law enforcement. Not until after the plea bargain was done?"

"After the hearing."

"Within minutes after the hearing right there at the courthouse."

"Correct."

"And in it you told them for the first time that your sister had been involved in the killing of your mother."

"Correct."

"And when you took that deal, your charge went from a first-degree murder to second-degree murder, correct?"

"Yes."

"At some point, you had known that the State could ask for the death penalty. And you knew that wasn't going to happen now?"

"Correct."

Robin jumped up and objected, which led into a long series of questions and answers, with Robin trying to prove that Rickie didn't make any sort of agreement to talk about me in exchange for a lesser sentence, and Diana implying, even though she had no proof of it, that there may have been some hints of some backdoor dealings. The rest of the afternoon was spent going over the same ground again and again, until finally both attorneys were satisfied that they had covered all the ground they needed to with my brother. Not a moment too soon, because I was emotionally exhausted and couldn't take much more of this.

Just before Diana finished with Rickie, she said, "Just a minute Your Honor," turned to Toni, and asked, "Did I get them all?" and they started counting on their fingers. Toni said, "Yep, you got 'em all, you're done with him." And Diana said, "Your Honor, I'm finished questioning him."

I said to her, "I missed something. What was the counting for?" She laughed and said, "Oh, Toni catches things I don't. After I gave my opening statement, she told me, 'You said he changed his story five times. Robin's going to come back, and there better be five different versions.' She wanted to make sure the testimony matched my opening statement."

CHAPTER 32

The Worst of It

The next day, Robin called Michael Vincent, the crime scene investigator who dug up Mom's body. He was so graphic that there was no doubt in my mind exactly what the scene looked like. "The victim was wrapped in two heavy-duty plastic trash bags with duct tape around the center. The one trash bag went from the head to the feet, and the second trash bag went from the feet to the head and it was duct-taped in the middle. She was facedown, with her head east and her feet west, with her legs bent at the knees, facing upward."

I knew the judge wanted no outbursts, but I just started bawling. That was *my mom* they were talking about. But at least I stayed quiet. I had to sit there and watch while Robin started displaying photos of the dig and he narrated, showing Mom's body wrapped in the bags, as it was unearthed.

Then Robin showed the jury Mom's actual jean jacket with the embroidered Disney characters on the back, encased in plastic for display. Susan and I had the same jackets. The three of us bought them the opening day of Animal Kingdom at Disney. The whole story of what fun we had that day, buying the jackets and going out to lunch, poured through my head.

The jacket was horribly stained, obviously soaked with body fluids, and there are no words to describe what it felt like to see it in person, other than every nerve in my body screamed out in protest against Robin's inhumane behavior. She deliberately left it sitting in front of me, leaning against the evidence table, just so I could sit there and stew in its horror. Diana whispered to me, "That's the reaction she wants. She wants you to get mad."

Robin asked, "Mr. Vincent, for what purpose was it packaged in this way?" and he replied, "It was packaged in this way in order to keep the smell contained. If I was to take it out of the plastic bag, I think we would have to clear the courtroom because it still has a bad smell to it. It's really saturated in there. I had dried this in the scalding hot sun but because of the decomposition liquid it just never goes away."

Robin entered the actual duct tape from around Mom's face, hands, and legs and Mom's stained shirt into evidence. It was all I could do to not vomit, as she and Mr. Vincent just tossed the items around casually, as if there was no meaning there. He kept talking about the smell, that he had to wrap the duct tape in plastic because of it. He seemed to be deliberately bringing it up, again and again and again. I could feel myself becoming numb. It had become too much, and I couldn't allow myself to feel anymore. Thank God his testimony was fairly short and Diana didn't ask him too many questions. After all, they didn't say anything about me being involved, and there was nothing for her to rebut.

Considering that Mom was wearing that jacket, and shorts and a T-shirt, when she died, I think she was either getting up in the morning and put the jacket on to go out with the cat, or came home from work and changed. She slept in shorts and a top. She didn't have pajamas, unless it was the middle of winter and she was in flannels. She was obviously not going to the movies if she was wearing those clothes. She would never go to a movie without jeans on. She didn't go anywhere without jeans on unless she was running to the grocery store across the street. Never. Unfortunately, there was no way of proving that.

Judge Lubet knew, before the medical examiner testified next, that he needed to say something to everyone in the courtroom. "All right, ladies and gentlemen, the next witness is going to take the stand in a few minutes. There are going to be photographs that might be disturbing. If you do not wish to see the photographs I suggest you leave the courtroom. The jury, of course, has no choice. I don't want any outbursts or disturbances, while this is going on."

Diana had warned me that this was going to be rough, and I had to be strong.

Robin called Dr. Sarah Irrgang to the stand, and she testified that Mom was asphyxiated. Her body was partially mummified and weighed only seventy-nine pounds when they found her. The mouth and nose area was covered by duct tape, which was wrapped around her head, and her wrists and ankles were bound. There was a Taser dart in the back of her jacket. The details began to get so gory that I had to stop listening and revert back to old coping mechanisms—I started counting the syllables of the words I was hearing. Robin asked about horrible things, like bugs and body fluids—things that were completely unnecessary to discuss, except to horrify me and the jury.

Robin asked, "How long would it take if someone was to cut off the air coming in through the mouth and the nose for someone to go unconscious?" and Dr. Irrgang replied, "If you put your hand over someone's mouth and nose, they will begin within a matter of a couple of minutes to have a shortage of oxygen and become light-headed and then faint."

I was devastated by the thought of Mom suffering for so long. I can't even fathom what that feels like. Somebody put a bullet in my father's head. He got off easy, and he was a vicious bastard. What did she do so bad that Rickie had to make her suffer? I don't understand the person he became.

Once the first photos were coming up, Toni grabbed one arm, and Diana grabbed the other, and both had Kleenex ready. I asked them, "How bad is it if I don't look?" and they both told me, "You don't have to. You just have to sit here and you can't be really loud." I kept my head down, for the most part, but it was hard not to look. It's just human nature. Even if you don't look up entirely, you do glance. You want to see what they're talking about, even if you desperately don't want to know. I was quietly hysterical. Diana patted my arm and said, "It will be okay. It will end soon. It'll be okay."

The photos were exceptionally graphic, pictures of her face, her scalp peeled back to expose her skull, and even her brain. Then they showed her laid out on the slab in the autopsy room. They showed the full body. I don't think I picked my head up the rest of the afternoon. I just cried the whole time. Previous days, when we broke and we'd stand up, I'd look at the jury. That day, I stood up, but I was still shaking and crying.

I know Robin was just doing her job, but I cannot conceive of deliberately torturing another human being like this. Innocent until proven guilty, my ass! All because a rookie detective wanted to prove himself as a hotshot homicide investigator in 2003, I was subjected to this torment.

I felt absolutely scraped raw. Over the course of my life, I'd been tortured by my father, beaten and sexually violated, and my own brother and sister conspired to have me arrested for murdering my beloved mom. And now I had been symbolically gagged, ordered to sit passively and watch as photos of my mother's decomposed face and body were tossed around like playing cards. Seriously, what else could I possibly be asked to endure? What other fresh hell could life possibly dish out?

We finished court at 6:00; I finished bawling at 6:30. I couldn't eat that night. Diana and Toni tried to encourage me, saying, "Come on, you have to participate. You have to look like you give a shit." I said, "I can't. I just don't care anymore. I just don't care. My sister thinks I could be that inhumane. It doesn't matter."

Toni and I went for a long walk that evening, and she said that was the hardest part of the trial, and now it would all be downhill. I said, "There's nothing downhill about those pictures. They're in my head for the rest of my life."

She said, "Yes, but the shock effect goes, the pain goes away, and you just go on."

I replied, "I don't know if the shock of those photos will ever go away. They show autopsies on TV and I turn my head, and that was my mother. I've been through a lot of things in my life; those pictures of that body are things I wish I didn't have in my head. There used to be a way I could pack things up in a little box and lock them up in my head, but that doesn't seem to work anymore."

Diana told me that just because it's obvious that Mom was murdered, it doesn't mean that the prosecution doesn't have a right to prove it. They didn't do anything out-of-bounds of what they have a right to do. What they wanted to do was horrify and gross out and affect the jury emotionally. They wanted to show awful pictures and freak me out. She said, "This is in every single murder case I've ever been a part of. Yes, that's what they do. To be honest, I know it felt like a lot to you, but in comparison it was a pretty lean presentation."

Then I got the good old "get your shit together" talk from Diana. She said, "Are you guilty?" I said no, and she said, "Then snap the fuck out of it." And then I finally realized, you know what? I'm fighting for my fucking life here. Hello, wake up!

CHAPTER 33

Homicide Hussey

There is a romance novelist in Florida who has a blog that features the writings of a certain Detective Mark Hussey, who works as a deputy sheriff in Orlando. He writes under the moniker "Homicide Hussey," and here is an example of the kinds of things he writes:

> I've found that each year I spend as a cop I get a little more cynical and a little less tolerant of stupidity . . . For some reason, cops consider themselves after a number of years to be a little better than anybody else. It's not a dig, it's just that we are required to keep our personal and professional lives free of problems . . . So after years of handling other people's problems it gets difficult to be objective and becomes more and more necessary to be-

little the common man and sometimes add to an already bad situation.[1]

I have no way of knowing if that's the same Detective Mark Hussey who went out of his way to belittle me and add to my already bad situation, but it's certainly obvious that the Homicide Hussey who came after me felt like he was better than me and found it difficult to be objective.

Hussey took the stand the next day—wearing a dark gray suit, an American flag tie, his sheriff's badge on a loop around his neck, and a miniature decorative gold sheriff's star badge on his lapel. He testified that he started as a homicide detective the month after Mom was killed, and took on this case in November 2003. He was assigned to the case as busywork. He told Robin that this was the case that he was spending all of his time on.

When Robin asked him, "From your first involvement in November, up until Marilyn Kananen was found, did you speak to Cheryl Bracken?" Hussey's face lit up. He chuckled and said fondly, "Almost daily."

"Were there some days when you talked to her more than once?" Robin asked.

"Yes, ma'am," Homicide Hussey responded, smiling.

"And would you describe Cheryl Bracken as fairly persistent?"

---

1 http://terryodell.blogspot.com/2009/06/homicide-hussey-cop speak.html

He nodded and laughed out loud, and replied, knowingly, "Yes, ma'am, I would."

"During that same time, going up to December 22, 2003, how many phone calls did you get from Stacey Kananen?"

Hussey's eyes shifted back and forth, and he said, curtly, "None."

"How many phone calls did you get from Richard Kananen?"

"None." I wrote on my legal pad, "*I had spoken to Cheryl weekly. Richard was telling me that he was speaking to police and IRS and SS frequently.*"

Robin continued, "Did you at one point make a phone call to Richard Kananen, to get him to come in and talk to you?"

"Yes, I did," Hussey said.

Hussey testified that he had sought out E-PASS[2] information from my mom's car ". . . to determine if there was any pattern for the use of the E-PASS and when that pattern came to an end." Robin entered that E-PASS record into evidence and displayed it on the wall behind the witness stand with the overhead projector. She asked Hussey, "Were you able to determine the last time that Marilyn's car would have used its E-PASS?"

Hussey turned around and looked at the screen behind him. "September 10, 2003, at 17:53 hours and 55 seconds."

---

2 E-PASS is the Orlando–Orange County Expressway Authority's electronic toll payment system.

"What was the significance of that in comparison to the time frame that you had in which she was reported missing?" Robin inquired.

"Well, she was reported missing the next morning. She did not arrive at work for her scheduled work shift. So last time that she went through the toll plaza, near her home, was after work on the afternoon prior."

When asked about that garage sale that I was already sick to death of hearing about, he testified, "I actually was off that day, but when you're working a homicide case, you're never off. So I just decided to go by and see what was going on." He saw that we were having a garage sale, and he recognized me from my driver's license photo. At that time, Robin asked Hussey to identify me in the courtroom, sitting between Diana and Toni. As he did so, I glared at him.

He said that we were selling Disney collectibles and that Susan was carrying a box out of the garage full of something that he couldn't see, and that she asked me, "What are we going to do with these?" and that I responded, "Mom wanted us to get rid of those." I wrote, "*Funny how Cheryl never told him that Susan and I worked for Disney and collected Disney.*"

Robin asked him about the checks and bank accounts, and nothing new was revealed. They were just reiterating testimony from previous witnesses from the banks. I wrote to Diana, "*Really feel like he didn't investigate the checks, he just decided that since one was made out to me, that I was guilty of stealing money so I must have killed my mother.*"

He told Robin that he talked to Rickie about coming in

for an interview on December 22, and Robin asked, "Did you ask him to bring anyone with him?" Hussey replied, "I asked him to bring his . . . well, he said he was going to bring his sister with him." I furiously scribbled on my legal pad, *"Thanks Richard for offering to take me with him to the Sheriff's Office. Yet Richard told me we were asked to come to Sheriff's Office to talk about my mother's missing."*

Robin took him through the story, again, of our morning interview at the sheriff's office and the subsequent suicide attempt. She asked him whether he let me know that I was a possible suspect, and he turned to the jury and said, smugly and officiously, "Yes, ma'am, I told her that there wasn't a statute of limitations on murder and that at some point I intended to prove that she was involved in this and I would be coming to arrest her."

Yes, I remember that day well. I wrote on my legal pad, *"It feels like Detective Hussey wanted me so bad in jail that he was going to believe anything to try to get me arrested."*

They then began talking about Rickie's plea agreement and subsequent interview with Hussey, wherein he told Hussey that I committed the murders. Robin asked if Rickie agreed to turn on me in exchange for special favors, and Hussey said, "At that point there wasn't anything we could offer him. He had already been sentenced. There was nothing we could have done for him at that point." Hussey neglected to mention that he and Robin had already arranged with Rickie, before the plea deal, to talk about me, so some sort of discussion had to have taken place. His turning on me wasn't a surprise to anyone on that side of the courtroom.

Finally, Diana had her turn to cross-examine the detective. One of her first questions ascertained that he was assigned this case for training purposes, that he was the "new guy on the block." It was bizarre watching his demeanor change, now that Diana was at bat. His breathing speeded up, his posture changed—he fidgeted in his seat—and his eyes started shifting back and forth, trying not to look at me. I even wrote on my pad, "*It is hard for me to look at Detective Hussey but he really can't look at me in the eye.*"

Diana asked him about how I came to be interviewed by the police in December, and he agreed that it was because I talked to the bank and was given his number. Because the account was frozen, I called him and he called me back. Her tone made it very clear that I had done nothing wrong; I had done exactly what I should have. I left a message for him with my name and my phone number. I obviously wasn't trying to hide anything.

She pressed on. "At no time during the pendency of Richard's case did you ever express concern that Stacey Kananen would perjure herself, or that you would be inviting false testimony by allowing her to testify against her brother, correct?"

Hussey shrugged, shook his head, and said, "That was not my call to make."

"You didn't know whether she was telling the truth or not. And it didn't bother you," Diana continued, "to have her testify in light of the suicide attempt because your mind was open to her having attempted to committing suicide due to the stresses of having been interrogated and finding out for the first time that her mother had been killed by her brother. Correct?"

He shook his head dismissively. "I have no idea why."

"Certainly that's a scenario that was highly possible, correct?" Diana asked.

Hussey replied, in a mildly condescending tone, "Anything's possible, counselor."

Diana got him to admit that there wasn't anything about Mom's murder that required a second person and then asked, "When you went to the jail on May 1, 2007, to talk to Mr. Kananen, you would have been well aware that he had given varying stories regarding the murder of his mother, correct?"

"That is true, yes ma'am."

"And," she continued, "you would certainly have reason to have some skepticism about what Richard Kananen would tell you, correct?" Hussey agreed. "And you had not followed closely the competency hearings regarding his mental health issues, is that right?" and Hussey replied, "No, I did not."

"But you knew that there had been questions raised as to his competency and mental wellness?" she asked, and he agreed, "Yes, I knew he had been evaluated." She got him to admit that he even visited Rickie at the mental health facility and got a look at him. "And at that time," Diana said, "he appeared unkempt and unbathed, his hair was grown out in a big shaggy mop, he had a big, full, not-shaved-in-many-weeks beard, and he had put his own feces on himself, correct?"

Hussey agreed about my brother's appearance but replied about the feces, "I had heard that. I didn't witness it. I heard that he was doing that, yes." Given Rickie's condition, Hussey said, he was unable to talk to him.

"So when you went in to interview him on May 1, 2007"—the day Rickie took his plea—"had you reviewed your report so you could take in any new version that Mr. Kananen told you and make some evaluation as to how likely it was?"

Hussey shifted his eyes and replied, "We were preparing for trial, so yes, I had reviewed the case."

"And he tells you initially at the start of the story of how Mom gets killed that he and Stacey and Marilyn go to a movie and dinner on the tenth of September, 2003. And he tells you that they go to the 6:00 showing of *Charlie's Angels* at the dollar theater on Colonial Drive."

"*Charlie's Angels II*, I believe," he corrected her, smiling.

"Did you check to see if that was playing at 6:00 on that day?" she inquired.

Hussey said, "I'm not sure. I don't remember."

"Well, you know already that Marilyn Kananen was not at a 6:00 movie on September 10, correct?"

He shook his head, confused, and said, "I don't . . . I don't know that. What . . ." He stopped talking and sat there twitching, as Diana crossed the courtroom toward the evidence table and shuffled through some papers, which she brought back with her to show Hussey.

"Well, you talked about what's been marked as State's Exhibit 31, the E-PASS transponder record, correct?"

Hussey just sat there.

"Do you recall talking about that?" Diana pressed, and he sprang back to life.

"Yes, I do."

"And you recall talking about the last transponder entry on September 10, 2003, at 5:53 in the afternoon being on her way home, where she would have been located at University and 417, correct?"

"That's correct," he admitted.

"Okay, so she wasn't sitting in a theater over on Colonial at seven minutes to 6:00, correct?"

"I would say you're right."

I loved Diana Tennis so much, at that moment, and had a hard time not grinning from ear to ear, but I was busting with glee, inside. I scrawled on my legal pad, *"Never questioned Richard about any of the story even if the evidence didn't support what he was told!"*

"In fact," Diana continued, "she's a good fifteen or twenty minutes from home, correct?"

"She's probably ten or fifteen minutes, yes."

"Okay. And so you knew from talking to these friends and neighbors and family members how regimented Marilyn Kananen was."

"A little bit." Hussey said, his eyes darting back and forth between me and Diana, "Yes, ma'am." He started breathing heavily as she continued.

"So she's not home until, call it 6:15." Diana plowed on as Hussey's discomfort became more pronounced. "You knew that she was somebody who wore work clothes to work, and not-work clothes to not work, correct?"

He had to admit, "I did find that out later, yes."

"So she would have had to, at the very least, change clothes, correct?" she asked, and he confirmed this. She continued, "And then they would have had to gotten to the theater. So a 6:00 movie just flat out didn't happen."

He nodded. "Probably."

"So, say there was a 7:00 movie. Do you know if there was a 7:00 movie?" He did not. "Do you know if *Charlie's Angels II* was playing on more than one screen?" He did not. "Alright, so maybe it was playing on more than one screen, maybe there's a 7:00, if not, who knows?" She began pacing the courtroom. "Let's say it's a two hour movie. Does that sound fair?" He nodded. "So let's say they go to a 7:00 movie and it let out at 9:00. He tells you they next have a sit down dinner at Fazoli's, correct? So that gets them home by ten? Quarter to ten?"

"Probably," Hussey agreed.

Diana went on, "The next day is the last working day Marilyn has before she's planning to take off Friday for her trip, correct? Now you know enough about Marilyn Kananen to know that she is not going to go out with her kids until 9:30, 10:00 at night on a work night, the day before her last day at work, correct?"

"I don't . . ."—Hussey stuttered—"I don't . . ." until Robin came to his rescue and said, in a bored voice, "Objection, speculative," and the judge sustained it.

Diana tried again. "Did you talk to any family members about whether it was likely that Marilyn Kananen would have gone out until 9:30, 10:00 at night on a work night?"

Hussey started to respond, "I don't recall . . ." and Robin popped up again, saying, "Objection, speculation."

Diana thought for a moment and rephrased. "Did you ever go back to Richard and say, 'I have E-PASS documents and your story is not adding up'?"

"No, I didn't," Hussey admitted.

Diana, having beaten that dead horse until there was nothing left to flog, moved on to ask Hussey about the Taser dart found in Mom's body. She said that the dart would have had two wires, but only one was found on Mom's body. Her implication was that perhaps the Taser malfunctioned and didn't actually take Mom down. It was grisly and I didn't want to think about the fight that would have ensued between the two of them if that was the case, but it did, once again, cast doubt on Rickie's story. Hussey couldn't dispute her theory—in fact, he admitted that he couldn't testify about how Tasers work.

Diana paused for a long moment and started pacing again. "Fair to say, that you never asked Richard Kananen *any questions* about whether his Taser story made any sense, given the physical evidence?"

"No, I didn't," Hussey confirmed.

After some questions about whether or not the duct tape was tested for DNA (it was not), she asked Hussey, "At the time that you went by to look at the garage sale, had you ever been in Susan and Stacey's home?" and he said he had not.

"So at the time you called Cheryl to say, 'Stacey is selling off your mom's stuff,' at that time you had never been inside their home."

Hussey replied, "That's not exactly what I said to her."

"Whatever you said, made her very, very upset, correct?"

He laughed and said, "Yes, ma'am, it did."

"And you did not give Cheryl a description, to actually determine whether any of the stuff you saw was from her mom. At the time you went by the garage sale, it was your understanding that Marilyn Kananen had a lot of Disney stuff. And were you under any understanding or knowledge about whether Stacey had a lot of Disney stuff?"

"No, I did not."

Eventually, Diana brought it full circle. "You would agree that the thing that changed between April 30 of 2007 and May 1 of 2007 that led you to filling out an affidavit for an arrest warrant for Stacey Kananen was your conversation with Richard Kananen?"

"It certainly was the main thrust, yes."

"You did not challenge him on any of the areas that I've asked you about here today, correct?"

"Correct."

"And part of that is because it wasn't your job to put your personal seal of approval on whether he was telling you the truth or not."

"That is true."

"I don't have anything further," she concluded. Diana had made her point. She was done with him.

CHAPTER 34

"SHE IS MAD NOW!"

The trial dragged on—we had been at this for a week and a half—and I was in absolute misery, 24–7. After we'd get out for the day—usually around 5:30 or 6:00—Susan, Diane, and I would go back to the hotel and I'd try to eat something, either room service or we'd grab something at a nearby restaurant. Sometimes we'd bring Chinese back to the room. I had no appetite, but I tried to choke down a few bites because I knew I had to keep something in my stomach. I was having a hard time sleeping, and the headache that had started on day one was relentless.

We didn't talk about the trial in the evenings much, because Susan had not testified yet. She was still being kept out in the hallway, outside the courtroom door. Mostly, I just tried to stay calm and deal with the pain between my ears. Between panic and constant headaches,

I'd go to the courtroom and Diana would ask, "Did you sleep last night?"

One morning I told her, "No, not really. I got an hour or two," and she replied, "Dear God, do something to sleep. You're starting to look crappy." There wasn't really anything I could do. I had quit drinking two weeks before the trial because I knew I had to be sober for this, I couldn't swallow pills, and I certainly wasn't going to take any liquid meds—the NyQuil suicide attempt had pretty much ruined that sort of thing for me. Besides, I didn't want to be groggy when I woke up, so I just tossed and turned every night, knowing it would be over soon.

The prosecution's witnesses weren't very damaging against me on their own, but Robin was certainly painting an overall picture of sneaky bank account activity. Robin pulled in Tom Vastrick, a handwriting analysis expert. It turns out that he helped us. Robin's expert testified that he was positive that I wrote the notes to Susan and Cheryl, which I never denied, and that it was only probable that I signed the check. And then he said about the flyer that I admitted to making the day after Mom's disappearance, "I was not able to determine whether or not she did it."

Robin had one more witness, Dr. Eric Mings, who testified that Rickie suffered from major depression with psychotic features, with hallucinations of our father visiting him in his cell, and was diagnosed at the hospital with schizoaffective disorder. He also said that Rickie told him that I helped him kill Mom.

With that, the State rested its case and it was Diana's turn. She called Susan as her first witness. Poor Susan was so nervous. I could see her cues; she was talking a little faster than normal, and her breathing was nerve-wracked, but once Diana gave her a little "relax, it will be okay" speech, she settled in and her testimony began.

First, Diana asked her about our family dynamic since we met in 1988, and Susan testified, in her mild New York accent, how we evolved into being very close: "We were all three of us were very close, Stacey and her mother, and myself and Marilyn. Through the years, Marilyn became almost—not the same kind of best friend Stacey was—but she was very close. I would call her a couple of times a week. We would do things, go to Disney all the time. We've gone to Disney conventions, out to eat almost every weekend."

Susan told the jury that we rarely saw Rickie—that he was always invited, if we knew where he was—but it was only occasionally that he was around. We really didn't see him much until he moved in with us. Diana asked, "If you didn't know him very well, why would you invite him to come live with Stacey?"

She shrugged and answered, matter-of-fact, "He's Stacey's older brother. My brother was living with us for six years"—she laughed—"so I said, 'Alright, your brother knows how to do this and do that,' and we did recently find out he was separated from his wife, living in a shanty mobile home. Stacey asked, 'Would you mind if I offer for my brother to live with us? He can help us fix the house up.'"

Diana asked, when Susan said we didn't charge him rent, "Was that because you didn't need it, or he didn't have it? Was he doing a substantial work that you thought was sufficient?"

Susan laughed and said, "Since my brother already lived with us for six years and didn't give us a nickel, and we didn't need it, we were doing fine. I don't believe in that with family anyway. Our theory was if Rickie moves in, instead of rent he can help us around the house and that's what he did. We would come home and dinner would be already made. He would buy groceries and make us dinner."

Susan testified that, in previous years, she and I always took the week of our birthdays off to celebrate with her mother, whose birthday was the same week, and that for the few years before 2003, we started going on a cruise together.

She told the jury that we decided against the cruise that year because of money and time off, but, she said, "A week or so before I got to thinking, well, maybe I'll still take my mother on a cruise if I can get a good deal."

She told the jury that she went on the cruise because her mother insisted. "I said perhaps I should not go on the cruise and maybe I should stay home, because I was just as close to Marilyn. I mean, she was not my mother, but she was almost like a mother to me. But my mother is very strong and my mother said that there was really nothing I could do. I wanted to be there for Stacey to be support but she said, 'She will be fine. The police will take care of it.'"

Diana had Susan describe Mom's strict regiment, going to bed and rising early, her house immaculate. "She would not leave anything out. She complained if Grandpa left a crumb on the table." She laughed, fondly remembering Mom and her ways, then remembered where she was. She glanced at the jury, smiling. "I don't mean to be silly, but she was always that way. She always wanted the counters clean, and when Grandpa was living there and he would make a sandwich or something, and if she saw a crumb, she would make a mumble and say, 'You would think he'd clean it up,'" she said, miming my mom furiously wiping. "But the guy's like, however old. He can't see these little tiny crumbs."

She testified that she and Rickie and I would often go to the movies, but we didn't go nearly as often with Mom. If we did go with her, we saw primarily Disney movies. Diana asked, "Had you and Stacey and Richard seen *Charlie's Angels*?" Susan said that we had and that Mom would not be likely to go see a movie like that.

I wrote on my legal pad, "*7 pm have shower and ready to rest for bed. Game night never more than 2 hours. Richard, Susan and Stacey went to movies frequently. Susan, Mom and I went to the movies on occasion.*"

"Did you see ever Rickie and Stacey and Marilyn go to the movies together?"

"No."

I wrote, "*Never saw Richard, Mom and I go to the movies together.*"

Diana asked about the events of December 22, the day of the suicide attempt and the finding of the bodies. Susan said she got home around 6:00 P.M. It wasn't a surprise to her to find two police officers waiting for her, she explained, "Because I had passed Marilyn's house, so I was already aware that there was a situation. I was frantic. The first thing I did—they were rattling whatever they were rattling to me—was where is Stacey and what happened? So I immediately was racing through the house to get to the answering machine to see if she had left me a message. And they followed me until I settled for half a minute so they could talk to me."

She said the officers told her that I was in the hospital. By the time they left, she was aware of what they found in our backyard. She and I both teared up at the memory of that night. She started telling about Betty Kelly coming over to fill in the hole and broke down into sobs. "I told her I didn't know how we were going to handle the back-yard. So she said she would send somebody over."

She continued crying and told Diana that she thought it would be better if we went and stayed with her mother. She wiped her eyes and testified about finding Rickie's manuscript in a file cabinet in his room, and turning it over to the police. Next thing both of us knew, we were witnesses for the State of Florida.

Diana asked, "Do you recall if there was discussion about the upcoming trial and the process that that would entail?"

"Robin Wilkinson asked Stacey what her feelings were as far as if the death penalty was on the table."

Robin leapt up from the table and said, in her conde-scending tone, "Objection, hearsay," and I saw Susan's face instantly switch to anger. I could see that she felt like Robin was accusing her of lying about something she damn well knew had happened. It was right then that Diana said, "I don't have anything further," and Susan was Robin's witness.

Robin started off as combative right out of the gate. "When you found out Marilyn was missing you would have been upset? And shortly after that you went on a cruise?"

"Unfortunately, yes, I did," Susan replied.

"And your partner at that time of approximately fifteen years, you left her behind. Did Stacey take a leave of absence from her work those three months that Marilyn was missing like her sister Cheryl did?" Robin asked.

"No, she did not," Susan said, archly. "She chose to be responsible and work to pay her bills."

Robin kept pushing. "While you were with Stacey did you see her pick up the phone and call the Orange County Sheriff's Office to find out what was going on in the investigation?"

"No, because Richard did."

"Ma'am, let me ask you this question one more time," Robin asked. "Did you ever see Stacey pick up the phone . . ." and Susan interrupted, "No, I never saw Stacey call the police department."

"How about Deputy Patrick, the one who came out that night? Did she pick up the phone and call him?"

Susan angrily enunciated her words very clearly. "I never saw Stacey call any police officer whatsoever."

Robin wisely changed the subject and started talking about Cheryl and Daniel, and family discussions about Mom quitting work so she could take Daniel. Susan was never really in on those conversations, but she was aware that they had taken place.

The questioning then led to why Susan didn't find it

odd that Rickie was taking things from Mom's house and storing them in our garage and in his room. Robin asked, "As you start to see item after item from Marilyn's home show up in yours, you don't think that's a little strange? Did you pick up the phone and call the police and say my lover's brother is clearing out his mother's home and it's all ending up here?"

I kept telling Diana, "She's going to lose her temper any minute now." And then she did. Now Susan was pissed. She's about the friendliest person I've ever met, but when you make her mad, look out. She is her mother's daughter.

"I didn't look at it that way," Susan snapped. "I looked at it as Marilyn's son was taking care of Marilyn's house. He is the older son. He was taking care of Marilyn's house." I wrote on my pad, "*SHE IS MAD NOW! LOOK OUT ROBIN.*"

She was just getting wound up. "He told me he was calling the police." She pounded on the witness stand railing. "He told me he was talking to the IRS. These are the things he told me. I felt confident that he was telling his sisters the same thing. I felt confident that the police were taking care of this."

Robin kept trying to interrupt, but Susan was on a roll. I smiled proudly and wrote on my pad, "*Give it to her, Susan!*" And she did. She kept going. "He told me he was putting things away to protect Marilyn so that when Marilyn would come back, if the house got sold, she would at least have her possessions. Stupidly, that made sense to me. I'm sorry. But I'm a simple person. That made sense to me. I wish I had the hindsight to know what happened but I didn't."

It's a good thing that Diana had so thoroughly taught me to maintain my composure, because it was all I could do to just sit there and grin broadly, instead of jumping up and fist-pumping, shouting, "You tell her, baby!"

Robin finally got a word in and asked, "You were the older person in the relationship with Stacey, correct? By a number of years? And you never stepped in there and checked any of this out about Marilyn's disappearance, although you're so close to her?"

Susan looked at her like she had two heads and said, "Why should I? The police were taking care of it. I'm not a police person. The police came to the house. The police took a report. The police are doing a missing person's report. I assumed the police do these things. I'm sorry. My mother was there and my mother told me the police would take care of it. I believed in the police department. I didn't know we had to do something."

You can't argue with that logic, can you?

CHAPTER 35

The Truth Is the Truth Is the Truth

Susan finished her testimony, and I was scheduled to take the stand next, on Friday morning, the end of the second week of the trial. I was terrified, but Diana and I had been preparing for three years. She suggested that I just pretend it was the two of us talking and not pay attention to them. It's all a painting. It's just us. Girl talk.

I was fine, all set to get it over with, until Judge Lubet talked to me directly on Thursday evening. He had me placed under oath and said, "Miss Kananen, it's been made known to me that tomorrow morning you are going to take the witness stand and testify on your behalf, is that correct?"

When I said yes, he replied, "I want you to understand several things. If this case doesn't go well for you, a year, two years, three years down the road, I don't want you coming back saying, 'My attorney forced me to testify, and I didn't want to.' Have you made the decision to testify after consulting with your attorney, and that is your decision alone? Did she explain to you all the possible consequences of you testifying?"

"Yes, Your Honor."

He continued to pound home the seriousness of what I was about to do, and he made it clear that he didn't think it was a good idea. He made me answer, over and over, that I knew what I was doing and made the decision to testify without coercion. After we finally got out of the courtroom, I frantically asked Diana, "What the hell? I was okay, until all of that!"

Diana said, in her calm-Stacey-down voice, "They do that to every defendant who wants to get on the stand. That's just status quo. Look, the popular defense lawyer theory is that you never have your client testify. That's one of those weird lawyer urban myths. But there are things you have to explain to that jury that I have no way of explaining. They have to hear it from you. The jury is told that they can't hold it against you for not testifying, but I think most of the time, they do anyway. They'll wonder, 'Why didn't she get up and tell me she didn't do it?'"

She told me to go back to my hotel and think about it—like I would be thinking about anything else. I didn't just think about it, though. I *agonized*. I paced the parking lot for hours, trying to decide. Was Diana wrong? Did we make a wrong decision? Is the judge telling me I don't really want to answer these questions? I ran the gamut that night. I finally decided maybe he's telling me not to testify because I've won and shouldn't mess with success. My decision was made.

Friday morning, I said to Diana, "Good morning. I'm not testifying," and she said, "Oh yes, you are! Don't give me that bullshit. I picked a jury based on your testifying. You've got to testify. You said, at the beginning of jury selection, that you wanted to tell your story. You gotta get on that stand now."

I was terrified of getting pissed off at Robin. I saw how she tore into Susan and made her lose her cool, but Diana reminded me that Robin would be uncomfortable because for four years I was her star witness and she knew it would be weird coming after me. Diana said, "Don't worry about it. I'm going to protect you from Robin."

I told her I felt like it was a mistake, and she said, "But what did you tell me? If we lose because you've told the truth, it's okay. You go to prison knowing you told the truth. If we lose because you didn't get on the stand, we have no appeal and you're screwed."

She fed my own words back to me, and I remembered saying them, during our many conversations. I remembered how much I trusted her judgment and advice over the years, how she managed to get the charges dropped in my father's death. I saw how she handled Hussey. I had to ask myself, "Do I trust Diana Tennis or do I not?"

I took the stand.

The tension in the room was palpable as I held up my right hand to solemnly swear to tell the truth, the whole truth, and nothing but the truth, so help me God. There was no backing out now.

Diana started out gently, asking about any previous testifying I might have done, which was her way of remind-
ing the jury that I testified at a hearing for my brother. She
asked whether the abuse stories that the jury had heard so
far were accurate, and I said yes, and when she asked what
kind of relationship I had with my siblings, I responded,
"I would say we were kind of distant. I don't think we ever
learned how to be close to each other because of all the
fighting between our parents. We were isolated when
someone moved out of the house. We wouldn't be able to
have much contact with each other."

It seemed that Cheryl thought I might have had it easier than she did, growing up, and she called me "the fair-
haired child." But from my perspective, all of us were
equally abused, including our mother. Diana asked,
"When your brother, Richard, says your mother sexually
abused him, was that your perception? Do you believe it?"

It was heartbreaking when I heard him say it during his
testimony, and it was heartbreaking now. I started crying
and said, "No." Diana brought me a tissue and I whispered to her, "Sorry."

She asked if I thought Mom failed in her job to protect
her children, and I replied, "No, I think my mother did
the best she could under the circumstances and the abuse
that she went through. My perception would be she was
very afraid for all of us. She was afraid to do anything
against what my father said."

Diana waited until I had calmed down a bit and said,
"I'm going to ask you a few questions about your childhood as they relate to this case. You heard the audiotape

of the conversation you had with law enforcement on December 22 of 2003. And the officer asked you repeatedly, why aren't you sticking up for yourself? Tell the jury, what did you learn when you were a child?"

I told them, "The more you fought back, the more you argued, the worse you got beaten or raped or whatever the abuse was of the day."

She then asked, "How'd you learn to deal with traumatic events as a child?" and I replied, "You kind of sat in a corner or sat by yourself. You were very quiet. You didn't discuss it. You didn't argue it. You didn't start an argument about it. You just kind of sat to yourself and kept it all inside."

Then came the big question: "Were you ever sexually abused by your father?" It was the question I dreaded. I knew it was coming, and I didn't want to do this. When I said yes, she said, "Tell the jury about one instance and how you dealt with it." I laughed a nervous laugh and smiled a nervous smile at her, thinking, "You're really gonna make me do this, aren't you?" and got on with it.

"Well, the one that I remember the most, that's the most poignant in my mind, was when we lived in Arkansas. My parents were having a fight and my father decided he was going to take me and my sister and leave. I must have been in sixth grade. He put us in the car, he went up to the town bar, got himself really polluted. Then he decided to go back home after the bar closed. It was two in the morning, one in the morning, and when we came in the house, my sister went to where we had our bunk beds. My brother was sleeping in the living room on a pullout sofa. He told my mother, 'You're not sleeping in the room with me. Stacey's going in the room with me.' We went in the bedroom, he locked the door, he pulled out a handgun . . ."

I had to pause. This was hard to say in front of so many people and cameras. I closed my eyes and forced myself to finish the story. ". . . and then he raped me with a gun in my . . . in my mouth." And then the tears came. I didn't want to cry, damn it.

Diana asked gently, "Did you fight back?" and I whispered, "No."

Out of the list of abuse stories I had given Diana, I got to pick the one I told in court. I wanted to make my sister hurt, too. She and I never talked about that night, when she and Mom got to go in that other bedroom and I got stuck going with him. We had never talked about that night, so I wanted her to hurt. That was my own way of making her realize that it's not all about her and it never has been.

Bless her, Diana changed the subject and asked about our new house and how often I saw Mom. I told her we talked on the phone often and at least once a week we'd go to dinner. I told the jury that I only saw Cheryl on game nights, and saw Rickie when he moved in with us. Otherwise, I didn't see him much. I told her, "When Susan and I bought our house, he helped us move in."

We talked about the night Mom disappeared. I told the story all the way through, about Rickie saying "it" must have taken her, and that he was waving a letter around from Social Security saying they needed to see our father.

We talked about Mom's house being in disarray, and

how out of character it was for her. We talked about the months following that day, how I thought Rickie was paying her bills and putting her stuff in storage to protect it. We talked about all of it, from my side of the story.

Diana then showed me a photo and asked, "Do you recognize the document laying on the dashboard of that vehicle?"

It was the suicide note to Susan, on the dashboard of my truck. The photo was taken after the police interrupted our suicide attempt. I said I did recognize it and that I wrote it. She then showed me the page with the two notes written to Cheryl. "When is the first time you would have been shown that note?" she asked, and I thought for a moment before replying, "Oh, goodness. I'm not sure of what the date was, but it was 2008, 2009."

"Is that a note that you recall writing in the truck on December 22, 2003?"

I did not recall writing it in the truck. Diana then said, "Now, I'm going to show you that notebook again, exhibit 36." It was the notebook she had found in the "stinky underworld of the sheriff's office," after the delay. "There appears to be in here a lot of pages with writing on them, including on this page, a note addressed to Susan with a 'See you later, Stacey,' referencing a cruise. Is that a note you wrote and did you ever give it to Susan?"

I told her that I did write it and said, "I may have left it on the counter. I may have closed it up in the notebook and not shown it to her."

"Do you know how long this notebook had been hanging around being written in?" she asked. I said, "Quite a while. From the looks of it, it came from our first house when we moved to the Okaloosa house, because it refers to the U-Haul we rented, the PODS we put some of our furniture in." I flipped through the pages, describing what I saw: "housekeeping—we had thought about calling to do a detail cleaning on our house before we moved. Different bill places, Bell South, Time Warner, we had to transfer everything from one house to the other."

"Did you take this notebook out of your house to the storage unit on December 22?"

"No."

"Do you know where your brother would have gotten it from?"

"It could have been anywhere in my house," I said.

"So going back to this note"—she pointed at the note to Cheryl, from that notebook, on the same page where Rickie had written his note to her, in the truck—"is that the sentiment in the note, the apology to Cheryl for something related to her kids and your mother, is that a sentiment or a feeling that you had that you wouldn't have expressed at the time?"

"I would have," I stated, "when I first heard about Cherokee School because I wouldn't want my mother to take the kids from Cheryl. Cheryl needed to raise her children."

"When you look at that writing, what is it about it that looks like it was written by you?"

"'I love you and the kids with all my heart.' 'With all my heart' is something I said to all my family." I could see Cheryl in the gallery, rolling her eyes.

"Is that a note that you would have written as an apology to your sister for having killed your mother?" Diana asked.

"No, absolutely not."

She continued, rapid-fire, "Did you kill your mother?"

"No."

"Did you help your brother kill your mother?"

"Absolutely not."

"Was that note in response to you killing your mother?"

"No, it was not."

"Would it have been unusual for you to write a note to someone, an apology, or about a tough subject that you did not send or give?"

"Not unusual. I wrote everything down when I was upset. I didn't speak to anybody. I didn't know how to say how I felt. It's not something we were taught when we were young. It's not something that was allowed to be done when we were young."

We wrapped up my testimony and I was desperately relieved. That note to Cheryl was pretty damning evidence, and Diana just blew it out of the water. Thank God the trial was postponed that first week, even if the delay did cause me considerable angst, because my incredible defense attorney never would have found that notebook.

Robin's turn was next, and I braced myself for her cross-examination, because she wasn't going to go easy on me, no matter how weird Diana said she might feel about coming after me. She had been attacking my integrity for two weeks, not to mention the fact that she thought so little of me that she charged me with two heinous crimes three years ago, and now here we were, face-to-face.

It would soon be up to the jury to decide. This had gone past her intimidating me now. I was facing the ultimate intimidation, in that courtroom. I thought, "You can't do any more to me. You can't take that little piece of humanity that I have left," and it was very small by the time I went to trial, let me tell you. I felt absolutely like I was going to lose, up until Hussey testified and Diana got ahold of him.

To say, however, that Robin was a total bitch is inaccurate because when I sat in her office right before my brother's trial was supposed to begin, she asked about my sexual abuse. I told her about Arkansas, the rape, and she cried. She couldn't talk to me on the way out of the office.

I don't think she wanted to do this trial, but it was her job. So to the best of her ability, and the only way she knew how, she played my brother and she did a good job with him. Just like anybody else paid to do a job, you do what your boss tells you. I really want to believe that about her. Hussey had a grudge against me, but I don't believe Robin did.

I think she got ugly because she had to, and everybody hated her for it, but if I look at the facts of the case, I don't think she was out to destroy me. I think she had to do what she had to do, but the uglier she got the more she turned the jury against herself.

Fortunately, by the time Robin had her turn, all of the witnesses had been on the stand and everything had already been discussed. I was the last witness, and Diana had made sure that she asked me everything she knew Robin would, and I had already responded fully, so she had a solid foundation to object and say, "Asked and answered." There wasn't much Robin could do.

She didn't throw me any surprises. I knew the case she had laid out against me: the checks, the bank accounts, the garage sale, et cetera. I won't say that I was confident, but I was ready. I had Susan sitting there in the gallery, along with my friends, all showing their support. Susan kissed the moonstone necklace I had given her years ago, to send a kiss to me, up there on the stand.

Robin tried to trip me up, and she tried to piss me off. She tried to catch me in lies, and she tried to ridicule me. We went through it all, start to finish, her condescension plain. The only time I really allowed myself to get upset was when she asked me about the suicide note, and that fateful line.

She said to me, "'We had a part in Mother's leaving.' That's 'we.' That's you and Rickie had a part in mother's leaving. You figured when this note was going be found, Miss Kananen, you would be dead."

I shot back, hopefully explaining that note for the last damned time, "I didn't know if I was going be alive or dead. My part in it was I put my brother in my house, on Okaloosa Avenue, put him ten or eleven houses down from my mother. I got him close to my family, close enough to screw everybody up. He messed with my nephew's head, messed with my sister. Got my sister upset with me and then I found out that he killed my mother and put her in my backyard. I should have never let that man move into my house."

She wasn't buying it. She said, "Daniel, your heart and soul, is why you killed your mom, right?"

I glared at her and said, "I never killed my mother."

CHAPTER 36

The Verdict

After my testimony ended, not a moment too soon because I was fried, closing arguments began. Robin went first. She spent a long time going over, again, what a liar I was. She repeated pretty much everything she said in her opening argument, laid out her whole case again, and made fun of the way I said "I don't know" about many things.

"I don't know," she sneered. "I don't know!" I didn't remember cashing that check. I didn't remember if I had used my name or Mom's when I called the bank. I didn't know where Cheryl's apology note had been written.

She mocked our handwriting expert and the flyer I made. She tried to take apart Diana's clever discovery of the notebook. "Do you really think that lo and behold Richard went through the notebook and somehow Stacey wrote this note back a month or so earlier when this letter came from Cheryl and he just happened to come upon that page? It just doesn't make sense. He told you the page was blank."

She addressed the fact that I was a witness for her case against Rickie but told the jury that I should have been arrested the same day as Rickie. "That is not your question to decide today. Your question to decide is plain and simple. Was Stacey Kananen involved in the murder of her mother? Was she a principal in this crime? Did she intend for this murder to happen? Did she actively participate? That's the question to decide.

"The fact that Stacey Kananen was ever put on a witness list doesn't mean we have to buy her story. And it doesn't mean we have to believe everything she said on the witness stand today. Ladies and gentlemen, use your common sense and look at how Stacey's story changes from when she's playing stupid with detectives to when she's talking to her partner in crime. The one thing that changed, May 1, 2007, was that Richard Kananen stopped protecting her."

I had a hard time not getting angry at what Robin was saying about me. It was bad enough I was on the stand for hours and then she got to attack me again. But that was all she could bring to her closing, to attack me. She couldn't bring any facts that said I was guilty; all she could do was mimic and mock me.

Diana brought facts to the table. How could my mother's car be in two places at once? How could Rickie spin five stories and anyone know which to believe? All Robin could do was say, "Oh, I don't know . . ." She didn't have any facts. If she had facts, that was the time for her to throw them out there like Diana did.

When Diana got up to rebut Robin's closing argument, she said, "Ladies and gentlemen, sarcasm doesn't mean you're right." And then she, once again, laid out the facts of her case and asked the jury to come back with a verdict of "Not Guilty."

We were released Friday, March 10, right around dinnertime, so Diana Tennis, Susan, Diane, and I, along with several people from the resort who stayed in Orlando for moral support, just in case the verdict came back that night, made our way down the street in downtown Orlando to eat at a little Italian restaurant. I couldn't eat. My stomach was in such knots, knowing this might be my last real meal, that I could not force myself to get anything down. I didn't know how else to sit there at dinner, just staring at the walls, and people were trying to get me to eat, trying to laugh and joke. I understood what they were trying to do, but I wasn't able to participate. I was surrounded by friends and family, and Susan and I just held hands and prayed. Then Diana got the call. The verdict was in.

We headed back to the courthouse immediately and Diana took me aside. She made everybody leave me and she walked me into the courtroom. She said, "If you have anything personal on you, hand it to Susan." This was becoming way too real. My insides felt like they had been thrown into a deep freeze. I took off my watch and necklace and handed them to Susan. I told her that Diana said to hold onto them until afterward.

By the time I got those words out of my mouth, several deputies had lined up there in the courtroom. I thought, "They must know something," and I freaked out. I freaked . . . out. I started to shake, and Diana and Toni each grabbed one of my hands. I whispered, "Why are they here?"

Diana said, "It's just procedure." I said, "Procedure my ass. I'm scared to death!" and Diana said, "You're supposed to be. That's a normal reaction."

I was not this scared when I got arrested, but that moment I was petrified with fear—*real* fear. I've never seen so many deputies, and all of them with handcuffs in hand. I sat there thinking, "Oh my God, oh my God, oh my God," and then Judge Lubet brought the jury in.

Everyone stood up, as we always did when the jury entered or exited. Susan was right behind me, in the front pew of the gallery, with Jeanice sitting beside her. Diane, our surrogate mom, sat behind Susan. I was the last to stand, because I couldn't feel my legs.

Judge Lubet gave another one of his speeches. "I don't want any cheering, screaming or yelling. This is a courtroom. It may be 10:30 at night but it's still a courtroom. Anybody who makes a ruckus is going to be escorted out by the deputies. Do we understand each other? Good."

Susan stood behind me with a tissue pressed to her mouth, eyes squeezed shut. I went dead inside. "This is it. This is the end. Just get it over with. Just get it over with.

Let's end it. Just send me to jail and get it over with." I didn't even have the energy to be nauseated. I could hear Susan sobbing quietly.

The jury was taking forever to be seated. Didn't they know my entire life was in their hands? God, I couldn't take the dead silence in the room as we waited, waited, waited for them to take their seats. Finally the bailiff said to us, "Be seated," and I was able to drop back into my chair. Now I felt like I could puke.

Judge Lubet said, "Alright Mr. Foreman, it's my understanding you've reached a verdict in this case," and the foreman replied, "Yes, Your Honor." The judge said, "Please make sure the form is signed and dated please, and that there's only one check mark on it. Fold it over and hand it to the court deputy."

The deputy walked the verdict over to the judge as my life passed before my eyes. I was able to see how everything that had ever happened to me had led to this moment, from being stranded on a floating deck in Lake Hebron, Maine, to the rape in Arkansas, to Mom's head being carved with a knife, to that horrible trip to Arizona and back. Father's disappearance, the happy years since, and then Mom's grisly murder. It all made sickening sense, somehow. Of course this is how it ended up. Of course. How could it have been otherwise? This is the story of my life.

The judge unfolded the paper and read. He passed it, folded, to the clerk, with no visible reaction on his face, and asked her to publish the verdict. She unfolded the paper and looked surprised. "In the Circuit Court of the Ninth Judicial Circuit for Orange County, Florida," she read as I closed my eyes, bracing for the worst, "Case Number 48-2007-CF-6901-O for Orange County, the State of Florida versus Stacey Kananen. Verdict as to Count One: We the jury find the defendant not guilty."

Stunned.

I just sat there. There had to be more. Another shoe was sure to drop.

"So say we all, this twelfth day of March, 2010," the clerk continued.

I finally felt it. Oh my God, not guilty. Not guilty. The two sweetest words ever. I allowed myself a small smile as Toni patted my back. Diana turned to me and said, "My God, we won!" and gave me the best hug of my life. I could feel her sobbing as I rested my head on her shoulder and just said, "Thank you." She gave me a heartfelt squeeze and released me. We looked each other in the eyes, and I loved her so much, right then. We laughed a little and then both broke down in sobs. Poor Susan was falling apart behind me. She is a loud crier, and I can only imagine how hard it was for her to keep quiet.

The judge polled the jury to make sure that the verdict was unanimous while we continued to cry. Diana was so sweet, obviously so moved and happy for me. Although the reason for our happiness was a horrid one, I felt light and free, for the first time in too many years. God, it was finally over.

They continued polling the jury, as we continued to cry, but Cheryl just sat there, staggered. She didn't move; she didn't blink. Finally, the judge said, "Miss Kananen, a jury of your peers has found you not guilty. At this time

I'm going to adjudicate you not guilty. You are released from all your bonds. Do you have a monitor on your ankle?"

"Yes, I do, Your Honor," I answered.

"Alright, it will be removed." He said to Jeanice, sitting behind me, "Can you remove that this evening?" and Jeanice said, "Yes, I can remove it now."

"You can wait for your paperwork if you want, otherwise you are free to go," the judge said.

"Thank you, Your Honor," I said. I hugged Diana again and whispered, "Thank you so much." We hugged and cried for a long minute as the judge thanked the jury for their time and consideration. Then I turned and hugged Toni, sobbing even harder. As she and I pulled apart and I sat back up in my chair, I couldn't hold it back anymore. I just started bawling, all the tears that had been pent up for so very long. I thought about my poor mom, my poor mentally ill brother, and even poor Cheryl. Poor all of us. What a hard life we'd had.

Finally, I had no more tears, and I wiped my eyes. The judge was still talking to the jury as I sat there sniffling. I took a deep breath, my first *free* deep breath, and said, "My God, it's over. Thank God, it's over."

"Court's adjourned, you're free to go," Judge Lubet said, and with that, it really was over.

EPILOGUE

Reach the Beach

I woke up Saturday morning in our Orlando hotel room, Susan asleep by my side in our bed, surrogate mom, Diane, sleeping in the other. Still groggy, I reached down to unplug the cord to my ankle bracelet because it would be done charging by now—I had to stay plugged in for twelve hours a night.

I felt around and couldn't find it. Suddenly, it dawned on me, "Hey, it's not there anymore!" After three years of vigilant awareness of that thing, it was no longer a concern. It felt weird, like getting used to wiggling a loose tooth and one day it's not there anymore.

Susan woke up then, and was in a bit of a hurry to get back to Hudson, to our home and our friends at GCR. Diane was looking forward to being in her own house again, as well. I told them, "I want to drive by my mother's house. Then we can go home." They thought I was crazy, but I insisted, "I just feel I need to do this."

When we got to Alachua Street, to the house where I had grown up and where my mother had died, I couldn't let Susan stop the car. I was crying too hard to get out and look around. I glanced as we drove by, and I was angry because the house was falling apart. Then we went by our old house around the corner on Okaloosa and saw that it was occupied. That felt right. I was glad to see that there was life happening there, that our personal tragedy didn't haunt our little home and that the new residents were taking care of it.

Then we drove by Cheryl's house and I saw my brother's truck there in the driveway; it had been given to Chris after Rickie's arrest. Mom's car was in Cheryl's possession, as well. I wondered if I could forgive my sister for believing I could help my brother strangle and bury our mother. She allowed me to watch her children and they spent many nights in my house. Only time will tell.

We didn't linger in Orlando. Wendell was calling Susan every twenty minutes, asking, "Are you on your way?" The folks at the resort had a party planned for my return. I loved them for it, but my heart just wasn't in party mode. While the verdict was a dream come true, I was shredded inside. He told Susan, "We have a whole parade waiting for you!" and I had to say, "I'm sorry. I'm going at my speed, for a change." It felt good to be able to say that, and to know that my wishes were being respected.

When we arrived back at Gulf Coast Resort, Wendell met us out on the main road, which almost three years earlier had been lined with police cars waiting to arrest me. This time, that same road was lined with golf carts and friends holding signs and waving banners. As we pulled in to the resort, they all fell in line behind us and formed a parade. We all gathered at the resort's common grounds, and there were hugs all around. Everyone wanted to see my ankle, sans bracelet.

Franda, the same woman who years earlier said that she was uncomfortable with my presence, and to whom I promised my story would be the truth, came up to me. She said, "My God, you said the same things in those hours of testimony that you said when you moved here. Nobody's that good, to not change their story at all if it's a lie. If the truth is the truth and you said it all along, I should have believed you seven years ago."

I told her, "Franda, the truth is the truth. The only thing that's ever going to be constant is the truth. You can't make up the stories because you can't remember them. And I didn't have to make up a story. I didn't do this."

When the trial aired later that summer on CNN's *In Session*, their commentators talked about "jury nullification," which means that the jury might have felt sorry for me because of the abuse. But Diana told me after the trial that Judge Lubet said the jury thought the police did a shitty, horrible job. They left holes all over the place, and the jury held the State to the standard of "beyond a reasonable doubt."

It was weird when the trial aired, months after the actual verdict. I didn't watch it—not only did I have to work, but I didn't want to relive it. But Susan checked the *In Session* blogs and Facebook page and saw the cruel things people were writing about me, like I cried crocodile tears while looking at my poor mother's autopsy photos, and that Mom was a horrible person for allowing the abuse.

It was awful. They obviously didn't consider that they were talking about real people. I didn't volunteer to be on a reality show, to invite the cameras into my personal business. This nightmare was foisted upon me against my will, and now my life was destroyed. I had lost my family, my promising career at Disney, my reputation, and now I couldn't even get a job outside of Gulf Coast Resort because every employer does background checks these days and, even with a not guilty verdict, it looks really bad to have a murder charge on your record.

Susan's father had died after marrying "the Bitch," and she was determined to get the resort and kick all of us out, so we both needed jobs. You try applying for work after having been on trial for murder on national TV! And those losses don't even touch what this whole thing cost, financially. Just the ankle bracelet and bonds alone drained us of almost $30,000.

The irony is that this whole thing started partially because of Mom's money, and now I needed money to rebuild my life. So I hired a probate attorney to retrieve any inheritance I might have coming. Sadly, Cheryl gave an interview saying, "Not two months after the trial ended, Stacey has hired an attorney to claim her part in my mother's estate. So much for really wanting to walk away from this. In an instant, it became so very crystal clear that, sickeningly, my mom *was* killed for the money." As it turned out, though, I got nothing because, as the executor of Mom's estate at the time, she spent it—I assume because she thought I'd be found guilty and not be entitled to any inheritance. I am now the executor, but unfortunately only Mom's house is left.

I did finally reconnect with Daniel almost a year after the trial. Susan found him on Facebook and sent him a private message. He cautiously responded, unsure whether he should communicate with us or not. We were his beloved aunts, and he missed us, but he had been told all these years that I was a murderer and he wasn't allowed to contact me. But now he was of legal age, and he was free to make his own decisions. It was slow going, but we did eventually manage to rebuild some semblance of a relationship.

He had an extremely hard row to hoe all those years and was having a really hard time with what happened in our family. His parents had divorced and he told me that Cheryl and Detective Hussey were now dating. He said that "Mark" offered to tell his little sisters all about their murderous Aunt Stacey.

The one thing, aside from Susan, that got me through the difficult time after the trial was therapy with a wonderful counselor, Jessica Deeb. Jessica has been a lifesaver, on numerous occasions. Working through and healing all of these horrible things has been both harder and more valuable than I ever would have dreamed, but I'm so much better off because of it. I had quit drinking before the trial. After it ended, I started drinking socially, but it was beginning to get a little heavier right before I started seeing Jessica. Susan told me, "If you're going to drink, you're going to have to find another counselor." I haven't had a drink since April 2010.

I sat in therapy one day after sending an e-mail to Jessica saying, "I'm bringing three pages. I need to read these to you, otherwise I'm a failure." I was only able to read two sentences out loud. I felt like such a wretch because that meant my father still controlled my life even though he was dead. It wasn't that the memories I was writing about were too painful to talk about; it was that I was never allowed to *tell* anyone and he still had that power over me.

So she read it, and I listened. I was proud of myself; I shook, but I didn't cry. I came close. Pain, anger, memories, emotions, never crying when I got raped, I wasn't allowed. I'd be killed. I'd just bite my tongue, bite my lip, stare at the ceiling. If you just lie there, they do their thing and then leave. It's over a lot faster. If I didn't cry when I got raped, I sure wasn't going to cry listening to Jessica read about it.

Even so, I left there telling myself I did not win. He was still winning, still able to control what came out of my mouth. But now, here I am writing about it, and telling the whole world that he no longer has that power.

I wrote this letter to him:

When I was very young, I had hoped for a dad. Someone to talk to, play games with, and teach me things. Instead, I got you. All three of your children have been damaged by the father that you were. You treated each and every one of us horribly. You owned us and we were just trying to stay alive.

Well, your son is in prison for the rest of his life. Your oldest daughter leads a life of personal destruction. I, on the other hand, am struggling daily to survive.

I have been struggling to find my way out of the life that you gave us. I am going to beat you in this head game you are playing still on me. I am going to find out how to live and feel emotions without you messing in my head. I have a right to be happy and to have a future and I intend to do just that.

I have a long road to go, to undo the things that I was taught. I will one day learn to cry for the loss of my mom and mourn the loss of my childhood. You took those emotions away from me at a young age and I will get them back.

I am in therapy and am learning to be my own person. I refuse to let you win inside my head. My thoughts of suicide are because of my thoughts of uselessness, thoughts you taught me. My drinking was to forget you and what you did to me. I am going to conquer those issues. I will beat you at your games.

I have the right to have a future. A good future—one without anger for my childhood—without needing to drink or wanting to die. I have a right to find happiness.

It is going to take time and a lot of work to change my mind processes. I have a great therapist who will teach me and help me until I beat this battle. You think that is weak—I tell you that it's strength.

The day will come that I will tell you to leave me for-ever. I will become that strong—I will win this battle. You will one day have no control in my mind or over my life. I will show you someday that I am not your weakest child. When that day comes, I will begin a new, free life full of happiness. I will have a right to feel all of my emo-tions. I will win this battle with the help of Jessica, my therapist and for now my strength.

Your daughter,
Stacey

I'm finally able to see that none of the abuse was my fault and that I am a person of worth. I do have something to say, and I do intend to make these tragedies not be in vain. I realize that I lived this life and learned these lessons for a reason. I have let go of so much hatred for my past and believe that my purpose is to help others in my future.

I feel that if you live your life in a fog of depression and despair you will never actually survive and prosper—you will just exist. I didn't come this far and survive what I did to remain in misery. My goal is to continue to heal and become stronger, to show others that abuse doesn't have to run your life, but it can show you compassion and a willingness to help others.

My brother, I feel, was the most emotionally damaged of all of us. He was the one who was never able to move past the pain of the abuse. He was the one who never found true happiness. He killed our parents, because he never stopped suffering. The memories, the pain, and the anger took over and he fell apart. One thing that I want everyone to realize is that I love my brother and I will always be sad that I didn't see his need for help. I wrote this letter to him:

Richard,

You are my brother and will always be my brother no matter what. We all had a childhood of horrors and each one of us has our own pain and confusion.

You are the oldest of all three of us; and I know during my trial neither one of us believed all of your abuse stories. I now know after a year in therapy that I have no right to judge what you say. You had so many more years of abuse before I was even born.

I do want to tell you that I believe in my heart we all wouldn't have lived to move to Florida if you had left the family after you turned 18. I think that you staying home, even though your abuse intensified, gave us a chance to grow up. You stood in between so many fights, so many times for us and even Mom.

I was happy but sad when you left: happy that you could try to find a life of joy, sad that my big brother, our protector, was gone. You had a lot of good years after that. Our father's death, although illegal, gave us all the opportunity to have many happy years together as a family. I am so sorry that during these years none of us realized the pain from the past that you were suffering. I wish that I could have helped you cope or find help. Maybe, then things would not have ended with Mom dying.

At this point in my life I do not hate you for all of the events after Mom died. I am learning to understand why those events happened, including my trial, and to accept that those events in time will make me stronger.

I hope for some day that you will be at peace with yourself. I know that I will never have the big brother that I once had; but I will always have a big brother. I miss you and grieve for the relationship we could have had.

Stacey

Cheryl was the one sibling that I was sure was going to make it. Her life seemed perfect at face value, but she sometimes struggled with her relationships with her children. With our childhood, none of us knew how to nurture; to have that soft, cry on a shoulder, kiss a skinned knee, give a good night kiss and hug relationship with children. I have great respect and admiration for my sister. I love her and always will. I hope someday that she and I can reunite and be a family again. A long time ago Cheryl gave me a pillow that says, "Chance made us sisters, but hearts made us friends." I hope someday to feel that connection with a sister that I miss more than I can even put into words.

It seems like it would be such a waste to let Mom's death be in vain, so I have dedicated my life to advocacy. It is my firm belief that if my family had been able to have access to the right kind of help, Mom would be alive today and Rickie wouldn't be in jail. It is my dream to found an organization designed to extend a nonjudgmental olive branch for those who want to quit the cycle of abuse. After all, the majority of abusers were once abused themselves: abuse is usually learned behavior—victims victimizing victims. Part of that learned behavior is shame. Both the abused and the abuser feel shame for the role they are playing. When one feels ashamed, one is not likely to ask for help to get out of the abusive situation. I would like to create an advocacy program that recognizes the courage that it takes to ask for help.

I want to find a way to do this compassionately and without judgment. No parent, like my mom, is going to ever admit that anything is wrong in the house because a) she's terrified that she's going to pay the price, and b) she'll be arrested for neglect.

Children are reluctant to ask for help because they fear that they will face even more abuse for telling family secrets, that their parents will end up in jail, and that they will end up in a foster home. And finally, abusive parents are reluctant to ask for help because asking for help is the same as admitting they are wrong, weak, or bad; they feel too far gone, that too much irreparable damage has been done, and that everyone else is to blame.

I want to help people who wish to escape the cycle of abuse—in a nonjudgmental way that keeps them out of the legal system before heinous crimes, like the ones my father committed, occur.

I wrote this letter to my mom, explaining what I want to do with my life:

Mom,

I am writing this letter to you even though I know you will never be able to physically read it. Our childhood is something that none of us ever talked about. We as a family unit never took the opportunity to heal from those horrors. That brought the horrifying end—your murder.

I have guilt about not protecting you from your son, my brother. I feel that after all that we as a family had been through I should have been there for you. I guess that I need to accept that not everyone can be saved from abuse.

I am now on a new journey in my life. A journey to heal myself and to try to find the strength and ability to help other abused children. I only wish that you could be on this journey beside me. No matter what we went through in the past, we together could have conquered so much now. I hope that from afar you are looking at me and going to find a way to help me heal from the pain of the past. I hope that you are smiling at me and giving me the strength to continue on my journey.

I miss you every day and not a day goes by that I don't try to figure out just where it all went wrong. Just how and if life for all of us should have been different. I know that there is a reason that our family has travelled this path. Maybe it is the journey that I want to begin. Maybe there is another reason.

Mom, I want to somehow find a peace inside me—to know that you are okay with my journey. I wish that you were with me. I wish that we as a family unit had found the strength and compassion to talk to each other about our past, to heal our wounds, to grow to be a family.

Please look out for Cheryl and her family. Keep them strong and try to show them to the truth someday, somehow.

I love you,
Stacey

Six months after the trial, on the seventh anniversary of Mom's death, Susan and I left the resort for the day, to get away for a while and honor her memory. She and I had been working all summer on our relationship, trying to rebuild it into the close friendship we had before tragedy tore us all apart. We still had a long way to go—a lot of damage had been done—but we were determined to not let outside forces break us up. Whether we stayed together or broke up, it would be our decision, not because the actions or words of others drove us apart. We decided to focus on what kept us together, and to try to nurture our strengths, instead of focusing on weaknesses. Part of that process was getting away from the resort once in a while, just to have some alone time. And this day held a specific meaning, so we drove past Clearwater Beach, just enjoying the drive.

We came to the end of the road, so we parked. As soon as we got out of the car, I realized, "We've been here with my mother." This was where we went on our last vacation with her. Susan and I sat there for a little bit, reminiscing, and then decided to get something to eat.

We got lost and turned around a few times, but we found our way back up to Clearwater just in time to eat something before we starved. We stopped at an Italian restaurant, and as we parked the car, we said to each other, "This is the restaurant we ate at with Mom!"

I got out of the car, pointed to the hotel across the street, and said, "That's the hotel we stayed in." In the restaurant, the hostess seated us at the same table where we sat with Mom. I'm a bit of a skeptic, but even I could not deny that these were some amazing coincidences. I felt like Mom was there with us that day, and a sense of peace and purpose came over me.

After an excellent meal, Susan and I were finally ready to go home. Out in the parking lot, which was directly across the street from the beach, we sat and watched the sun set over the Gulf of Mexico. I saw a couple of little girls, about the ages that Cheryl and I were that day at Lake Hebron, laughing and playing in the surf with their dad, and the memories—superimposed over the joy these girls were feeling, with their doting father—brought bittersweet tears to my eyes.

If only . . .

A NOTE

from Stacey Lannert

God grant me the serenity to accept the things I cannot change; courage to change the things I can, and wisdom to know the difference.

—FROM "THE SERENITY PRAYER" BY REINHOLD NIEBUHR

As I grow older, I become more appreciative of the Serenity Prayer. It is a reminder that we cannot change everything— we cannot change most things—and we must come to accept this fact. For those of us who have lived through violent and difficult childhoods, it is easy to want to remember that we grew up differently than we did. It's easy for us to keep wishing we had something different. But we must not. We must come to terms with the permanence of what has happened. We must accept our lives for what they were. The future, however, is an entirely different story. The future is the wide-open sky. We can change it, and we have the ability to make it better for others.

America teems with child abuse that is violent, sexual, and verbal. The problem is pandemic, but we can help to eradicate it. For so long, abuse against children has been hidden in the shadows. It's what happens behind closed doors. Too often, keeping up the family image is tantamount. No one wants to be the person who tarnishes a reputation. So adults who suffered horrific childhoods sometimes remain silent. They feel alone and isolated. I was one of those adults once. I coped in whatever way I could. I didn't realize that there were more people just like me.

I was not alone.

More than thirty-nine million Americans have suffered from childhood abuse. Thirty-nine million! The only way we can change the rampant spread of harm is to raise our voices, erase the shame, and educate those who are unaffected. Over the course of many years, I came forth with my story. I started to tell the truth about what happened to me. To my own surprise, I found sympathy and outstretched arms. Eventually, the truth set me free literally and figuratively.

It wasn't easy. Too often, victims are further victimized by careless sentiments from people who don't understand. We hear words like, "If that happened to me, I would have done this or that." Or they blame us with words such as, "Why didn't you leave or tell?" People have a tendency to place themselves in the role of the victim, but they cannot imagine the horrors of child abuse unless they have lived it. These kinds of statements and questions create blame and shame. We must not victimize the victim in this way. Together, we can erase shame. Together, we can create a support system so people will speak up and abusers will be held accountable.

Stacey Kananen's story is both horrific and inspiring. She survived a childhood nightmare and was later falsely accused of patricide and matricide. She was thrown unwillingly into the glare of the public spotlight. Her life and her lifestyle were put on display for the public to judge and critique. Yet somehow she found the strength to shed the role of victim and help others who have been hurt.

Everyone has suffered from something in our lives—some more than others. People deal with their pain differently. Many try to ignore it or drown it in denial. A select few stand up and raise their voices in an attempt to make a difference. Stacey is one of those people. She has risen above the judgment of herself and others. Bravely, she takes us down the unimaginable twists and turns of her inconceivable life. She tells the truth. And her childhood is no longer the land of nightmares. Instead, it is a battleground where she fought for her sanity and won. Stacey is an inspiration, and I admire her ability to reflect upon her past with such candor. Her story, like all of our stories, will empower others.

Stacey Lannert, author of
Redemption: A Story of Sisterhood, Survival,
and Finding Freedom Behind Bars

ACKNOWLEDGMENTS

I have so many people to thank, but I absolutely must thank Susan Cowan first. Without her believing in me and standing by my side, this story would never have come to life. The support she has given me has been unconditional, and she has been my rock since 2003.

I must also thank my legal team, Diana Tennis, Toni Maloney, Claudia Lee, Jeanice Chevere, and John Von Achen. Without all of these wonderful people who had never met me until my arrest in 2003, I would not be sharing my story in the efforts to try to change the lives of many. A murder trial is more stressful than those who have never experienced it can imagine.

Thank you to Linda Langton, Chuck Hurewitz, Shannon Jamieson Vazquez, and Adrienne Avila. Without all of you, this project would still be on the drawing board.

Thanks to Stacey Lannert and Kristen Kemp, who made contributions to this book and gave me strength to continue. One of my inspirations for the changes I want to make when it comes to child abuse is the life Stacey Lannert had. Her author and friend Kristen helped me to see that with the right person you can share your story. Thank you for your support.

My therapist, Jessica Deeb, has been a special person in this process. Without her untiring hours of working with me for over two years now, I would have never had the courage to write this book. She has been and will remain a great support for me.

Last, but most certainly not least, is a special thanks for Lisa Bonnice for the tireless hours we worked on getting the story told so she could write it. So many times I said, "I don't want to talk about this," even though I knew we needed to. She was there at the trial, one of my staunchest supporters, besides Susan. There may have been other people who wanted to write this, but in my heart I believe I chose the best person. Her objectivity and respect for my family and our lives were more than I could have hoped for.

To my family, those here and those not with us any-more, I hope someday for healing and for a day of peace. To my grandfather, thank you for watching out for me. To my mom, I hope that you have finally found peace and joy, since you were never allowed those during your marriage. May you know that all of your children and grandchildren love and miss you.

Stacey M. Kananen

I would like to thank Stacey's legal defense team: Diana Tennis, Toni Maloney, Claudia Lee, John Von Achen, and Jeanice Chevere, for meeting with me and telling their parts of this story. I also want to thank Linda Langton, our agent; Chuck Hurewitz, our attorney; and Shannon Jamieson Vazquez and Adrienne Avila at The Berkley Publish Group for making this happen. Jessica Deeb, Stacey's therapist, was very helpful in allowing me to interview her. And special thanks go to Stacey Anne Lannert and Kristen Kemp for their contributions.

Personally, I give thanks to my family for being so supportive: Kristina and Mike for the office space/elbow room, Stacy for the editorial feedback, Mom for the spare bedroom, and Jeff for being Jeff. Thanks, Dad, for watching over me from "the other side," and thank you to Francis de Sales, patron saint of authors, for getting me through the toughest times of writing this harrowing story. Monica Shank, thanks for your assistance in the early stages of this project!

Susan Cowan deserves a shout-out, as well, because she was a big part of this project, in a lot of ways. But I especially want to thank Stacey M. Kananen for choosing me to write this book with her. I'm honored for her trust in me to be the one to share this journey with her.

Lisa Bonnice